First World War
and Army of Occupation
War Diary
France, Belgium and Germany

33 DIVISION
19 Infantry Brigade
Royal Welsh Fusiliers 2nd Battalion,
Royal Fusiliers (City of London Regiment) 18th and 20th Battalion,
Brigade Trench Mortar Battery
and Brigade Machine Gun Company
1 November 1915 - 31 January 1918

WO95/2423

The Naval & Military Press Ltd
www.nmarchive.com
Published in association with The National Archives

Published by

The Naval & Military Press Ltd

Unit 10 Ridgewood Industrial Park,

Uckfield, East Sussex,

TN22 5QE England

Tel: +44 (0) 1825 749494

www.naval-military-press.com

www.nmarchive.com

This diary has been reprinted in facsimile from the original. Any imperfections are inevitably reproduced and the quality may fall short of modern type and cartographic standards.

© **Crown Copyright**
Images reproduced by permission of The National Archives, London, England, 2015.

Contents

Document type	Place/Title	Date From	Date To
Heading	33rd Division 19th Infy Bde 2nd Bn Roy. Welsh Fus. Dec 1915-Dec 1918 Jan From 2 Division Same Bde To 38 Div 115 Bde 42 1918		
Heading	2/Div Welsh Fusrs Dec Vol XVII		
War Diary	Quesnoy.	01/12/1915	05/12/1915
War Diary	Givenchy	06/12/1915	09/12/1915
War Diary	Bethune	10/12/1915	11/12/1915
War Diary	Cornet Bourdois	12/12/1915	26/12/1915
War Diary	Bethune	27/12/1915	27/12/1915
War Diary	Beuvry.	28/12/1915	31/12/1915
Heading	2/R. Welsh Fus Jan Vol XVIII		
War Diary	Beuvry	01/01/1916	15/01/1916
War Diary	Annequin	16/01/1916	20/01/1916
War Diary	Cuinchy	21/01/1916	27/01/1916
War Diary	Annequin	28/01/1916	29/01/1916
War Diary	Fouquereuil	30/01/1916	05/02/1916
War Diary	Annequin Fosse	06/02/1916	06/02/1916
War Diary	Cambrin	07/02/1916	11/02/1916
War Diary	Annequin South	12/02/1916	18/02/1916
War Diary	Cambrin	19/02/1916	21/02/1916
War Diary	Bethune	22/02/1916	29/02/1916
War Diary	Annequin North	01/03/1916	05/03/1916
War Diary	Cuinchy	06/03/1916	10/03/1916
War Diary	Annequin North	11/03/1916	13/03/1916
War Diary	Cuinchy	14/03/1916	16/03/1916
War Diary	Bethune	17/03/1916	24/03/1916
War Diary	Beuvry	25/03/1916	28/03/1916
War Diary	Cambrin	29/03/1916	31/03/1916
War Diary	Auchy Left Sub Section	01/04/1916	02/04/1916
War Diary	Beuvry	03/04/1916	06/04/1916
War Diary	Auchy Left Sub Section	07/04/1916	10/04/1916
War Diary	Annezin	11/04/1916	18/04/1916
War Diary	Annequin	19/04/1916	22/04/1916
War Diary	Cuinchyright Sub Section	23/04/1916	26/04/1916
War Diary	Annequin	27/04/1916	30/04/1916
War Diary	Cuinchy Right	01/05/1916	04/05/1916
War Diary	Bethune	05/05/1916	16/05/1916
War Diary	Auchy Right	17/05/1916	22/05/1916
War Diary	Beuvry	23/05/1916	29/05/1916
War Diary	Auchy Right	30/05/1916	03/06/1916
War Diary	Annequin S	04/06/1916	09/06/1916
War Diary	Fouquereuil	10/06/1916	11/06/1916
War Diary	Bethune	12/06/1916	17/06/1916
War Diary	Gorre	18/06/1916	20/06/1916
War Diary	Givenchy Left.	22/06/1916	27/06/1916
War Diary	Le Preol	28/06/1916	30/06/1916
Heading	19th Inf. Bde. 33rd Div. War Diary 2nd Battn. The Royal Welsh Fusiliers. July 1916		
War Diary	Le Preol	01/07/1916	04/07/1916
War Diary	Givenchy Left	05/07/1916	08/07/1916

War Diary	Fouquieres	09/07/1916	09/07/1916
War Diary	Longeau	10/07/1916	10/07/1916
War Diary	Cardonnette	11/07/1916	11/07/1916
War Diary	Daours	12/07/1916	12/07/1916
War Diary	Buire	13/07/1916	14/07/1916
War Diary	Meaulte	15/07/1916	15/07/1916
War Diary	Mametz Wood	16/07/1916	18/07/1916
War Diary	Bazentine-Le-Petit	19/07/1916	19/07/1916
War Diary	Flat Iron Copse	20/07/1916	20/07/1916
War Diary	Bois Des Foureaux	20/07/1916	20/07/1916
War Diary	High Wood (Bois-Des-Foureaux)	20/07/1916	21/07/1916
War Diary	Mametz Wood	21/07/1916	21/07/1916
War Diary	Buire-Sur-L'Ancre	21/07/1916	31/07/1916
Heading	19th Brigade. 33rd Division. 2nd Battalion Royal Welsh Fusiliers August 1916		
War Diary	Buire-Sur L'Ancre	01/08/1916	01/08/1916
War Diary	Ancre	02/08/1916	06/08/1916
War Diary	Becordel	07/08/1916	13/08/1916
War Diary	Fricourt Wood	14/08/1916	18/08/1916
War Diary	High Wood	19/08/1916	22/08/1916
War Diary	Bazentin Le Grand	23/08/1916	26/08/1916
War Diary	High Wood	27/08/1916	27/08/1916
War Diary	Fricourt Wood	28/08/1916	29/08/1916
War Diary	Montauban Alley	30/08/1916	30/08/1916
War Diary	Becordel	31/08/1916	31/08/1916
War Diary	Ribemont	01/09/1916	01/09/1916
War Diary	Rainneville	02/09/1916	02/09/1916
War Diary	Bernaville	03/09/1916	04/09/1916
War Diary	Bonnieres & Beauvoir	05/09/1916	05/09/1916
War Diary	Blangermont	06/09/1916	08/09/1916
War Diary	Ivergny	10/09/1916	10/09/1916
War Diary	Humber Camp	11/09/1916	11/09/1916
War Diary	Bienvillers Au Bois	12/09/1916	21/09/1916
War Diary	Bienvillers	22/09/1916	27/09/1916
War Diary	Hannescamps	28/09/1916	29/09/1916
War Diary	Souastre	30/09/1916	30/09/1916
War Diary	Lucheux	01/10/1916	19/10/1916
War Diary	Mericourt L'Abbe	20/10/1916	20/10/1916
War Diary	Meault	21/10/1916	21/10/1916
War Diary	Trones Wood	22/10/1916	22/10/1916
War Diary	Serpentine Trench	23/10/1916	23/10/1916
War Diary	Les Boeufs Trenches	24/10/1916	27/10/1916
War Diary	Guillemont	28/10/1916	29/10/1916
War Diary	Behveen Trones and Bernafay Woods	30/10/1916	30/10/1916
War Diary	Briqueterie	31/10/1916	08/11/1916
War Diary	Meaulte	09/11/1916	12/11/1916
War Diary	Forceville Neuville	13/11/1916	30/11/1916
War Diary	Briqeterie	02/11/1916	02/11/1916
War Diary	Les Boeufs	03/11/1916	03/11/1916
War Diary	Grdilb	04/11/1916	29/11/1916
War Diary	Forceville and Neuville	01/12/1916	09/12/1916
War Diary	Camp III Suzanne	10/12/1916	14/12/1916
War Diary	Camp B. 14. Maurepas	15/12/1916	16/12/1916
War Diary	Maurepas	17/12/1916	18/12/1916
War Diary	Trenches St Pierre Vaast under	19/12/1916	22/12/1916
War Diary	Camp 21 Suzanne	23/12/1916	27/12/1916

War Diary	Vauchelles Les Quesnoy	28/12/1916	16/01/1917
War Diary	Bray	17/01/1917	19/01/1917
War Diary	Suzanne	20/01/1917	20/01/1917
War Diary	Clery Sector	21/01/1917	31/01/1917
War Diary	Suzanne	01/02/1917	08/02/1917
War Diary	Bethune Road Sector	09/02/1917	12/02/1917
War Diary	Howitzer Wood	13/02/1917	16/02/1917
War Diary	Bethune Road Sector	17/02/1917	20/02/1917
War Diary	P.C. Madame	21/02/1917	23/02/1917
War Diary	Suzanne	24/02/1917	03/03/1917
War Diary	Right Sector	04/03/1917	08/03/1917
War Diary	Frise Bend	09/03/1917	09/03/1917
War Diary	Suzanne	10/03/1917	10/03/1917
War Diary	Camp 13.V	11/03/1917	31/03/1917
War Diary	Camp 13	01/04/1917	01/04/1917
War Diary	Corbie	02/04/1917	02/04/1917
War Diary	Villers-Bocage.	03/04/1917	03/04/1917
War Diary	Beuval	04/03/1917	05/04/1917
War Diary	Lucheux	06/04/1917	06/04/1917
War Diary	Saulty	07/04/1917	07/04/1917
War Diary	Basseux	08/04/1917	11/04/1917
War Diary	M. 35 C	12/04/1917	12/04/1917
War Diary	Henin	13/04/1917	14/04/1917
War Diary	Hindenburg	15/04/1917	15/04/1917
War Diary	Line	16/04/1917	17/04/1917
War Diary	M.35-C	18/04/1917	19/04/1917
War Diary	Trenches	20/04/1917	21/04/1917
War Diary	Mercatel	22/04/1917	22/04/1917
War Diary	Trenches	23/04/1917	23/04/1917
War Diary	Boiry Becquerelle	24/04/1917	25/04/1917
War Diary	Blairville	26/04/1917	26/04/1917
War Diary	Basseux.	27/04/1917	02/05/1917
War Diary	Adinfer	03/05/1917	11/05/1917
War Diary	Moyenneville	12/05/1917	14/05/1917
War Diary	St. Ledger	15/05/1917	18/05/1917
War Diary	R. Sub Sector	19/05/1917	19/05/1917
War Diary	T. 30.a	20/05/1917	21/05/1917
War Diary	Hindenburg Front Line	22/05/1917	22/05/1917
War Diary	T. 20.d.	23/05/1917	26/05/1917
War Diary	T. 20.d.	21/05/1917	21/05/1917
War Diary	Front Line	27/05/1917	28/05/1917
War Diary	Moyenville	29/05/1917	30/05/1917
War Diary	Basseux.	31/05/1917	31/05/1917
War Diary	Bailleulval	01/06/1917	18/06/1917
War Diary	Moyenneville	19/06/1917	19/06/1917
War Diary	Trenches	20/06/1917	24/06/1917
War Diary	Moyenneville	25/06/1917	25/06/1917
War Diary	Trenches	26/06/1917	30/06/1917
War Diary	Monchy-Au-Bois	01/07/1917	01/07/1917
War Diary	Acheux.	02/07/1917	02/07/1917
War Diary	Talmas	03/07/1917	03/07/1917
War Diary	Belloy-Sur-Somme	04/07/1917	04/07/1917
War Diary	Airaines	05/07/1917	31/07/1917
War Diary	Bray Dunes	01/08/1917	14/08/1917
War Diary	Oost Dunkerque	15/08/1917	16/08/1917
War Diary	Trenches	17/08/1917	27/08/1917

War Diary	La Panne		28/08/1917	28/08/1917
War Diary	Coudekerke Branch		29/08/1917	30/08/1917
War Diary	Moulle		31/08/1917	14/09/1917
War Diary	Wulverdinghe		15/09/1917	15/09/1917
War Diary	Steenvoorde		16/09/1917	16/09/1917
War Diary	Thieushouk		17/09/1917	19/09/1917
War Diary	Kenora Camp		20/09/1917	24/09/1917
War Diary	Trenches		25/09/1917	27/09/1917
War Diary	Dickebusch.		28/09/1917	28/09/1917
War Diary	Blarlinghem Area		29/09/1917	30/09/1917
Miscellaneous	Message Map.			
Miscellaneous	Message Form.			
War Diary	Blaringhem		01/10/1917	05/10/1917
War Diary	Acquin		06/10/1917	06/10/1917
War Diary	Kortepyp Camp		07/10/1917	07/10/1917
War Diary	Messines		08/10/1917	12/10/1917
War Diary	Front Line		13/10/1917	14/10/1917
War Diary	Neuve Eglise.		15/10/1917	18/10/1917
War Diary	Ypres		19/10/1917	25/10/1917
War Diary	Bulford Camp		26/10/1917	30/10/1917
War Diary	Support Trenches Left Sub-Sector		31/10/1917	31/10/1917
War Diary	Support Trenches		01/11/1917	02/11/1917
War Diary	Front Line		03/11/1917	07/11/1917
War Diary	Bulford Camp		08/11/1917	13/11/1917
War Diary	Line Of March		14/11/1917	14/11/1917
War Diary	Strazelle		15/11/1917	16/11/1917
War Diary	Line Of March		17/11/1917	17/11/1917
War Diary	White Chateau		18/11/1917	18/11/1917
War Diary	Potijze		19/11/1917	23/11/1917
War Diary	Paschendael		24/11/1917	30/11/1917
War Diary	Brandhoek		01/12/1917	06/12/1917
War Diary	Menin Gate		07/12/1917	10/12/1917
War Diary	Watou Area		11/12/1917	16/12/1917
War Diary	Watou Area		16/12/1917	21/12/1917
War Diary	Poperinghe		22/12/1917	27/12/1917
War Diary	Poperinghe		28/12/1917	29/12/1917
War Diary	Watou		30/12/1917	31/12/1917
War Diary	Watou Area		01/01/1918	02/01/1918
War Diary	Brandhoek		03/01/1918	04/01/1918
War Diary	Hamburg		05/01/1918	05/01/1918
War Diary	Passchendaele		06/01/1918	09/01/1918
War Diary	Ypres		10/01/1918	10/01/1918
War Diary	Brandhoek		11/01/1918	13/01/1918
War Diary	Whitby Camp		14/01/1918	26/01/1918
War Diary	Longuenesse		28/01/1918	31/01/1918
Heading	33rd Division 19th Infy Bde 18th Bn Royal Fusiliers Nov 1915-Feb 1916			
Heading	98th Brigade 33rd Division Disembarked Calais 14.11.15 Battalion transferred to 19th Infantry Brigade 27.11.15 18th Battalion Royal Fusiliers November 1915 Feb 1916			
War Diary	Tidworth		01/11/1915	13/11/1915
War Diary	Boulogne		14/11/1915	15/11/1915
War Diary	Thiennes		16/11/1915	16/11/1915
War Diary	Tannay		17/11/1915	18/11/1915
War Diary	Robecq		19/11/1915	19/11/1915

War Diary	Bethune	20/11/1915	20/11/1915
War Diary	Vermelles	21/11/1915	22/11/1915
War Diary	Annequin South	23/11/1915	25/11/1915
War Diary	Bethune	26/11/1915	30/11/1915
Heading	33rd Div 19th Bde. from 98th		
War Diary	Bethune	01/12/1915	01/12/1915
War Diary	Givenchy Section	02/12/1915	06/12/1915
War Diary	Essars	07/12/1918	10/12/1918
War Diary	Fontes	11/12/1915	27/12/1915
War Diary	Bethune	28/12/1915	28/12/1915
War Diary	Annequin Fosse	29/12/1915	29/12/1915
War Diary	Trenches Z 2	30/12/1915	31/12/1915
War Diary	Cambrin Trenches Z2 Sub Section	01/01/1916	04/01/1916
War Diary	Annequin South	05/01/1916	08/01/1916
War Diary	Fouquereuil	09/01/1916	14/01/1916
War Diary	Annequin North	15/01/1916	15/01/1916
War Diary	A.I. Sector	16/01/1916	23/01/1916
War Diary	Beuvry North	24/01/1916	28/01/1916
War Diary	B I Section	29/01/1916	30/01/1916
War Diary	Bethune	31/01/1916	31/01/1916
War Diary	Rue d'Aire Bethune	01/02/1916	06/02/1916
War Diary	Annequin S.	07/02/1916	11/02/1916
War Diary	Z.O.	12/02/1916	14/02/1916
War Diary	Bethune	15/02/1916	16/02/1916
War Diary	Z.O.	17/02/1916	22/02/1916
War Diary	Bethune	23/02/1916	26/02/1916
War Diary	Campagne	27/02/1916	29/02/1916
Heading	18th Royal Fus. Vol. 3		
Heading	33rd Division 19th Infy Bde. 20th Bn. Royal Fusiliers Nov 1916-Feb 1918 Disbanded 15.2.18		
Heading	19th Brigade 33rd Division Battalion disembarked Calais 14.11.15 Battalion transferred to 19th Brigade 27.11.15 20th Battalion Royal Fusiliers November 1915		
War Diary	Boulogne	14/11/1915	16/11/1915
War Diary	Thennes	19/11/1915	19/11/1915
War Diary	L'Ecleme	20/11/1915	20/11/1915
War Diary	Bethune	21/11/1915	21/11/1915
War Diary	Cambrin	22/11/1915	22/11/1915
War Diary	S. Annequin	23/11/1915	23/11/1915
War Diary	N. Annequin	24/11/1915	26/11/1915
War Diary	Bethune	27/11/1915	01/12/1915
War Diary	E.6.a.c.	04/12/1915	04/12/1915
War Diary	E.6.a.c. A.2	06/12/1915	06/12/1915
War Diary	A2	07/12/1915	10/12/1915
War Diary	Bethune	12/12/1915	12/12/1915
War Diary	Ham-En-Artois	14/12/1915	27/12/1915
War Diary	Bethune	28/12/1915	30/12/1915
War Diary	S. Annequin F 29 B	01/01/1916	04/01/1916
War Diary	Trenches Royal 14 Gun Street	05/01/1916	09/01/1916
War Diary	Bethune	10/01/1916	14/01/1916
War Diary	A 14 B	15/01/1916	19/01/1916
War Diary	Beuvry (a)	20/01/1916	23/01/1916
War Diary	A. 21.b-d	24/01/1916	29/01/1916
War Diary	Bethune	29/01/1916	31/01/1916
War Diary	Bethune (Ecole Michelet)	01/02/1916	07/02/1916
War Diary	Annequin Fosse F.29.d	07/02/1916	12/02/1916

War Diary	Z 2	13/02/1916	16/02/1916
War Diary	Annequin Fosse F. 29.d.	17/02/1916	19/02/1916
War Diary	Z 2	19/02/1916	22/02/1916
War Diary	Beuvry North	22/02/1916	22/02/1916
War Diary	F. 14.a.8.2	23/02/1916	29/02/1916
War Diary	A. 15.a.b.	29/02/1916	29/02/1916
War Diary	B I Subsection A. 15.a.b. (Trench map Area E)	01/03/1916	08/03/1916
War Diary	Lequesnoy	08/03/1916	08/03/1916
War Diary	F.8.b.71	08/03/1916	12/03/1916
War Diary	A. 21. b. & d	12/03/1916	17/03/1916
War Diary	Bethune	17/03/1916	25/03/1916
War Diary	Annequin South	26/03/1916	28/03/1916
War Diary	G. 4.a. & A.27.d.	28/03/1916	31/03/1916
War Diary	Auchy Right Subsection G.4. & and A. 27.d.	01/04/1916	01/04/1916
War Diary	Bethune	02/04/1916	04/04/1916
War Diary	Annequin South	04/04/1916	07/04/1916
War Diary	Auchy Right	07/04/1916	07/04/1916
War Diary	G. 4.b. and A. 27.d	07/04/1916	10/04/1916
War Diary	Bethune	11/04/1916	18/04/1916
War Diary	Le Quesnoy F.8.b.6.1	18/04/1916	18/04/1916
War Diary	Le Quesnoy (f.8.b.61)	19/04/1916	21/04/1916
War Diary	Cuinchy Left Subsection (Brick Stacks)	22/04/1916	22/04/1916
War Diary	Boyau 32 to La Basee Canal	22/04/1916	22/04/1916
War Diary	A. 21. B. 8.2. to A. 16.c.0.6	23/04/1916	26/04/1916
War Diary	Le Quesnoy F.g.b.2.8	27/04/1916	30/04/1916
War Diary	Coinchy left subsection (Bricks Tanks)	30/04/1916	30/04/1916
War Diary	Boyau 32. to La Bass Le Canal A. 21. B. 8.2.to A.16.c.0.6.	30/04/1916	04/05/1916
War Diary	Bethune (Rue d'aire)	05/05/1916	16/05/1916
War Diary	Auchy Left Sub Section Buyan 8 to Boyan 20 Both inclusive A. 27.d.8.7 to A.21.d.55.00	17/05/1916	22/05/1916
War Diary	Annequin South	23/05/1916	27/05/1916
War Diary	Auchy Left sub Section Buyan 8 to Boyan 20 A.27.d.8.7 to A.21.d.55.00	28/05/1916	29/05/1916
War Diary	A. 27.d.6.9	29/05/1916	30/05/1916
War Diary	Auchy Left Subsection Boyan 8 to Boyan 20 A. 27.d.8.7. to A.21.d.5.5.00	01/06/1916	02/06/1916
War Diary	Beuvry	02/06/1916	07/06/1916
War Diary	Oblinghem	08/06/1916	08/06/1916
War Diary	W. 20.c. and 26.a.	09/06/1917	17/06/1917
War Diary	Beuvry (North)	18/06/1916	20/06/1916
War Diary	Givenchy right Boyan 36 to Boyan 53 A. 22.a.0.s. to A.15.b.8.9	22/06/1916	22/06/1916
War Diary	Givenchy right subsection A. 22.a.0.6 to A. 15.b.8.9	23/06/1916	26/06/1916
War Diary	Village Line	26/06/1916	26/06/1916
War Diary	A.8.9.14.15	26/06/1916	27/06/1916
Heading	19th Inf Bde. 33rd Div. War Diary 20th Battn. The Royal Fusiliers. July 1916		
War Diary	Village Line	01/07/1916	02/07/1916
War Diary	Givenchy Right Subsection A. 22.a.6.0. to A.9.d.0.9.	02/07/1916	08/07/1916
War Diary	Annezin	08/07/1916	10/07/1916
War Diary	Poulainville	10/07/1916	10/07/1916
War Diary	Vecquemont	11/07/1916	11/07/1916
War Diary	Buire Sur L'Ancre	12/07/1916	14/07/1916
War Diary	Meaulte	14/07/1916	14/07/1916
War Diary	Mametz Wood	15/07/1916	16/07/1916

War Diary	Bazentin	16/07/1916	16/07/1916
War Diary	Mametz Wood	16/07/1916	17/07/1916
War Diary	Bazentin	18/07/1916	20/07/1916
War Diary	High Wood	20/07/1916	20/07/1916
War Diary	(Map Reference Martinpuich Area)	20/07/1916	20/07/1916
War Diary	Mametz Wood	21/07/1916	21/07/1916
War Diary	Buire Sur L'Ancre	22/07/1916	22/07/1916
War Diary	L'Ancre	23/07/1916	31/07/1916
Heading	19th Brigade. 33rd Division. 20th Battalion Royal Fusiliers August 1916		
War Diary	Buire Fus	01/08/1916	01/08/1916
War Diary	L'Ancre	05/08/1916	06/08/1916
War Diary	Meaulte E. 12. A.	07/08/1916	12/08/1916
War Diary	Mametz Wood	13/08/1916	13/08/1916
War Diary	S. 19.b. 5.5	14/08/1916	17/08/1916
War Diary	S. 9.c.9.0	18/08/1916	18/08/1916
War Diary	S. 10.b.60.75 to S. 10.b. 8.5	18/08/1916	18/08/1916
War Diary	S.9.c.9.0	19/08/1916	19/08/1916
War Diary	S.19.b.5.5	20/08/1916	22/08/1916
War Diary	Front Line	22/08/1916	22/08/1916
War Diary	S. 4.c.05.30 to S. 10.d.9.9	23/08/1916	26/08/1916
War Diary	Mametz Wood Sig b 5.5	27/08/1916	27/08/1916
War Diary	Montauban Alley A 16. 7.5. to S 26. c. 9.4. 28.	28/08/1916	28/08/1916
War Diary	Fricourt Wood	29/08/1916	30/08/1916
War Diary	Ribemont	30/08/1916	01/09/1916
War Diary	Molliens Au Bois	02/09/1916	02/09/1916
War Diary	Bernaville	03/09/1916	04/09/1916
War Diary	Bonnieres	05/09/1916	05/09/1916
War Diary	Oeuf	06/09/1916	06/09/1916
War Diary	Croisette	07/09/1916	08/09/1916
War Diary	Sibiville	09/09/1916	09/09/1916
War Diary	Le Souich	10/09/1916	10/09/1916
War Diary	Bienvillers Au Bois Pommiers	11/09/1916	12/09/1916
War Diary	Hannescamps	13/09/1916	13/09/1916
War Diary	Z section left subsection	16/09/1916	16/09/1916
War Diary	Bienvillers Au Bois	16/09/1916	21/09/1916
War Diary	Hannescamps	21/09/1916	21/09/1916
War Diary	Z section left subsection	22/09/1916	26/09/1916
War Diary	Bienvillers Au Bois	27/09/1916	28/09/1916
War Diary	Humber Camp	29/09/1916	30/09/1916
War Diary	Boullens	01/10/1916	10/10/1916
War Diary	Lucheux	11/10/1916	18/10/1916
War Diary	Ville-Sur-L'Ancre	18/10/1916	20/10/1916
War Diary	Citadel F. 21. B. (Albert Combined Sheet)	21/10/1916	21/10/1916
War Diary	Straight Trench T.R.D.C. 3 To T. 8.d.8.6	23/10/1916	25/10/1916
War Diary	Trench Map 57.c. S.W. T.5.a.b.8 To T.5.a.7.7	25/10/1916	27/10/1916
War Diary	T.9	28/10/1916	28/10/1916
War Diary	Albert Combined Left A. 2.d. 4.0.	30/10/1916	31/10/1916
War Diary	Albert Combined Sheet A. 2.d.4.0	01/11/1916	01/11/1916
War Diary	Carnoy	02/11/1916	02/11/1916
War Diary	Les Boeufs	03/11/1916	07/11/1916
War Diary	Briqueterie Camp A4b.3.7	08/11/1916	08/11/1916
War Diary	Meaulte	09/11/1916	11/11/1916
War Diary	Albert Combined Sheet 1/400000.	12/11/1916	12/11/1916
War Diary	Merelessart	12/11/1916	30/11/1916
War Diary	Merelessart	25/11/1916	06/12/1916

War Diary	Albert Combined Sheet 1/40.000	08/12/1916	08/12/1916
War Diary	Morlancourt	08/12/1916	08/12/1916
War Diary	Camp 112 L. 2.a 9.9	09/12/1916	09/12/1916
War Diary	Camp III L. 2.b.	10/12/1916	11/12/1916
War Diary	Priez Farm B.b.a. 4.4	14/12/1916	17/12/1916
War Diary	SE Of Rancourt. C.2.d.3.5 to C.3.c. 9.5	18/12/1916	20/12/1916
War Diary	Camp 21. L. 3.c.3.4	22/12/1916	31/12/1916
War Diary	Yaucourt Bussus (Sheet 14 Abbeville 1; 100,000)	01/01/1917	19/01/1917
War Diary	Camp 12 (K. 27 D)	19/01/1917	19/01/1917
War Diary	Albert Combined Sheet 1.400000	20/01/1917	20/01/1917
War Diary	Camp 13 (K. 22. c.)	20/01/1917	20/01/1917
War Diary	Camp 18 (G.10.d)	22/01/1917	22/01/1917
War Diary	Map. 62c. N.W. Edition	23/01/1917	23/01/1917
War Diary	Howitzer Wood (H. 3.b.5.1). Reserve Battalion Right Brigade.	23/01/1917	23/01/1917
War Diary	Right Sector (Right Instruction) H. 18.b.6.5. to I. 7.b.8.9. B H. 12. b.9.2	24/01/1917	26/01/1917
War Diary	Map 62.c. N.W. extra 4 Right Sector Right Subsection H. 18. B.6.5. to I, 7.b.8.9 B HQ. H. 12.b.9.2	27/01/1917	28/01/1917
War Diary	Right Brigade Reserve	28/01/1917	28/01/1917
War Diary	Frise Bend G. 18.b. Central	28/01/1917	28/01/1917
War Diary	Howitzer Wood Ommiecourt	29/01/1917	31/01/1917
War Diary	Map 62c. N.W. 1/20000 Edition H	01/02/1917	01/02/1917
War Diary	Frise Bend (G 18b Central)	02/02/1917	03/02/1917
War Diary	Camp 19 (G. 16.a.8.8)	04/02/1917	07/02/1917
War Diary	Left. Brigade Sector Right Instruction (C2.b. b.1.7 to. I. 2a.4.6	08/02/1917	11/02/1917
War Diary	Support Battalion to Left Brigade Road Wood (C. 25.A. C)	12/02/1917	15/02/1917
War Diary	Left Brigade Sector Right Sub Section	16/02/1917	16/02/1917
War Diary	Map 62c NW 1/20000 Edition 4 Left Brigade Sector Right Sub Section	16/02/1917	19/02/1917
War Diary	Howitzer Wood (H. 3.b)	21/02/1917	21/02/1917
War Diary	Suzanne (G 8.C)	23/02/1917	23/02/1917
War Diary	Suzanne (G.8.C)	22/02/1917	22/02/1917
War Diary	Map 62c N.W. 1/20000 Suzanne	01/03/1917	02/03/1917
War Diary	Frise Bend	03/03/1917	03/03/1917
War Diary	Clery Sector B.H.Q. At H.12.b.8.3	04/03/1917	07/03/1917
War Diary	In Support to Clery Sector B.H.Q. At H.6.a.7.6	08/03/1917	09/03/1917
War Diary	Ref Map. 62c N.W. 1/20000	10/03/1917	31/03/1917
War Diary	Camp 12 K.33.b.55	14/03/1917	19/03/1917
War Diary	Map Amiens 1/100.000	01/04/1917	01/04/1917
War Diary	Camp 12 Chipilly	01/04/1917	02/04/1917
War Diary	Corbie	03/04/1917	03/04/1917
War Diary	Bertangles	04/04/1917	04/04/1917
War Diary	Map Lens 1/100,000 Beauval	05/04/1917	05/04/1917
War Diary	Lucheux	06/04/1917	07/04/1917
War Diary	Humbercamp	08/04/1917	08/04/1917
War Diary	Bailleulval	09/04/1917	10/04/1917
War Diary	Bailleulmont	11/04/1917	11/04/1917
War Diary	Boisleux Au Mont	12/04/1917	12/04/1917
War Diary	In The Line	13/04/1917	16/04/1917
War Diary	Boyelles	22/04/1917	23/04/1917
War Diary	In Bde Reserve	24/04/1917	25/04/1917
War Diary	Boiry Becquerelle	26/04/1917	26/04/1917
War Diary	Boyelles	27/04/1917	27/04/1917

War Diary	Bailleulval	28/04/1917	30/04/1917
War Diary	In The Line	16/04/1917	17/04/1917
War Diary	Neuville Vitasse	18/04/1917	20/04/1917
War Diary	In The Line	21/04/1917	21/04/1917
War Diary	Bailleuval	01/05/1917	02/05/1917
War Diary	Adinfer	03/05/1917	12/05/1917
War Diary	Moyenville	13/05/1917	15/05/1917
War Diary	Line	16/05/1917	25/05/1917
War Diary	T22.a. & C	26/05/1917	30/05/1917
War Diary	Moyenville	31/05/1917	31/05/1917
War Diary	Ref. Map. Lens/ II Bellacourt	01/06/1917	18/06/1917
War Diary	Ref. Map. 51.B. S.W.	18/06/1917	18/06/1917
War Diary	Camp "A" Moyenneville A.5.a.2.4	19/06/1917	19/06/1917
War Diary	Ref. Map 51 R. S.W. In The Line	19/06/1917	19/06/1917
War Diary	In The Line	20/06/1917	25/06/1917
War Diary	Camp "C" Moyenneville (S. 28.d.3.9).	25/06/1917	28/06/1917
War Diary	Ref./Map. Lens II	29/06/1917	29/06/1917
War Diary	Monchy Au Bois	30/06/1917	02/07/1917
War Diary	Arqueves	03/07/1917	03/07/1917
War Diary	Naours	04/07/1917	04/07/1917
War Diary	Yzeux	05/07/1917	05/07/1917
War Diary	Airaines	06/07/1917	31/07/1917
War Diary	Ref. Map. Dunkerque	01/08/1917	01/08/1917
War Diary	Dunkerque	01/08/1917	01/08/1917
War Diary	Bray. Dunes.	02/08/1917	15/08/1917
War Diary	Oost Dunkerque	16/08/1917	16/08/1917
War Diary	Ref. Map. Lombartzyde 1/20:000	15/08/1917	15/08/1917
War Diary	Oost Dunkerque	16/08/1917	16/08/1917
War Diary	In The Line	17/08/1917	28/08/1917
War Diary	Ref. Map. Dunkerque I.A	28/08/1917	29/08/1917
War Diary	L.A. Panne	29/08/1917	29/08/1917
War Diary	P.K. Synthe	30/08/1917	31/08/1917
War Diary	Ref. Map. Hazebrouck 5a	01/09/1917	01/09/1917
War Diary	Houlle	01/09/1917	15/09/1917
War Diary	Lederzeele	16/09/1917	16/09/1917
War Diary	Steenvoorde	17/09/1917	17/09/1917
War Diary	Thieushouk	18/09/1917	20/09/1917
War Diary	Westoutre	21/09/1917	24/09/1917
War Diary	Ref. Map. Ypres. Edn. 3 1/10,000	25/09/1917	25/09/1917
War Diary	Ref. Map. Polygon Wood Edn. la	26/09/1917	28/09/1917
War Diary	Ref. Map. Hazebrouck 5a 1/100,000	29/09/1917	30/09/1917
War Diary	Ref Map Sheet 36 A 1/40,000	01/10/1917	01/10/1917
War Diary	Le Croquet	02/10/1917	03/10/1917
War Diary	Ref Map Hazebrouck 5a	04/10/1917	04/10/1917
War Diary	Vlamertinghe	04/10/1917	04/10/1917
War Diary	Ref Map Sheet 28 NW 1/20,000	04/10/1917	04/10/1917
War Diary	Vlamertinghe	05/10/1917	08/10/1917
War Diary	Ref Map Sheet 28 N.W. 1/20,000	09/10/1917	09/10/1917
War Diary	Vlamertinghe	10/10/1917	11/10/1917
War Diary	Ypres	12/10/1917	17/10/1917
War Diary	Ref. Map Hazebrouck 5.A. 1/100,000	17/10/1917	17/10/1917
War Diary	Neuve Eglise	17/10/1917	20/10/1917
War Diary	Ref. Map Sheet 28 S.W.	21/10/1917	31/10/1917
War Diary	Sheet 28 S.W. In Reserve	01/11/1917	02/11/1917
War Diary	In The Line	03/11/1917	04/11/1917
War Diary	Ref Map Sheet 28 S.W	04/11/1917	13/11/1917

War Diary	Strazeele Ref Maps Sheet 27 S.E. Sheet 36 A	14/11/1917	16/11/1917
War Diary	Ref. Map Sheet 28	17/11/1917	17/11/1917
War Diary	Potijze	18/11/1917	19/11/1917
War Diary	Ref Map Sheet 28	20/11/1917	20/11/1917
War Diary	Ref Map Zonnebeke 7a	24/11/1917	30/11/1917
War Diary	Ref Map Sheet 28 Brandhoek	01/12/1917	06/12/1917
War Diary	Potijzerd In Bde Reserve	07/12/1917	10/12/1917
War Diary	Ref Map Sheet 27 Watou	11/12/1917	20/12/1917
War Diary	Ref Map Sheet 28 Poperinghe	21/12/1917	28/12/1917
War Diary	Ref Map Sheet 27 Watou	29/12/1917	31/12/1917
War Diary		29/12/1917	29/12/1917
War Diary		10/12/1917	24/12/1917
War Diary		22/12/1917	22/12/1917
War Diary		11/12/1917	11/12/1917
War Diary		06/12/1917	29/12/1917
War Diary	Watou Sheet 27	01/01/1918	02/01/1918
War Diary	Brandhoek Sheet 28	03/01/1918	03/01/1918
War Diary	In Support Seine	04/01/1918	04/01/1918
War Diary	Right Sub-Sector Hamburg	05/01/1918	05/01/1918
War Diary	Ref. Map Sheet 28 Right Sub Sector	06/01/1918	09/01/1918
War Diary	Whitby Camp	09/01/1918	09/01/1918
War Diary	Brandhoek	10/01/1918	13/01/1918
War Diary	Ypres Brigade Support	14/01/1918	20/01/1918
War Diary	Seine In Support	21/01/1918	24/01/1918
War Diary	Ref. Map. Sheet 28 Alnwick Camp	25/01/1918	25/01/1918
War Diary	Ref. Map. Sheet 27a. St. Martin Au Laert	27/01/1918	31/01/1918
War Diary	Ref. Map Sheet 27A. S.E. St. Martin au. Laert.	01/02/1918	15/02/1918
War Diary	Ref. Map Sheet 27A S.E. St Martin au Laert.	15/02/1918	15/02/1918
Heading	20th Royal Fus Vol 3 Jan 16		
Heading	33rd Division 19th Infy Bde Trench Mortar Bty Jly-Aug 1916		
Heading	19th Brigade 33rd Division. 19th Brigade Light Trench Mortar Battery July 1916		
War Diary	Givenchy	01/07/1916	19/07/1916
War Diary	Mametz Wood	19/07/1916	31/07/1916
Heading	19th Brigade. 33rd Division. 19th Brigade Light Trench Mortar Battery August 1916		
War Diary	Buire	01/08/1916	12/08/1916
War Diary	Forcourt	13/08/1916	15/08/1916
War Diary	Highwood	16/08/1916	27/08/1916
War Diary	Fricourt	28/08/1916	31/08/1916
Heading	33rd Division 19th Infy Bde 19th Machine Gun Coy. Feb 1916-Jan 1918		
War Diary	In The Field	24/02/1916	30/06/1916
Heading	19th Inf. Bde. 33rd Div. War Diary 19th Machine Gun Company July 1916		
War Diary	In The Field	03/07/1916	31/07/1916
Heading	19th Brigade 33rd Division 19th Brigade Machine Gun Company August 1916		
War Diary	In The Field	01/08/1916	31/08/1916
War Diary	Field	01/09/1916	11/09/1916
War Diary	In The Field	11/09/1916	31/10/1916
Heading	War Diary Of 19th Machine Gun Company From 1st Nov 1916 To 30 Nov 1916		
War Diary	In The Field	01/11/1916	31/12/1916

Heading	War Diary of 19th Machine Gun Company From 1st Jan 1917 To Jan 31st 1917 Vol 12		
War Diary	In The Field	01/01/1917	06/01/1917
War Diary	Field	07/01/1918	31/01/1918
Heading	War Diary 19 M.G Coy From 19th M.G Coy To Headquarters 33rd Div. Vol 13		
War Diary	In The Field	01/02/1917	28/02/1917
Heading	19th Machine Gun Company War Diary for March 1917 Vol 14		
War Diary	In The Field	02/03/1917	06/03/1917
War Diary	Field	07/03/1917	31/03/1917
Heading	War Diary of 19th Machine Gun Company From 1/4/17 To 30/4/17 Vol 15		
War Diary	Field	01/04/1917	26/04/1917
War Diary	In The Field	27/04/1917	30/04/1917
Heading	19th Machine Gun Company War Diary for May 1917 Vol 16		
War Diary	Field	01/05/1917	05/06/1917
War Diary	In The Field	06/06/1917	31/07/1917
Heading	War Diary Of 19th Machine Gun Company From 1-9-17 to 30-9-17 Vol 20		
War Diary	In The Field	01/09/1917	31/10/1917
Heading	War Diary 19th Machine Gun Company Vol 22		
War Diary	In The Field	01/11/1917	30/11/1917
Heading	War Diary 19th Machine Gun Coy. Vol 23		
War Diary	Gotile	01/12/1917	10/12/1917
War Diary	Steenvoorde Beauvoorde Wood	11/12/1917	18/12/1917
War Diary	Steenvoorde	19/12/1917	23/12/1917
War Diary	Beauvoorde Wood	24/12/1917	31/12/1917
War Diary	Steenvoorde	01/01/1918	02/01/1918
War Diary	Brandhoek	03/01/1918	03/01/1918
War Diary	Potijze	04/01/1918	04/01/1918
War Diary	In The Line	05/01/1918	08/01/1918
War Diary	Potijze	09/01/1918	12/01/1918
War Diary	In The Field	13/01/1918	16/01/1918
War Diary	Potijze	17/01/1918	19/01/1918
War Diary	In The Line	20/01/1918	24/01/1918
War Diary	Potijze	25/01/1918	28/01/1918
War Diary	Val D'Acquin	29/01/1918	31/01/1918
Heading	33rd Div 20th Roy. Fus from 98 Vol 2		
Heading	2 R Welsh Fus Vol XX		
Heading	2 R Welsh Fus Vol XXI		

33RD DIVISION
19TH INFY BDE

2ND BN ROY. WELSH FUS.

DEC 1915 - DEC 1917 1918 JAN

FROM 2 DIVISION
SAME BDE

TO 38 DIV. 115 BDE   4.2.1918

19/33

2/Royal Welch Fus.

See.
Vol. XVII

171/793

17.N.

Whittlesea

Dec 15
pre 17

XXXIII Just 5 W

2nd Batt. Royal Welch Fusiliers.   Army Form C. 2118.

WAR DIARY
or
INTELLIGENCE SUMMARY.
(Erase heading not required.)

Hour, Date, Place	Summary of Events and Information	Remarks and references to Appendices
1. December 1915 QUESNOY	Moved from OBINGHEM to QUESNOY.	
2nd "	Remained in billets. Very wet.	Imt
3rd "	ditto	Imt
4th "	ditto	Imt
5th "	Very wet.	Imt
6th " GIVENCHY.	Relieved 1. Cameronians WINDY CORNER.	Imt
7th "	Variable weather. Comparative quiet.	Imt
8th "	Mine exploded front of 5. Scottish Rifles few casualties. 1 man wounded.	Imt
9th "	Weather bad. 3 slightly wounded.	Imt
10th " BETHUNE.	Relieved by Buffs & E. Surreys. Billets in Tobacco Factory. BETHUNE. 1 man wounded.	Imt
11th "	In billets Tobacco Factory.	Imt
12th " CORNET BOURDOIS.	Moved into billets at CORNET BOURDOIS. land flooded.	Imt
13th "	Fine weather, land partly under water.	Imt
14th "	In billets.	Imt

Army Form C. 2118.

WAR DIARY
or
INTELLIGENCE SUMMARY.

(Erase heading not required.)

Instructions regarding War Diaries and Intelligence Summaries are contained in F. S. Regs., Part II. and the Staff Manual respectively. Title pages will be prepared in manuscript.

Hour, Date, Place	Summary of Events and Information	Remarks and references to Appendices
15 December 1915 CORBIE BOURDOIS	In Billets.	Ind
16 "	In Billets. Brigade Route March.	Ind
17 "	In Billets.	Ind
18 "	In Billets.	Ind
19 "	In Billets.	Ind
20 "	In Billets. 19th Battalion passed through	
21 "	on march to ROBECQ.	Ind
21 "	In Billets — much rain.	Ind
22 "	In Billets — very wet.	Ind
23 "	In Billets — rain, heavy floods.	Ind
24 "	In Billets. In reply to a telegram despatched	Ind

23rd running as follows:—
The Equerry to H.M. The King,
Buckingham Palace,
London

all ranks of Royal Welch Fusiliers wish

Army Form C. 2118.

WAR DIARY
or
INTELLIGENCE SUMMARY.
(Erase heading not required.)

Instructions regarding War Diaries and Intelligence Summaries are contained in F. S. Regs., Part II. and the Staff Manual respectively. Title pages will be prepared in manuscript.

Hour, Date, Place	Summary of Events and Information	Remarks and references to Appendices
24th December 1915 CORNET BOURDOIS. (continued).	Their Colonel-in-Chief and Her Majesty a Merry Xmas and a Happy New Year. Commanding Officer.	
	The following was received "Thank you for the message to the Queen and myself. My best wishes to all ranks for 1916. George R.I. Colonel-in-Chief."	Ind
25th December 1915.	Christmas Day. 11 a.m. Church Parade. 12.30 p.m. Commanding Officer visited dinners.	
" " "	In billets.	Ind
26th " "	In billets.	Ind
27th " BETHUNE.	9.30 a.m. moved to fresh billets in RUE MICHELET BETHUNE.	
28th " BEUVRY.	10.30 a.m. moved to fresh billets in BEUVRY.	Ind
" " "	7.45 a.m. "A" and "C" Companies went in trenches Sub section Z.1. at CAMBRIN. On our right 18th.	Ind Ind

WAR DIARY
or
INTELLIGENCE SUMMARY.
(Erase heading not required.)

Army Form C. 2118.

Instructions regarding War Diaries and Intelligence Summaries are contained in F. S. Regs., Part II. and the Staff Manual respectively. Title pages will be prepared in manuscript.

Hour, Date, Place	Summary of Events and Information	Remarks and references to Appendices
29 December 1915. BEURY. (continued)	Royal Fusiliers on our Left. H. Cameronians. No 10154 Pte Tracey was killed from machine gun fire while wiring.	Init Init
30th December 1915	Quiet day.	
31st	Quiet day. One man wounded by sniper in evening at 4 pm an enquiry was received asking to the manner in which our front line to be cooperated with rifle and Lewis Gun fire. Enquiry reply.	Init

Formond Captain
Comdg 3rd Bn. Roy. Welch Fusiliers.

In the Field
January 1916.

18. V.
8 sheets

2nd Bn. Royal Welch Fusiliers

Army Form C. 2118.

WAR DIARY
or
INTELLIGENCE SUMMARY.
(Erase heading not required.)

Hour, Date, Place	Summary of Events and Information	Remarks and references to Appendices
1st January, 1916, BEUVRY.	Quiet day.	
2nd January, 1916. — "	CAMBRIN heavily shelled, Brigade Head Quarters in particular. A working party of "D" Company which was engaged on sandbagging Brigade Head Quarters and suffered the following casualties. Three men killed and three wounded. One man belonging to the Sapping Platoon billetted in CAMBRIN was also wounded.	
3rd January 1916. — "	Quiet on our immediate front, but CUINCHY was very heavily shelled.	
4th January 1916. — "	"A" and "C" Companies relieved by "B" and "D" Companies from BEUVRY.	
5th January, 1916. — "	Quiet day.	
6th January, 1916. — "	Quiet day.	
7th January, 1916.	Garrison of SIMS and ARTHURS KEEPS relieved by 2 platoons of "A" and "C" Companies respectively.	

Army Form C. 2118.

WAR DIARY
or
INTELLIGENCE SUMMARY.
(Erase heading not required.)

Instructions regarding War Diaries and Intelligence Summaries are contained in F. S. Regs., Part II. and the Staff Manual respectively. Title pages will be prepared in manuscript.

Hour, Date, Place	Summary of Events and Information	Remarks and references to Appendices
8th January, 1916 BEUVRY	Heavy shelling of CAMBRIN in the morning. At 3-30 p.m. Captain E. B. Benison arrived at Head Quarter trenches and took over command of the Battalion. Lieut Colonel I de L. Williams having been evacuated sick to England. Half Battalion in BEUVRY moved from BEUVRY S. to BEUVRY N. Reinforcement of 28 other ranks. The following with machine gun & disabled Major E. S. Owen, D.S.O. Captain W.L. Stanway, Captain C. Mordy, Lieut. J. C. Dunn, R.A.M.C., Lieut S. Hales, Sergeant Major J. Davies, Company Sergeant Major W. Fox, and Corporal Bate. No. 8800	
9th January, 1916 —	Battalion so far as in trenches relieved at 6-30. a.m. & Left Company and ARTHURSKEEP by 2/1st Royal Fusiliers Right Company by	

Army Form C. 2118.

WAR DIARY
or
INTELLIGENCE SUMMARY.
(Erase heading not required.)

Instructions regarding War Diaries and Intelligence Summaries are contained in F. S. Regs., Part II. and the Staff Manual respectively. Title pages will be prepared in manuscript.

Hour, Date, Place	Summary of Events and Information	Remarks and references to Appendices
9th January 1916 BEUPRY	1st Middlesex Regt. SIMS KEEP by 19th Royal Fusiliers, and joined the remainder of the Battalion at BEUPRY-N. in Billets.	ARC3
10th January 1916, BEUPRY	"	ARC3
11th January 1916	"	ARC3
12th January 1916	"	ARC3
13th January 1916	In billets	ARC3
14th January 1916	In billets	ARC3
15th January 1916	In billets. Route March BETHUNE-OBLINGHEM-ANNEQUIN(N) relieving 18th Royal Fusiliers at 5.p.m. The following honours were awarded to members of the Battalion:- Military Cross:- Captain W.H. Stoway, Captain F. Moody and Sergeant Major J. Davis. Distinguished Conduct Medal:- 2nd Lieut: J. McKay, Sergeant Heaney, Lance Corporal A. Westcott, and Private J. Moss.	ARC3

Army Form C. 2118.

Army Form C. 2118.

WAR DIARY
or
INTELLIGENCE SUMMARY.
(Erase heading not required.)

Instructions regarding War Diaries and Intelligence Summaries are contained in F. S. Regs., Part II. and the Staff Manual respectively. Title pages will be prepared in manuscript.

Hour, Date, Place	Summary of Events and Information	Remarks and references to Appendices
16th January, 1916. ANNEQUIN.	In billets. Working parties all day.	ER03
17th January, 1916. — " —	In billets	ER03
18th January, 1916. — " —	In billets	ER03
19th January, 1916. — " —	In billets	ER03
20th January, 1916. — " —	Relieved 1st Camerons in CUINCHY trenches in sub-section immediately south of the canal.	ER03
21st January, 1916. CUINCHY.	Enemy minen werfer very active in the morning. Reinforcement of 21 other ranks.	ER03
22nd January, 1916. — " —	Very heavy trench mortaring by the enemy during the morning.	ER03
23rd January, 1916. — " —	Fairly quiet day. Combined artillery and Lewis Gun fire at 9 p.m. by us. A German working party just south of the canal.	ER03
24th January, 1916. — " —	Except for some trench mortaring in the morning, quiet day.	ER03

Army Form C. 2118.

WAR DIARY
or
INTELLIGENCE SUMMARY.
(Erase heading not required.)

Hour, Date, Place	Summary of Events and Information	Remarks and references to Appendices
25th January 1916. CUINCHY.	During the evening 2nd Lieut. ELFR Kelly and 5 grenadiers went out to see if the enemy was wiring some new stakes which looked observed the day before. The enemy were found and heavy bombed. Three at least were accounted for and groans were heard. The artillery by previous arrangement, cooperated with accuracy.	ZZC3
26th January 1916 — " —	Hostile minen werfers and trench mortars very active. Much damage done to trenches. Hostile Artillery also active. Casualty Captain A.P.R. Robertson killed by minen werfer.	ZZC3
27th January 1916 — " —	Hostile minen werfer etc. again very active, also enemy artillery. The Battalion moved into ANNEQUIN NORTH.	ZZC3

Army Form C. 2118.

WAR DIARY
or
INTELLIGENCE SUMMARY.
(Erase heading not required.)

Hour, Date, Place	Summary of Events and Information	Remarks and references to Appendices
28th January 1916. ANNEQUIN(B)	In billets	A203
29th January 1916 — "	The Battalion moved into billets at FOUQUEREUIL.	BR13
30th January 1916. FOUQUEREUIL.	In billets.	BR03
31st January 1916 — "	In billets. Lieut. Col. O. de L. Williams arrived back and took over command of the Battalion. Lieut. Col. E. B. Benison left to take over command of the 21st Bn. Royal Fusiliers.	A203

Ol Williams
Lieut. Colonel.
Commandg. 2nd Bn. Royal Welch Fus.rs

In the Field
1st February 1916

Army Form C. 2118.

2nd Bn Royal Welch Fus.

WAR DIARY
or
INTELLIGENCE SUMMARY.
(Erase heading not required.)

Instructions regarding War Diaries and Intelligence Summaries are contained in F.S. Regs., Part II. and the Staff Manual respectively. Title pages will be prepared in manuscript.

Hour, Date, Place	Summary of Events and Information	Remarks and references to Appendices
1st February, 1916. FOUQUEREUIL.	In billets.	
2nd February, 1916. " "	In Billets.	
3rd February, 1916. " "	In Billets.	
4th " " " "	In Billets.	
5th " " " "	In billets at ANNEQUIN FOSSE. An assault was carried out on a mine crater in subsection Z 2 by "B" Company, under Captain W.A. Starway, Lieut J.W. Owen, 2/Lieut G.W. Beuterse & Lieut & R.S.R. Rolling. Commenced at 9-45 p.m. Our Bombers were very effective. The Bayonet men consolidated. The Enemy retaliated with bombs, rifle grenades, trench mortars, rifle fire and shell fire. Consolidation continued until 4 a.m. when relieved by another party under 2/Lieut J.R.C. Barrett & 2/Lieut R.A. Hatters. Enemy loophole plates were forced in the lip of the crater taken, enabling them to fire at a range of 35 yards and enfilade. Steel helmets were	

Army Form C. 2118/11.

Army Form C. 2118.

WAR DIARY
or
INTELLIGENCE SUMMARY.
(Erase heading not required.)

Instructions regarding War Diaries and Intelligence Summaries are contained in F. S. Regs., Part II. and the Staff Manual respectively. Title pages will be prepared in manuscript.

Hour, Date, Place	Summary of Events and Information	Remarks and references to Appendices
6th February, 1916. ANNEQUIN FOSSE	Very satisfactory. Casualties. Lt. J. M. Olver wounded. 2/Lt. S. R. R. Rolling slightly wounded, 8 other ranks killed, 28 other ranks wounded.	
	Consolidation of craters continued. Lt. Colonel O. De L. Williams D.S.O. took over command of 10th Infy. Brigade.	JMN
7th February, 1916. CAMBRIN	In Trenches, relieved 1st "Queens". Consolidation of craters continued. Crater handed over to 5/Scottish Rifles. 2nd Lieut. W. J. M. Williams killed. Lieut. H. M. Smith & 2nd Lieut. J. O. Caldwell wounded. 2nd Lieut. S. R. F. R. Rolling & 2nd Lieut. S. Harris to hospital.	JMN
8th February, 1916. — . —	Trenches. Fine weather. 2nd Lieut. McStay wounded on patrol.	JMN
9th February, 1916. — . —	Trenches. Fine weather. Patrol went out under 2nd Lieut. R. H. Morris who was grazed. The following from the Major General, 33rd Division. - 10-2-16.	JMN

Army Form C. 2118.

WAR DIARY
or
INTELLIGENCE SUMMARY.
(Erase heading not required.)

Instructions regarding War Diaries and Intelligence Summaries are contained in F. S. Regs., Part II. and the Staff Manual respectively. Title pages will be prepared in manuscript.

Hour, Date, Place	Summary of Events and Information	Remarks and references to Appendices
10th February 1916, CAMBRIN	The Major General considers the determination shown by the patrol of 2nd Royal Welsh Fusiliers who reconnoitred German trench near MAD POINT worthy of the tradition of the regiment and wishes all concerned to know this. In trenches	
11th " "	Relieved by 18th Royal Fusiliers, and went to billets in ANNEQUIN SOUTH. Lieut W. Williams slightly wounded	
12th " " ANNEQUIN SOUTH	In billets.	
13th " "	In billets.	
14th " "	In billets. 2nd Lieut A. M. Smith rejoined.	
15th " "	In billets.	
16th " "	In billets. 1 other rank killed.	
18th " "	Relieved 1st Cameronians in Z.1 (A.27d. A.27.2.) following suit. message received from Brig. General, 1st Corps:- With reference to the report of the capture and consideration of	

Army Form C. 2118.

WAR DIARY
or
INTELLIGENCE SUMMARY.
(Erase heading not required.)

Instructions regarding War Diaries and Intelligence Summaries are contained in F. S. Regs., Part II. and the Staff Manual respectively. Title pages will be prepared in manuscript.

Hour, Date, Place	Summary of Events and Information	Remarks and references to Appendices
	The craters by "C" Company on the 5th February. The Corps Commander considers that the operation was well organized and gallantly carried out and that it reflects the greatest credit on Lt-Colonel O. de L. Williams, D.S.O. & Captain Stanway and all concerned. He wishes them to be informed of the satisfaction he felt on reading of their exploit." AAA Ends.	
19th February, 1916. CAMBRIN.	On trenches. One other rank wounded. One other rank killed.	JCW
20th —"— —"—	In trenches. British Aeroplane brought down by rifle fire	JCW
21st —"— —"—	near CUINCHY CHURCH.	
—"— —"— BETHUNE.	Relieved by 19th Royal Fusiliers.	
22nd —"— —"—	In billets. MONTMORENCY BARRACKS.	JCW
23rd —"— —"—	In billets	JCW
24th —"— —"—	In billets	JCW
25th —"— —"—	In billets. Captain J. C. Wynne-Edwards struck off the strength. (Sick on leave.) The following message	JCW

Form/C. 2118/11

WAR DIARY
or
INTELLIGENCE SUMMARY.
(Erase heading not required.)

Army Form C. 2118.

Hour, Date, Place	Summary of Events and Information	Remarks and references to Appendices
26th February 1916. BETHUNE.	Received:— Following from 33rd Division. "The Commander in Chief has awarded decorations to the following Officers N.C.O's and men AAA. Military Cross. 2nd Lieut. C.R.J. Rolling AAA. Distinguished Conduct Medals. 9339 Cpl. J. Bate, 7851 Cpl. A. Aden, 6584, Pte. R. Richards, 10390 Pte. E. Barrett. 19740 Pte. Nuttall AAA General Officer Commanding 33rd Division sends congratulations AAA General Officer Commanding 19th Infantry Brigade sends congratulations.	
27th " " "	Lieut R.J.A. Bowles and Lieut L.J. Wolff joined.	Fine
28th " " "	In Billets.	Fine
28th " " "	In Billets.	Fine
29th " " "	In Billets.	Fine
	In Billets.	Fine

J B W Williams
Lt Colonel
Comdg 1/5 R Welsh Fus

1st March 1916.

Confidential.

2nd Bn. Royal Welch Fusiliers.

Army Form C. 2118.

WAR DIARY
of
INTELLIGENCE SUMMARY.
(Erase heading not required.)

Instructions regarding War Diaries and Intelligence Summaries are contained in F.S. Regs., Part II. and the Staff Manual respectively. Title pages will be prepared in manuscript.

Hour, Date, Place	Summary of Events and Information	Remarks and references to Appendices
1st March 1915 D. ANNEQUIN NORTH	Moved to ANNEQUIN NORTH to relieve 1st Cameronians.	Jm
2nd "	In Billets.	Jm
3rd "	1st R. Bns. 2nd Gjerk Dellies relieved 1st Black	Jm
4th "	In Billets.	Jm
5th "	In Billets.	Jm
6th "	Trenches relieved 1st Cameronians, evening quiet.	Jm
7th " QUINCHY	Trenches quiet. We exploded a mine at 5.45 p.m. a 30 yds South of LA BASSÉE Road & 50 yds outside our wire.	Jm
8th "	(1 Cameron) 1 Other Rank wounded.	
9th "	Trenches.	Jm
10th "	Trenches. 2 Other Ranks wounded.	Jm
11th "	Trenches. 2nd Gjerk Exeter arrived.	Jm
12th " ANNEQUIN NORTH	Relieved by 1st Cameronians. 1 Other Rank wounded.	Jm
13th "	In Billets.	Jm
14th "	In Billets.	Jm
15th " QUINCHY	Trenches O.2.	Jm

Army Form C. 2118.

WAR DIARY
or
INTELLIGENCE SUMMARY.
(Erase heading not required.)

Instructions regarding War Diaries and Intelligence Summaries are contained in F. S. Regs., Part II. and the Staff Manual respectively. Title pages will be prepared in manuscript.

Hour, Date, Place	Summary of Events and Information	Remarks and references to Appendices
15th ... 1915 OUIMCHY	Trenches 1 other Rank killed.	
16	Relieved by 4th Kings. 5 other Ranks wounded.	
17th BETHUNE	Billeted in Montmorency Barracks. Casuals 2 O.R. Wagons	
	Sports Arrival.	
	in Billets.	
19	in Billets. Capt A R Edmonds & 2nd Lieut Whipp arrived	
20	in Billets.	
	in Billets. Inspection by 2nd in command & 1 new officers arrived	
	in Billets.	
22	in Billets. 2nd Lieut R. Gardiner and J arrived	
23	in Billets. Bataillon R.W. Levinshirds	
	in Billets.	
	in Billets	
BEUVRY to Festubert. BEUVRY One Company with ?
	Barricades at WIMPOLE ST	
25	in Billets	
	in Billets	

(9 29 6) W 2794 100,000 8/14 H W V Form C. 2118/11

WAR DIARY
or
INTELLIGENCE SUMMARY.
(Erase heading not required.)

Army Form C. 2118

Hour, Date, Place	Summary of Events and Information	Remarks and references to Appendices
28th March 1916 BEUVRY.	In Billets.	Jw
29 CAMBRIN.	Relieved 1st Cameronians in AUCHY Left. 2 Other	Jw
30th " "	Ranks slightly wounded. In Trenches	Jw
31st " "	In Trenches.	Jw

HMWilliams Lieut. Colonel
Comdg. 2nd Bn. Royal Welch Fusiliers.

1st April 1916.

Loyal North Lancs ~Confidential~

Army Form C. 2118.

WAR DIARY
or
INTELLIGENCE SUMMARY.
(Erase heading not required.)

Instructions regarding War Diaries and Intelligence Summaries are contained in F.S. Regs., Part II. and the Staff Manual respectively. Title pages will be prepared in manuscript.

Hour, Date, Place	Summary of Events and Information	Remarks and references to Appendices
1st April 1916 BUSHNEY huts	The trenches Captain & J Jones reported his arrival.	
	2 Other Ranks wounded.	Feu
	In trenches. 2nd Lieut. & Foster and 8 Other ranks went	Feu
	out at 2 a.m. and bombed enemy sap East of MIDNIGHT	
	CRATER. The raid was successful as groans were heard	
	and the party returned in safety.	
3rd	In billets at BEUVRY.	Feu
4	In billets.	Feu
5	In billets.	Feu
6	Relieved 1st Ba[tt]. the Cameronians in AUCHY LEFT Sub-section.	Feu
AUCHY LEFT Sub-section	In trenches.	Feu
6	Mine blown up by us at 2 a.m. 8 Other Ranks wounded. Two	Feu
	small raids were carried out simultaneously. The right	
	one under 2nd Lieut. J.R.E. Barrett bombed an enemy sap, and	
	the left one under 2nd Lieut. & Foster did likewise.	
7	Mine blown up by the enemy at 8.30 a.m. 1 Other Rank	Feu
	killed and 7 Other Ranks wounded.	

Forms C. 2118/11.

Army Form C. 2118.

WAR DIARY
INTELLIGENCE SUMMARY.
(Erase heading not required.)

Instructions regarding War Diaries and Intelligence Summaries are contained in F.S. Regs., Part II. and the Staff Manual respectively. Title pages will be prepared in manuscript.

Hour, Date, Place		Summary of Events and Information	Remarks and references to Appendices
10th April 1916	AUCHY LEFT Sub-section	Relieved by 2nd Bn. Argyle & Sutherland Highlanders.	—
11th	ANNEZIN	In billets.	—
12th	— " —	In billets.	—
13th	— " —	In billets.	—
14th	— " —	In billets.	—
15th	— " —	In billets. Commanding Officer's route march.	—
16th	— " —	In billets. Sunday Church Parade.	—
17th	— " —	In billets.	—
18th	— " —	Moved to fresh billets at ANNEQUIN.	—
19th	ANNEQUIN	In billets.	—
20th	— " —	In billets.	—
21st	— " —	In billets.	—
22nd	— " —	Relieved 5th Bn. Scottish Rifles in CUINCHY RIGHT Sub-section	—
23rd	CUINCHY RIGHT Sub-section	In trenches. 1 Other Rank killed, 1 Other Rank wounded.	—

WAR DIARY

INTELLIGENCE SUMMARY.

(Erase heading not required.)

Army Form C. 2118.

Instructions regarding War Diaries and Intelligence Summaries are contained in F.S. Regs., Part II. and the Staff Manual respectively. Title pages will be prepared in manuscript.

Hour, Date, Place	Summary of Events and Information	Remarks and references to Appendices
24th April, 1916. CUNCHY RIGHT Sub-section	Nil	
25th " "	Raid carried out in two places on CUINCHY Right. The right party under Lieut D. W. Morgan and 2nd Lieut R.A. Morris, 30 Other Ranks. The left party, 2nd Lieut C.R. J. R. Bolling, 2nd Lieut J.R. Corning and 25 Other Ranks. Both parties left the lines at 10 p.m. after a 15 minutes bombardment. The Northern party entered the enemy trench a few yards South of LA BASSEE Road. This party captured a German anti-gas apparatus and a rifle, and accounted for several of the enemy. The Southern party was held up by enemy wire and only a few of the party entered the trench. Casualties:- 4 Officers; Lieut D.W. Morgan, 2nd Lieut C.R. J.R. Bolling, 2nd Lieut R.A. Morris, wounded. 2nd Lieut J.R. Corning slightly wounded. 3 Other Ranks Missing; believed killed. 18 Other Ranks wounded.	Nil
26th " "	Relieved by 5th Leinster Rifles. In billets at ANNEQUIN.	Nil

WAR DIARY
INTELLIGENCE SUMMARY.
(Erase heading not required.)

Army Form C. 2118.

Hour, Date, Place	Summary of Events and Information	Remarks and references to Appendices
27th April, 1916. ANNEQUIN.	In billets.	Fine
28th " "	In billets. Gas smelt at 4 a.m. 1 Other Rank wounded.	Fine
29th " "	In billets. 2 Other ranks wounded.	Fine
30th " "	Relieved 5th Scottish Rifles. CUINCHY RIGHT. 1 Other Rank died of wounds.	Fine

O.S. Flower
Lieut-Colonel.
Commanding 2nd Bn. Royal Welch Fusiliers

1st May, 1916.

Confidential.

3rd Bde Royal Welch Fusiliers. 2 Bn W W Fus

WAR DIARY
of
INTELLIGENCE SUMMARY

Army Form C. 2118

(Erase heading not required.)

Instructions regarding War Diaries and Intelligence Summaries are contained in F. S. Regs., Part II. and the Staff Manual respectively. Title Pages will be prepared in manuscript.

22-N
3 sheets

Place	Date	Hour	Summary of Events and Information	Remarks and references to Appendices
CUINCHY RIGHT	1-5-16		In trenches. Four Other ranks, wounded, slightly, at duty.	9 Appx 3
— " —	2-5-16		In trenches.	9 Appx
— " —	3-5-16		In trenches.	9 Appx
— " —	4-5-16		Enemy trench mortars bombarded South of LA BASSEE Road at 3.30 a.m. Relieved by 4 Bn. Suffolk Regt.	9 Appx
BETHUNE	5-5-16		In billets at MONTMORENCY BARRACKS. Captain A.M. Blair rejoined from hospital.	9 Appx
— " —	6-5-16		In billets.	9 Appx
— " —	7-5-16		In billets.	9 Appx
— " —	8-5-16		In billets.	9 Appx
— " —	9-5-16		In billets.	9 Appx
— " —	10-5-16		In billets. Brigade route march.	9 Appx
— " —	11-5-16		In billets. Captain J.U. Higginson. Lieut. 9 & H Radford rejoined from hospital.	9 Appx
— " —	12-5-16		In billets.	9 Appx
— " —	13-5-16		In billets.	9 Appx

Army Form C. 2118

WAR DIARY
INTELLIGENCE SUMMARY
(Erase heading not required.)

Instructions regarding War Diaries and Intelligence Summaries are contained in F. S. Regs., Part II. and the Staff Manual respectively. Title Pages will be prepared in manuscript.

Place	Date	Hour	Summary of Events and Information	Remarks and references to Appendices
BETHUNE	14-5-16	—	In billets.	9/4345
"	15-5-16	—	In billets.	9/4345
"	16-5-16	—	Relieved 2nd Bn. Worcester Regt. in AUCHY RIGHT.	9/4345
AUCHY RIGHT	17-5-16	—	In trenches. Two other ranks killed. Four other ranks wounded.	9/4345
"	18-5-16	—	In trenches. Two other ranks wounded.	9/4345
"	19-5-16	—	In trenches. Three other ranks wounded. 2nd Lieut. A.E. Banks wounded.	9/4345
"	20-5-16	—	In trenches. Two other ranks wounded.	9/4345
"	21-5-16	—	In trenches. Two other ranks killed.	9/4345
"	22-5-16	—	Relieved by 15th Scottish Rifles. One other rank wounded.	9/4345
BEUVRY	23-5-16	—	In billets.	9/4345
"	24-5-16	—	In billets.	9/4345
"	25-5-16	—	In billets. One other rank wounded.	9/4345
"	26-5-16	—	In billets. Captain C. Price Edwards arrived. Two other ranks wounded.	9/4345
"	27-5-16	—	In billets.	9/4345

Army Form C. 2118

WAR DIARY
of
INTELLIGENCE SUMMARY
(Erase heading not required.)

Instructions regarding War Diaries and Intelligence Summaries are contained in F. S. Regs., Part II. and the Staff Manual respectively. Title Pages will be prepared in manuscript.

Place	Date	Hour	Summary of Events and Information	Remarks and references to Appendices
BEUVRY	28-5-16	—	In billets. Relief postponed.	9/x/15
—	29-5-16	—	Relieved 1/5th Scottish Rifles in AUCHY RIGHT.	9/x/15
AUCHY RIGHT	30-5-16	—	In trenches. One other rank killed. One other rank wounded. 1 Company 2/5 Warwick Regt. attached.	9/x/15
—	31-5-16	—	In trenches. 37 Other ranks arrived. One other rank wounded. Enemy rifle grenades fairly active during the morning. Enemy were bombarded during the night.	9/x/15

1st June, 1916

J.R. Minshull ___
Lieut-Colonel,
Commdg. 2nd Bn Royal Welsh Fusiliers.

WAR DIARY
INTELLIGENCE SUMMARY

(Erase heading not required.)

Army Form C. 2118

2 R W F

Vol 23

Place	Date	Hour	Summary of Events and Information	Remarks and references to Appendices
AUCHY RIGHT.	1-6-16	-	In trenches. Everything quiet. 2 Other Ranks wounded.	—
—"—	2-6-16	-	In trenches. 2 Other Ranks killed. 2 Other Ranks wounded.	—
—"—	3-6-16	-	Relieved by 1/5th Scottish Rifles. 10 killed at ANNEQUIN SOUTH.	—
ANNEQUIN S.	4-6-16	-	In billets.	—
—"—	5-6-16	-	In billets.	—
—"—	6-6-16	-	In billets. 2nd Lieut. J.A. Crosland & 2nd Lieut. E.J. Rowland joined.	—
—"—	7-6-16	-	In billets. 2nd Lieut. A.G. Ford & 2nd Lieut. R.A.R. Hollingbery joined.	—
—"—	8-6-16	-	In billets. Lieut. Col. O. de L. Williams, D.S.O. left to assume temporary command of the 92nd Infantry Brigade. 1 Other Rank wounded, slightly, at duty.	—
—"—	9-6-16	-	Relieved by 9th Highland Light Infantry.	—
BEUVRY	10-6-16	-	In billets. 2nd Lieut. A.K. Jones wounded.	—
—"—	11-6-16	-	Relieved 2nd Argyll & Sutherland Hdrs in Rue D'Aire, BETHUNE.	—
BETHUNE.	12-6-16	-	In billets.	—
—"—	13-6-16	-	In billets.	—
—"—	14-6-16	-	In billets. Major C.H.R. Crawshay assumes temporary command of the Battalion.	—

Army Form C. 2118

WAR DIARY
or
INTELLIGENCE SUMMARY
(Erase heading not required.)

Instructions regarding War Diaries and Intelligence Summaries are contained in F. S. Regs., Part II. and the Staff Manual respectively. Title Pages will be prepared in manuscript.

Place	Date	Hour	Summary of Events and Information	Remarks and references to Appendices
BETHUNE.	15-6-16	—	In billets.	—
—"—	16-6-16	—	In billets.	—
—"—	17-6-16	—	Relieved A/5th Black Watch in GORRE.	—
GORRE	18-6-16	—	In billets.	—
—"—	19-6-16	—	In billets.	—
—"—	20-6-16	—	Relieved 4th Suffolk Regt. in GIVENCHY LEFT. 5 Other Ranks wounded during relief.	—
GIVENCHY LEFT.	22-6-16	—	At 2-5 a.m. the enemy exploded a mine on the Right of GIVENCHY LEFT, sender "B" Company's front line, wrecking completely about 80 yards of the line and doing considerable damage to the support line. At the same time a very intense bombardment was put up by the enemy on the front line, support line & Battalion Headquarters, of all calibres up to 8". This lasting for 1½ hours, after which, the enemy attacked about 150 men and entered our front trench, but were promptly ovicted by the small remnant of 'B' Company left after the mine explosion and bombardment. Casualties. 1 Officer killed, 2nd Lieut A. C. Banks, who killed 4 Germans before	—

WAR DIARY
or
INTELLIGENCE SUMMARY
(Erase heading not required.)

Army Form C. 2118

Place	Date	Hour	Summary of Events and Information	Remarks and references to Appendices
GIVENCHY LEFT	22-6-16		before being killed, 3 Officers missing; Captain A. M. Blair since recovered, having been found buried by debris for 24 hours, Captain C. Prise Edwards, and 2nd Lieut J. A. Crosland also Company Sergeant-Major P. Pattison and 25 other Ranks missing, 34 other Ranks wounded and 8 Other Ranks killed. 'B' Company relieved by 'A' Company, 1st tomorrow. The following messages were received:— To 19th Infantry Brigade. "The Major General instructs me to say that he has heard with pride of the fine conduct and bearing of the 2nd Bn. Royal Welsh Fusiliers under most trying circumstances last night, and he wishes his appreciation to be expressed to the Battalion." "The Corps Commander also desires to warmly congratulate them." (Sd) A. Symons, Lieut-Colonel General Staff. To 2nd Bn. Royal Welsh Fusiliers.	

WAR DIARY
INTELLIGENCE SUMMARY
(Erase heading not required.)

Army Form C. 2118

Instructions regarding War Diaries and Intelligence Summaries are contained in F. S. Regs., Part II. and the Staff Manual respectively. Title Pages will be prepared in manuscript.

Place	Date	Hour	Summary of Events and Information	Remarks and references to Appendices
GIVENCHY LEFT	22-6-16		Forwarded aaa. The Brigadier wishes to again and his congratulations and to say how proud he is of the conduct of the Battalion. (Sd) E. H. Faris, Major. 19th Infantry Brigade. The following Officers, Non-commissioned Officers and men showed determined courage in driving the enemy out and in the consolidation:— Captain W. A. Stannway, Lieut. J. L. W. Craig, Lieut. W. Williams, No. 8749 Sergeant P. Roderick, 8672 Sergeant C. Rush, 9147 Corporal D. Davis, 9198 Private J. Lane, 36481 Lance Corporal B. Knight, 8043 Private W. Walsh, 11275 Private A. Jones, 10344 Private 916 Dyce, 9468 Private F. Bond, 8320 Private T. Morgan.	Tim
GIVENCHY LEFT	24/6/16		Quiet. Consolidation in progress. 10 Other ranks wounded.	Tim
	24.6.16		Consolidation continued. 3 Other ranks wounded (includes 1 Other Rank died of wounds)	Tim
	25.6.16		Consolidation continued. All damage to C and D Companys' trenches repaired. 1 Other rank wounded.	Tim

Army Form C. 2118

WAR DIARY
or
INTELLIGENCE SUMMARY
(Erase heading not required.)

Instructions regarding War Diaries and Intelligence Summaries are contained in F. S. Regs., Part II. and the Staff Manual respectively. Title Pages will be prepared in manuscript.

Place	Date	Hour	Summary of Events and Information	Remarks and references to Appendices
GIVENCHY LEFT	26.6.16		In trenches. 2 Other Ranks wounded	JCu
—"—	27.6.16		In trenches. 6 Other Ranks wounded (includes 1 Other Rank died of wounds.)	JCu
—"—			Relieved by 1/5th Scottish Rifles. To billets in LE PREOL	JCu
LE PREOL	28.6.16		In billets.	JCu
—"—	29.6.16		In billets.	JCu
—"—	30.6.16		In billets.	JCu

C. Cannon
Major.

Comdg. 2nd Bn. Royal Welsh Fusiliers.

19th Inf.Bde.
33rd Div.

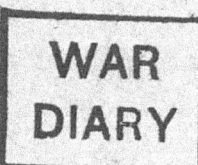

2nd BATTN. THE ROYAL WELCH FUSILIERS.

J U L Y

1 9 1 6

WAR DIARY
or
INTELLIGENCE SUMMARY

Place	Date	Hour	Summary of Events and Information	Remarks and references to Appendices
LE PREOL	1.7.16	—	In billets. Captain W.A. Stanway granted temporary command of 1/6th Cheshire Regt. with temporary rank of Lieut. Colonel. 1 Other ranks wounded.	Jun
LE PREOL	2.7.16	—	In billets.	Jun
" "	3.7.16	—	Relieved the 5th Scottish Rifles in GIVENCHY LEFT. Captains J. Ormrod and R.J. Rigg left for England. 2 Other ranks wounded.	Jun
" "	4.7.16	—	In trenches. Lieut. Colonel W.A. Stanway left for 1/6 Cheshire Regt. The following awards for the night 21/22nd June were published:– Distinguished Service Order;– Captain W.A. Stanway. Military Crosses;– Lieut. & A/Capt J.L. W. Craig, Lieut. W.B. Williams. C.M.G. to D.C.M.;– No. 8749 Sgt. Yp. Kavenor. Distinguished Conduct Medals:– No. 8672 Sgt. E. Rush, No. 9798 Pte J. Lane. Military Medals:– 10344 Pte. 96 Gye. 8043 Pte. 96 Walsh, 9147 Cpl. D. Davies, 36481 L/Cpl. J. Knight, 11245 Pte. A. Jones, 9468 L/Cpl. J. Bond, 8320 Pte. G. Morgan. 3 Other ranks wounded.	Jun
GIVENCHY LEFT	5.7.16	—	A raid on the hostile trenches known as the "WARREN" was successfully carried out.	Jun

WAR DIARY
INTELLIGENCE SUMMARY
(Erase heading not required.)

Army Form C. 2118

Place	Date	Hour	Summary of Events and Information	Remarks and references to Appendices
CUINCHY LEFT	6·7·16	—	carried out by 'A' Company and our Captain J.P. Higgenson & 'D' Company under Captain P. Hoey. After a consids. bombardment of the salient by trench mortar artillery and rifle grenades, with an expenditure of 4000 rounds in 3½ hours, 'A' Company on the left and 'D' Company on the right, assaulted the enemy trenches and the continuation of staying in them 2 hours and in that time to completely wreck the enemy mining system, dug-outs, trench mortar emplacements, etc. This was more than fulfilled as, between A and D Companies 39 prisoners were captured, & dead brought in, 14 identity discs taken off others, and many others known to have been killed and wounded. In addition, 1 machine gun, 1 trench mortar, much equipment, food, correspondence, knicknacks and rifles were captured. The enemy first line was entered and destroyed by us. The following congratulatory messages have been received. "From I.A.Q. Seymour aha. Please convey to 2nd R.W. Fus.rs the	Jun

Army Form C. 2118.

WAR DIARY
INTELLIGENCE SUMMARY.
(Erase heading not required.)

Place	Date	Hour	Summary of Events and Information	Remarks and references to Appendices
GIVENCHY LEFT.	5.7.16		Commander-in-chief's congratulations on their very successful raid last night aaa Raids of this sort are of great material assistance to the main operations aaa ends aaa "Following were received from General Haking aaa Please convey to 1st battalion Cameronians and all ranks 2nd RWF my heartiest congratulations on their splendid raid last night aaa ends aaa "Following were received by 33rd Division begins aaa G.O.C. 1st Army wires his congratulations conveyed to all ranks who took part in the raid last night at GIVENCHY aaa ends aaa. "Following letter from General H.J.S. Landon 33rd Division :- "I was delighted to hear of the complete success of the operations last night and warmly congratulate Major Crawshay and the RWF who have got their own back well. (Sd) H.J.S. Landon, Maj. Gen. The following from the Brigadier General:- "The Brigadier wishes to convey to you and all ranks of your battalion his congratulations on your splendid work last night aaa He considers the attack could not	

Army Form C. 2118.

WAR DIARY
of
INTELLIGENCE SUMMARY.
(Erase heading not required.)

Instructions regarding War Diaries and Intelligence Summaries are contained in F. S. Regs., Part II. and the Staff Manual respectively. Title pages will be prepared in manuscript.

Place	Date	Hour	Summary of Events and Information	Remarks and references to Appendices
GIVENCHY LEFT	5.7.16		have been carried out letter and that all your arrangements were first rate.	
----	6.7.16		Casualties:- 2nd Lieut R.A.R. Hollingbery & 10 Other Ranks killed. 1 Other Rank missing, 2nd Lieut A.H. Smith (1st Bn. Loyal North Lancs. Regt. attached) and 47 Other Ranks wounded.	
----	6.7.16		In trenches. Captain R. von R. Graves & 11 Other Ranks joined.	
----	7.7.16		In trenches. Normal. A large Prussian Werfer was also destroyed by us on the 5th July. The following message was received through G.O.C., 33rd Division. (Translation.) "Dear General,	

T.J134. Wt. W708—776. 500000. 4/15. Sir J. C. & S.

Army Form C. 2118

WAR DIARY
of
INTELLIGENCE SUMMARY
(Erase heading not required.)

Place	Date	Hour	Summary of Events and Information	Remarks and references to Appendices
GUENCHY LEFT	7-7-16		I have just received your "Communique" of the 6th instant, and I am glad to see that the 33rd Division is continuing its brilliant success in vigorous raids on the enemy trenches. The Royal Welsh Fusiliers have distinguished themselves once more. The "Bosches" opposite you have neither to leisure nor rest and I am exceedingly glad to shout "Bravo". Please accept my best congratulations and ever friendly compliments. (Sd) S. de Wignacourt General Casualties:— 1 Other rank wounded (Attached to the Trench Mortar Bty.)	Tu
	8-7-16		Relieved by 4/5th Bn. The Black Watch and marched to billets at FOUQUIERES. At 6 p.m. we blew a fairly large mine on "D" Company's front which apparently did some damage to the enemy's front line, but also wrecked a portion of our own 2nd line & took over temporary command of "B" Company.	Tu
FOUQUIERES	9-7-16		The Battalion entrained at FOUQUEREUIL Station at midnight, complete with 1st & 9th line transport. Strength 20 Officers 626 Other Ranks.	Tu

Army Form C. 2118

WAR DIARY
or
INTELLIGENCE SUMMARY
(Erase heading not required.)

Instructions regarding War Diaries and Intelligence Summaries are contained in F. S. Regs., Part II. and the Staff Manual respectively. Title Pages will be prepared in manuscript.

Place	Date	Hour	Summary of Events and Information	Remarks and references to Appendices
LONGEAU	10-7-16		Arrived at LONGEAU near AMIENS at 7 a.m. and marched to CARDONNETTE. 6 miles.	
CARDONNETTE	11-7-16		Marched to DAOURS at 7 a.m. and were in billets in a factory on the canal. 4 miles.	
DAOURS	12-7-16		Marched to BUIRE-SUR-L'ANCRE about 8 miles and went under canvas. 2nd Lieuts. A. W. Foreshew, G. W. Foss and O. the Roberts joined.	
BUIRE	13-7-16		Under canvas. Several Officers rode over to see 1st Battalion Hampshire at MEAULTE, about 4 miles away.	
"	14-7-16		Left BUIRE at 11.30 a.m. and marched to MEAULTE and bivouacked about 3/4 mile East of the Village. The Brigade was lightly shelled about 8.30 p.m. No casualties.	
MEAULTE	15-7-16		Left bivouac about 5 a.m. marched through ERICOURT and halted at S.E. corner of MAMETZ WOOD. Spent the day in clearing S.E. portion of the Wood. 1 Other rank killed, 1 Other rank wounded. The Battalion was in Brigade Reserve.	
MAMETZ WOOD	16-7-16		Moved about R. Thiepval [?]. The Brigade being in the [line]	

Army Form C. 2118

WAR DIARY
or
INTELLIGENCE SUMMARY
(Erase heading not required.)

Instructions regarding War Diaries and Intelligence Summaries are contained in F. S. Regs., Part II. and the Staff Manual respectively. Title Pages will be prepared in manuscript.

Place	Date	Hour	Summary of Events and Information	Remarks and references to Appendices
MAMETZ WOOD	16-7-16		line, having relieved the 100th Brigade. Spent the day in digging in comfortably. Casualties: 1 Other rank killed, 1 Other rank missing believed killed 4 Other ranks wounded 2 Other ranks to hospital.	Ten
	17-7-16		Battalion in MAMETZ WOOD in Divisional Reserve. Casualties - Sec Lieut J. F. W. Craig wounded, 2 Other ranks killed 13 Other ranks wounded.	Ten
	18-7-16		Aroused at midnight 17/18 and moved to BAZENTINE-LE-PETIT and lent to 98th Brigade. Relieved 4th Kings in front of the village with our right on the Cemetery and left on the MARTINPUICH Road. Battalion was shelled heavily for about 6 hours from noon. Casualties: 5 Other ranks killed, 32 Other ranks wounded.	Ten
BAZENTINE-LE-PETIT	19-7-16		Quiet. Battalion Headquarters now established in a deep dug-out in the village. Relieved by 4th Kings about 10 p.m. and bivouacked near Brigade Headquarters in MAMETZ WOOD. Aroused at about midnight and moved to a position in Brigade Reserve in front of FLAT-IRON COPSE	Ten

WAR DIARY
INTELLIGENCE SUMMARY
(Erase heading not required.)

Army Form C. 2118

Place	Date	Hour	Summary of Events and Information	Remarks and references to Appendices
FRATRICIDE COPSE	20-7-16		The Battalion was heavily shelled from 3am. to 8am., then intermittently until noon, when we were under orders to go up to HIGH WOOD (BOIS DES FOURBEAUX) what the Brigade had only been able to partially capture. The Cameronians & 2nd Scottish Rifles and 20th Royal Fusiliers sustaining heavy losses.	
BOIS-DES-FOUREAUX			High Wood was reached about 2 pm, and our attack succeeded in capturing and clearing the wood, including the Strong Point in the N.W. Corner. Owing to the presence of machine guns on the SWITCH, a defensive line was dug 100 yards within the N. edge of the wood. At about 9 pm the O.C. 20th Royal Fusiliers reported that the enemy were counter-attacking defensive line. At about 10 pm the enemy heavily shelled the edges of the wood. Casualties:- 2nd Lieut. E. Craft & 98 Other ranks Killed. Lieut. R.J.A. Bowles, wounded; died of wounds. Captain R. von R. Crave, Captain Phinney, Lieut. E.G.B. C.R. Headley Killed.	

Army Form C. 2118

WAR DIARY or INTELLIGENCE SUMMARY

(Erase heading not required.)

Instructions regarding War Diaries and Intelligence Summaries are contained in F.S. Regs., Part II. and the Staff Manual respectively. Title Pages will be prepared in manuscript.

Place	Date	Hour	Summary of Events and Information	Remarks and references to Appendices
HIGH WOOD (BOIS DE FOURCAUX)	20-7-16	1	Barksworth, Lieut. 96 O. Parry, Lieut R. Gambier-Parry, 2nd Lieut. A.S. Ford. 2nd Lieut. Roberts, G.W. Lowe, 2nd Lt. F. Crockett wounded. 29 Other Ranks killed, 180 Other Ranks wounded & 29 Other Ranks missing.	True
—	21-7-16	1	At about 1 a.m. 2 Companies 1st Bn. The Queens Regt. and 1 Company 1st Bn. R.R. Corps relieved us and the Battalion marched back to Trévaux under MAMETZ WOOD. Quiet morning. At about 3 p.m. we	True
MAMETZ WOOD			started to march back to BUIRE-SUR-L'ANCRE via FRICOURT. Reinforcement	
BUIRE-SUR-L'ANCRE			of Lieut. A.E. Goldsmith, 2nd Lieut. E.G. Hunnicliffe, P.S. Wilson, G.W. Jagger and 111 Other Ranks joined. The following Officers, Warrant Officers, N.C.O.s and men distinguished themselves during the Action:- Captain P. Moody, Captain J.E. Higginson, Lieut R.J.A. Bowles, Lieut & Adjutant J.C. Mann, 2nd Lieut & Coster, 2nd Lieut J.R. Conway, 2nd Lieut A.J. Crockett, 2nd Lieut G.W. Lowe, 2nd Lieut E.J. Rowland. No. 9595 T/C J. Berry, 9011 Pte J. Duckett, 11053 Pte B. Hughes, 7962 Pte G. Walsh, 9644 J. Evans, 9358 Sgt D. Roberts-Morgan, 9901 Cpl J. Dorsey, 8434 Cpl W. Keate, 9366 Cpl L. Evans,	

WAR DIARY
or
INTELLIGENCE SUMMARY
(Erase heading not required.)

Army Form C. 2118

Place	Date	Hour	Summary of Events and Information	Remarks and references to Appendices
Bout-Sur-Ancre	21-7-16		911 Sgt W Roberts, 8797 Sgt A Owen, 9332 Pte T Richards, 5575 68 W A Musson, 10424 Pte A Fox, 9042 Pte E Jones, 8749, Pte P Roderick, 36653 Pte R Jones, 8122 Pte T Cook, 11960 Cpl L Spencer, 10438 Sgt S Davis, 9836 Pte J Hughes, 17286 Cpl R Worrall, 6804 Pte J Haley, 9119 Cpl A Howell, 8369, Pte D Evans, 10404 Pte A Jones, 8718 Pte Vickery, 859 L896 J Powell, 9200 Sgt E Jones, 8510 Sgt E Jones, 8391 Sgt E Stoton, 4921 Cpl J Williams, 9709 Cpl W Shearby, 8102 Pte J Haywood, 31042 Pte J Bellup, 2077 Pte J Brown, 3282 J Jones, 5369 Pte A Callear, 5686 Pte E Remek, 6938 Pte Pierpoint, 3763 Pte J Evans, 8813, Pte A Jenkins	See
—	22-7-16		In tents Reorganizing began.	See
—	23-7-16		Still reorganizing	See
—	24-7-16		Still reorganizing	See
—	25-7-16		Still reorganizing. Reinforcement of 62 Other Ranks joined	See
—	26-7-16		Still reorganizing. 2nd Lieuts A J Harris & A Robertson joined	See
—	27-7-16		Still reorganizing.	See

WAR DIARY or INTELLIGENCE SUMMARY

Army Form C. 2118

(Erase heading not required.)

Place	Date	Hour	Summary of Events and Information	Remarks and references to Appendices
BUIRE-SUR-L'ANCRE	27-7-16	-	Still reorganizing.	J.Cur
"	28-7-16	-	Still reorganizing. Inspected by Brigadier General Mayne, D.S.O.	J.Cur
"	29-7-16	-	Still reorganizing. The following N.C.O's and men were awarded Military Medals for good work and gallantry on July 20th. 8797, Sgt. A. Owen, 8434 Cpl. Heale, 9901 Cpl. J. Dodson, 9595, L/C J. Berry, 8418, Pte J. Pickering, 4077, Pte J. Brown, 6864, Pte J. Healy, 9332 Pte J. Richards, 9644 Pte J. Evans, 10438 Sgt. E. Davis, 9119 Cpl. A. Ussell, 9356 Sgt. D. Roberts-Morgan, 8813, Pte A. Jenkins, 36938 Pte A. Reyport. 9836 Pte J. Hughes, 11209 Sgt. E. Jones 16575 Sgt. J. Snider. Also the following Officer, Warrant Officer, N.C.O's and men were awarded decorations for gallantry at GIVENCHY Raid July 5/6 th. 2nd Lieut E. Foster Military Cross. 682. C.S.M. W. Fox, Military Cross, 9385 Sgt. D. Roberts-Morgan, & 8037 Pte W. Buckley Distinguished Conduct Medals 8683, Sgt. A. Franks & 8216 Pte. Ed Thorets. Military Medals. 125 O.R. joined.	J.Cur
"	30-7-16	-	Distribution of Medal Ribbons by General Landon to men who displayed gallantry on 20th July! Onft of 21 Other Ranks joined Battalion Went March. 119 Other Ranks joined	J.Cur
"	31-7-16	1/8/16		

C. Murray. Major,
Comdg. 2nd Bn Royal Welsh Fusiliers.

19th Brigade.
33rd Division.

2nd BATTALION

ROYAL WELCH FUSILIERS

AUGUST 1 9 1 6

Army Form C. 2118.

2nd R. Royal Welsh Fusiliers

WAR DIARY
INTELLIGENCE SUMMARY
(Erase heading not required.)

2nd Welsh Fus

Vol 25

Instructions regarding War Diaries and Intelligence Summaries are contained in F. S. Regs., Part II. and the Staff Manual respectively. Title Pages will be prepared in manuscript.

Place	Date	Hour	Summary of Events and Information	Remarks and references to Appendices
BOUZINCOURT	1-8-16		Still reorganizing	
ANCRE	2-8-16		Still reorganizing. 2nd Lieut C.P.J.R. Dolling rejoined.	
"	3-8-16		Still reorganizing	
"	4-8-16		Still reorganizing.	
"	5-8-16		Still reorganizing	
"	6-8-16		Moved to BECORDEL AREA at 10-5 p.m. from BOUZINCOURT-SUR-L'ANCRE	
BECORDEL	7-8-16		No move. Training of reinforcements continued	
"	8-8-16		Continued training. Captain E.T. Higgins awarded the Military Cross for gallantry.	
"	9-8-16		Training continued. The following were awarded Military Crosses for gallantry:- Captain G.L. Orton, R.W. to & attached 2nd Bn. Royal Welch Fusiliers and Company Sergeant-Major J. Beech "D" Company. Regimental S.M. F.H. Brown & L.S.M. W.H. Fox received Commissions	
"	10-8-16		Training continued.	
"	11-8-16		Continued training. Other ranks returned wilts on working-party.	
"	12-8-16		Continued training.	
"	13-8-16		Battalion moved to FRICOURT WOOD at 2 a.m. 1 O.R. killed & 2 Wounded	
FRICOURT WOOD	14-8-16		Quiet day. The enemy sent over several heavy shells. 1 O.R. was killed	

WAR DIARY or INTELLIGENCE SUMMARY

Army Form C. 2118.

(Erase heading not required.)

Instructions regarding War Diaries and Intelligence Summaries are contained in F. S. Regs., Part II. and the Staff Manual respectively. Title Pages will be prepared in manuscript.

Place	Date	Hour	Summary of Events and Information	Remarks and references to Appendices
ERQUIN WOOD	15.8.16		In bivouac. 2 Other ranks wounded.	
"	16.8.16		In bivouac. 1 Other rank wounded.	
"	17.8.16		In bivouac.	
"	18.8.16		Moved into trenches in HIGH (FOUREAUX) WOOD, relieving 2nd Bn. Argyll & Sutherland Highlanders. Quiet journey to the trenches. 6 Other ranks wounded.	
HIGH WOOD	19.8.16		Reinforcement of 5 R.C.s joined. 3 Other ranks wounded. Enemy bombardment by the enemy started about 9 a.m. followed by a raid which was easily repulsed. 2nd Lieut. H. St. G. Slingsby wounded at duty. 14 Other ranks killed and 9 Other ranks wounded. Another attack at night after a heavy bombardment was repulsed. 2nd Lieut. G.R.J.R. Selby and 2nd Lieut. P.B. Wilson killed. 6 Other ranks killed and 9 Other ranks wounded.	
"	20.8.16		The enemy opened a heavy bombardment which lasted all day. 6 Other ranks killed, 20 Other ranks wounded and 2 Other ranks wounded slightly at duty.	
"	21.8.16		Relieved by the Cameronians at 5 a.m. and went back into the BAZENTIN-LE-GRAND line. Reinforcement of 8 R.C.s. 6 Other ranks killed. 3 Other ranks wounded.	

Army Form C. 2118.

WAR DIARY
or
INTELLIGENCE SUMMARY
(Erase heading not required.)

Instructions regarding War Diaries and Intelligence Summaries are contained in F. S. Regs., Part II. and the Staff Manual respectively. Title Pages will be prepared in manuscript.

Place	Date	Hour	Summary of Events and Information	Remarks and references to Appendices
BAZENTIN-LE-GRAND	23-8-16		Enemy working parties. The line was shelled fairly heavily. 1 other rank wounded.	
—	24-8-16		Continuous working parties. Heavy shelled in the evening. 1 other rank killed and 3 other ranks wounded.	
—	25-8-16		BAZENTIN Line again heavily shelled in the evening. 2nd Lieut J.P.L. Prescott (11th Royal West Kent Regt. attd.) and 2 other ranks wounded. Relieved the Bavarians at 3-35 a.m. in HIGH WOOD. The 1st Bn Gloster Regt. 1st Queens on our left and 15th Scottish Rifles on our right. Our snipers killed one of the enemy who was walking in the open. Fairly quiet. 4 other ranks wounded.	
HIGH WOOD	26/8/16		One hundred (100) of the support trench was shelled during the afternoon. Relieved by 1st Bn The Blackwatch & Queens at 8 p.m. to Bivouac in FRICOURT WOOD. 6 other ranks wounded.	
FRICOURT WOOD	27/8/16		In Bivouac. 2 other ranks missing. The uncommissioned officers for commissions 2/Lt R.H. Newman, 2/Lts O.B. Williams, E.C. Lopes, P.E. Lind and E.R. St. John.	
—	28/8/16		Relieved 20th Royal Fusiliers in MONTAUBAN ALLEY. Company in support to 98th Infantry Brigade. The undermentioned officers joined: 2/Lts H Savage, J.F.G Raw, R. Jones, D. Phillips, and B.J. Bradley.	
MONTAUBAN ALLEY	29-8-16		Shelled Heavy Rain. Very wet and muddy.	

Army Form C. 2118.

WAR DIARY
or
INTELLIGENCE SUMMARY

(Erase heading not required.)

Instructions regarding War Diaries and Intelligence Summaries are contained in F. S. Regs., Part II. and the Staff Manual respectively. Title Pages will be prepared in manuscript.

Place	Date	Hour	Summary of Events and Information	Remarks and references to Appendices
BECOURDEL	31-8-16		Arrived into billets at RIBEMONT.	

Sturm
Lieut. Colonel
Commanding 2nd Bn. Royal Welsh Fusiliers

WAR DIARY
INTELLIGENCE SUMMARY

Army Form C. 2118.

2/W Jus Vol 26

25a
N.

Place	Date	Hour	Summary of Events and Information	Remarks and references to Appendices
RIBEMONT	1-9-16		Moved into billets at RAINNEVILLE.	
RAINNEVILLE	2-9-16		Moved from RAINNEVILLE to BERNAVILLE (16½ miles Route March), very hot.	
BERNAVILLE	3-9-16		Rested at BERNAVILLE. Companies overhauled & cleaned up kits and equipment. Fine day.	
"	4-9-16		Marched to BONNIERES and BEAUVOIR - "A" & "D" Companies quartered in BONNIERES, "C" & "B" Companies & Headquarters in BEAUVOIR (advance 9½ miles) Cool day and a little rain.	
BONNIERES & BEAUVOIR	5-9-16		Marched to BLANGERMONT (distance 7½ miles) - fine day.	
BLANGERMONT	6-9-16		Rested at BLANGERMONT - cleaned up - parades - fine day. The undermentioned officers arrived :- Lieut R.B.J.Greaves, 2nd Lieut H.H.Annear, 2nd Lieut R.C.Shelley.	
" "	7-9-16		Still at BLANGERMONT - cleaned up - parades - fine day	
" "	8-9-16		Marched to MONCHEAUX - (distance 8 miles) - fine day	
MONCHEAUX	9-9-16		Marched to IVERGNY (distance 6½ miles) - cleaning up and parades during rest of day - fine day.	
IVERGNY	10-9-16		Marched to HUMBERCAMP (distance 11½ miles) - fine day. The undermentioned N.C.O's & men joined :- Lcpl Prince & Lcpl Owen & 13 O.R.	

WAR DIARY
or
INTELLIGENCE SUMMARY

Army Form C. 2118.

(Erase heading not required.)

2nd Battalion Royal Militia Fusiliers   Confidential

Instructions regarding War Diaries and Intelligence Summaries are contained in F. S. Regs., Part II. and the Staff Manual respectively. Title Pages will be prepared in manuscript.

Places	Date	Hour	Summary of Events and Information	Remarks and references to Appendices
HUMBERCAMP	11-9-16	1	Took over Brigade Reserve from 1st Scottish Rifles (The Cameronians) at 8.45 p.m. at BIENVILLERS-AU-BOIS at 8.45 p.m. weather fine. Billets good. 2nd Lieut Eric B'tay Captain Dunn RAMC & 24 OR left for 7 days at Seaside. 2nd Lieut Sykes "C" Coy sent to 19th Field Ambulance sick. The undermentioned officers joined Battalion: Cuthbert (and took over "B" Coy) 2nd Lieuts T. Williams, H. A. Edwards & C.A. Nair. Lieut J.C. Kann rejoined from 98th Brigade Headquarters as received as Brig. Adjutant.	98. Inf. Bde A.Co.H.F.
BIENVILLERS -AU-BOIS	12-9-16		In Brigade Reserve. Captain Higginson proceeded on 10 days leave to the United Kingdom. 95 OR joined from Base. weather fine. day quiet.	98. Inf. Bde A.Co.H.F.
	13-9-16		Still in Brigade Reserve at BIENVILLERS. 2nd Lieut Sykes returned to England sick.	98. Inf. Bde A.Co.H.F.
	14-9-16		Still in Brigade Reserve at BIENVILLERS	98. Inf. Bde A.Co.H.F.
	15-9-16		Still in Brigade Reserve at BIENVILLERS	98. Inf. Bde A.Co.H.F.
	16-9-16		The Battalion went into trenches at Left Subsection. Section Z. Battalion Head-Quarters at HANNESCAMPS. Took over from 20th Battalion Royal Fusiliers, who took over our billets.	98. Inf. Bde A.Co.H.F.
	17-9-16		Still in trenches - Germans shelled a little. 1 O.R. wounded.	98. Inf. Bde A.Co.H.F.
	18-9-16		Still in trenches -- do --	98. Inf. Bde A.Co.H.F.
	19-9-16		Still in trenches -- do --	98. Inf. Bde A.Co.H.F.
	20-9-16		Still in trenches -- do --	98. Inf. Bde A.Co.H.F.
	21-9-16		Relieved by 20th Battalion Royal Fusiliers at 8.0 p.m. and returned to previous billets in BIENVILLERS in Brigade support. 9 OR wounded 1 OR joined.	98. Inf. Bde A.Co.H.F.

2449 Wt. W14957/M90 750,000 1/16 J.B.C. & A. Forms/C.2118/12.

2nd Bn Royal Welch Fusiliers

WAR DIARY
or
INTELLIGENCE SUMMARY

Army Form C. 2118.

Confidential

(Erase heading not required.)

Instructions regarding War Diaries and Intelligence Summaries are contained in F.S. Regs., Part II. and the Staff Manual respectively. Title Pages will be prepared in manuscript.

Place	Date	Hour	Summary of Events and Information	Remarks and references to Appendices
BIENVILLERS	22.9.16		Still in Brigade support at BIENVILLERS	S.R. Auth. Copt
"	23.9.16		Still in Brigade support at —do—	S.R. Auth. Copt
"	24.9.16		Still in Brigade support at —do—	S.R. Auth. Copt
"	25.9.16		Still in Brigade support at —do— 10.0 P. rained	S.R. det. Copt
"	26.9.16		Still in Brigade support at —do—	S.R. det. Copt
"	27.9.16		Relieved 20th Battalion Royal Fusiliers (who relieved us). Went into trenches Left Subsection, Section Z. Battalion Headquarters at HANNESCAMPS	
HANNESCAMPS	28.9.16		In trenches, Left Subsection, Section Z. very quiet.	S.R. Auth. Copt
"	29.9.16		Relieved during the day by 4th West Riding Regiment. Battalion marched to SOUASTRE 3½ miles and the men billeted in good huts.	S.R. Auth. Copt
SOUASTRE	30.9.16		Battalion moved to LUCHEUX. Good marching day. Good billets. 9½ miles. Capture J.M. Hignon 2nd Lieut R.W. Fus. 30/9/16	S.R. Auth. Copt

Crawford
Lieut-Colonel
Commanding 2nd Battalion Royal Welch Fusiliers

Confidential.

WAR DIARY

INTELLIGENCE SUMMARY

Army Form C. 2118.

19/3/

VOL 27

2nd Bn. Royal Welch Fusiliers.

26.N
9 sheets

Place	Date	Hour	Summary of Events and Information	Remarks and references to Appendices
LUCHEUX	1/16		At LUCHEUX. Fine day. Church Parade with 2 Coy's. The Cameronians. Generals Pinney (Comdg 33rd Divn) Mayne (Comdg 19th Infy Bde) and Staff present. Lectured by General Pinney after Parade Service.	Fine
LUCHEUX	2/16		At LUCHEUX. Wet day. Companies undergoing training.	Rain
LUCHEUX	3/16		At LUCHEUX. Training.	Rain
LUCHEUX	4/16		At LUCHEUX. Training.	Rain
LUCHEUX	5/16		At LUCHEUX. Training.	Rain
LUCHEUX	6/16		At LUCHEUX. Training.	Rain
LUCHEUX	7/16		At LUCHEUX. Training. Trenches at HEBUTERNE visited.	Rain
LUCHEUX	8/16		At LUCHEUX. Training. Trenches at HEBUTERNE visited.	Rain
LUCHEUX	9/16		At LUCHEUX. Training. Trenches at HEBUTERNE visited.	Rain
LUCHEUX	10/16		At LUCHEUX. Training.	Rain
LUCHEUX	11/16		At LUCHEUX. Training.	Rain
LUCHEUX	12/16		At LUCHEUX. Training.	Rain

Army Form C. 2118.

WAR DIARY
or
INTELLIGENCE SUMMARY

(Erase heading not required.)

Instructions regarding War Diaries and Intelligence Summaries are contained in F. S. Regs., Part II. and the Staff Manual respectively. Title Pages will be prepared in manuscript.

Place	Date	Hour	Summary of Events and Information	Remarks and references to Appendices
LUCHEUX.	13/10/16		At LUCHEUX. Training.	
LUCHEUX.	14/10/16		At LUCHEUX. Training.	
LUCHEUX.	15/10/16		At LUCHEUX. Training.	
LUCHEUX.	16/10/16		At LUCHEUX. Training.	
LUCHEUX.	17/10/16		At LUCHEUX. Training.	
LUCHEUX.	18/10/16		Transport moved to BEAUCOURT.	
LUCHEUX.	19/10/16		The Battalion moved by Bus to MERICOURT L'ABBÉ arrived at 2 a.m. 20th.	
MERICOURT L'ABBÉ.	20/10/16		At MERICOURT L'ABBÉ.	
MEAULT.	21/10/16		The Battalion moved to MEAULT and encamped in tents and huts. very cold night.	
TRONES WOOD.	22/10/16		The Battalion moved up to TRONES WOOD and lay in old and battered trenches - very cold.	

Army Form C. 2118.

WAR DIARY
or
INTELLIGENCE SUMMARY

(Erase heading not required.)

Instructions regarding War Diaries and Intelligence Summaries are contained in F. S. Regs., Part II. and the Staff Manual respectively. Title Pages will be prepared in manuscript.

Place	Date	Hour	Summary of Events and Information	Remarks and references to Appendices
SERPEN- TINE TRENCH	10 23/9/16		The Battalion moved at 1.30.a.m. for SERPENTINE TRENCH between GINCHY and LES BOEUFS, the 19th Brigade in Divisional Reserve. The 2nd Bn. Roy.Welch Fus: were in reserve with the 20th Roy.Fus: to the 1st Brigade of the 4th Division.	E.Q. d.h
			At 2p.m. the 4th Division attacked the line of trenches between LES BOEUFS and LE TRANSLOY. The bombardment had been heavy all day intensifying to a high degree from 2p.m. onwards. At 5.45.p.m. the bombardment quietened slightly. The German shelling of the SERPENTINE TRENCH was light during the whole day.	E.Q. d.h E.Q. d.h
LES BOEUFS TRENCHES.	19 24/9/16		The Battalion moved to LES BOEUFS Trenches leaving SERPENTINE TRENCH at 5.p.m. and relieving 1st Hants Regt: and 1st Rifle Bde at 10.30.p.m. Trenches occupied as follows:—	E.Q. d.h

Front Line { "A" Coy: "C" Coy: FROSTY TRENCH.
              "D" Coy: "C" Coy: ANTELOPE TRENCH East of FLANK AVENUE.
              "B" Coy: ANTELOPE TRENCH West of FLANK AVENUE.
              "B" Coy: ANDREWS POST TRENCH.

Army Form C. 2118.

WAR DIARY
INTELLIGENCE SUMMARY
(Erase heading not required.)

Place	Date	Hour	Summary of Events and Information	Remarks and references to Appendices
LES BOEUFS TRENCHES.	24/76 10		N.B. "B" Coy in touch with the French Army on our immediate right.	
	(continued).		Support { "D" Coy: in GERMAN TRENCH. "A" Coy: in MUGGY TRENCH. Battalion Headquarters and Headquarters on SUNKEN ROAD. Continuous shelling and sniping during the night. Troops on Left — 20th Royal Fusiliers. Troops on Right — 125th G.R. French Army. Casualties — Killed 4 O.R. Wounded 7 O.R. Wounded at duty 1 O.R.	
LES BOEUFS TRENCHES.	25/76 10		Still in LES BOEUFS TRENCHES. Continuous artillery activity and sniping on both sides. Casualties — Killed 1 O.R. Wounded 13 O.R. Wounded at duty 2 O.R. Missing 2 O.R.	

Army Form C. 2118.

WAR DIARY
INTELLIGENCE SUMMARY
(Erase heading not required.)

Place	Date	Hour	Summary of Events and Information	Remarks and references to Appendices
LES BOEUFS TRENCHES.	26/16	a.m.	Shelled LES BOEUFS TRENCHES. Orders received from Brigade at 11.50 p.m. to clear FROSTY and ANTELOPE Trenches as the French on our right contemplated an attack on BORITSKA TRENCH and we were to bombard DENDROP and BORITSKA trenches immediately on left of French objective. Trench zero time given was 9 a.m. at which time our guns would bombard DENDROP and BORITSKA trenches and by which time "C" Coy and ½ "B" Coy should be clear of their line. ½ "B" Coy and ½ "C" Coy evacuated and the Battalion was on following position by 7.0 a.m. ½ "B" Coy:- ANDREWS POST TRENCH. "C" Coy & ½ "B" Coy:- GERMAN TRENCH. ½ "B" Coy & "A" Coy:- MUGGY TRENCH. The French attack did not take place however our bombardment on DENDROP and BORITSKA trenches were badly knocked about. FROSTY and ANTELOPE trenches were dropping very short and ½ "C" Coy & ½ "B" Coy went back to their original position.	J.R.Gath

WAR DIARY or INTELLIGENCE SUMMARY

Army Form C. 2118.

Place	Date	Hour	Summary of Events and Information	Remarks and references to Appendices
LES BOEUFS TRENCHES. (Continued)	26/10/16		During the night our Sapping Platoon dug 30 yards N. from East end of FROSTY trench in endeavour to connect with 21th Royal Fusiliers who were on our left and who were digging in a Southerly direction to meet us. We had already effected cut 25 yards in front of FROSTY TRENCH. Artillery and sniping on both sides active during night. Casualties:— Killed 3. O.R. Wounded 9. O.R. Wounded at duty Lieut R.C.J. Greaves and 2 O.R. Accidentally Wounded 1 O.R.	R.O.A.R.
LES BOEUFS TRENCHES.	27/10/16		Still in LES BOEUFS TRENCHES. The Trench again prepared attack which was put off on Oct. 26th. We received the same orders as to clearing our first line trenches as on October 26th which we complied with. Our action was again to be the same. The Trench again put off the attack but our guns will bombard DEWDROP and BORITSKA Trenches as arranged. At 4.30. p.m. "C" Coy. and ½ "B" Coy. returned to their original Trenches which had been again badly knocked about by our	

Army Form C. 2118.

WAR DIARY
or
INTELLIGENCE SUMMARY
(Erase heading not required.)

Instructions regarding War Diaries and Intelligence Summaries are contained in F.S. Regs., Part II. and the Staff Manual respectively. Title Pages will be prepared in manuscript.

Place	Date	Hour	Summary of Events and Information	Remarks and references to Appendices
LES BOEUFS TR.	19		from Artillery during this bombardment on DENDROP and BORITSKA trenches.	
TRENCHES (continued)			At 1 p.m. we had received an order that we would be relieved by the Cameronians. This relief took place and was completed by 2.30 a.m. on the 26th. The weather conditions during the whole time had been bad, the trenches were very wet and muddy and in the early stage of construction. Carrying parties were very heavy ration and water parties having to go three miles from the line over ground much cut up by shell holes and in a bad state owing to the rain. Rain. There were many wounded and dead of the 11th Brigade in the Sector left from previous attacks by that Brigade. During the four the Regiment evacuated about 20 wounded of the 11th Brigade and buried as many of their dead as was possible. We had contemplated and arranged for an attack each night on the German line of Ph. site our shot or each occasion we were unable to carry the attacks out owing to the of mentioned reasons. Trenches out owing to the of mentioned reasons. There was considerable Artillery activity today on both sides. Casualties:— Killed 3 O.R. Wounded 9 O.R. Wounded at duty 3 O.R. Missing 2 O.R.	

WAR DIARY
INTELLIGENCE SUMMARY

(Erase heading not required.)

Army Form C. 2118.

Place	Date	Hour	Summary of Events and Information	Remarks and references to Appendices
GUILLE-MONT	28/7/16		The Battalion on completion of relief by the Cameronians moved to and took over the shell holes at GUILLEMONT which had been previously occupied by the Cameronians. The night was very wet. The cover inadequate. Casualties:- Accidentally wounded 1 O.R.	
GUILLE-MONT	29/7/16		The Battalion still in shell holes at GUILLEMONT. The day was spent in cleaning up and making cover for the men. A very fine day. "A" Coy was ordered to move at 1.30 a.m on the 30th to reinforce the Cameronians. Casualties:- missing 1 O.R.	
Between TRONES and BERNAFAY woods	30/7/16		"A" Coy moved at 1.30 a.m to reinforce the Cameronians who were in the Right Sub-section of LES BOEUFS sector of trenches. The Battalion moved to bivouac between TRONES and BERNAFAY Woods. The Regiment exchanged quarters with the 1st Queens Regt of the 100th Brigade. The 19th Brigade came out of the line today. Very wet and muddy. Cover for the men in new Bivouacs very bad indeed. Casualties:- Killed 3 O.R. Wounded 3 O.R.	

Army Form C. 2118.

WAR DIARY
or
INTELLIGENCE SUMMARY
(Erase heading not required.)

Instructions regarding War Diaries and Intelligence Summaries are contained in F. S. Regs., Part II. and the Staff Manual respectively. Title Pages will be prepared in manuscript.

Place	Date	Hour	Summary of Events and Information	Remarks and references to Appendices
BRIQUETERIE	31/10/16		"A" Coy: arrived from LES BOEUFS Trenches at 3.30.a.m. The day was fine. Orders received to move again into fresh bivouacs at BRIQUETERIE. We took over from 2/5th Scottish Rifles, 4th Bri. The Kings took over our bivouac from us. Our present quarters are bad as regards mud but the men are in tents and have blankets for the first time since leaving TROMES - and on the 23rd	

M. arten

C Crawley
Lieut: Colonel
Comdg. 2nd Bon. Roy: Welch Fusiliers.

21 November 1916.

2nd Bn. Royal Welch Fusiliers

Confidential
Army Form C. 2118.

WAR DIARY
INTELLIGENCE SUMMARY.
(Erase heading not required.)

Place	Date	Hour	Summary of Events and Information	Remarks and references to Appendices
BRIQUETERIE	2.11.16 3.11.16		At BRIQUETERIE - Heavy trench. The battalion moved in to the line & took over the Right subsection of the sector of the LES BOEUFS line, from the 1st Middlesex of the 98th I.B. Relief was completed at 7.40 p.m. The battalion was disposed as follows:- Right Coy "B" SUMMER TRENCH & Jingling 5. Wing points & mehr each, two coys of KINDY TRENCH. Left Coy "D" in DEWDROP TRENCH "A" Coy in KINDY TRENCH Support "C" Coy in JOHN BULL TRENCH on our Left 20th R.F. - on our Right KRR of 98th Bde.	
	4.11.16		Still in trenches. Light subsection of Left sector of LES BOEUFS line. A warning order received. General attack of French, 6th Army & British 4th & 5th Armies and similar instructions for 4th to be placed by 19th I Bde received. Heavy hostile shelling between 4.30 p.m. & 5.15 p.m. real of the day inconsequent only "C" Coy moved up to DEWDROP & by night "D" on the night of the 4th/5th. An attempt was made by 2/Loversedge a party of bombers from "B" Coy to dislodge a party of Germans occupying a position likely to cause great annoyance to the daylight attack of this was unsuccessful & heavy casualties incurred. The battalion or received orders was to go forward to a line roughly 230 yards in advance of SUMMER TRENCH & tie in. The 20th R.F. on our Left was to establish a touching back up to SUNKEN ROAD so as to establish connection by between our (2nd R.W.F.) new line and ORION TRENCH which the 17th Divn. were to attack on our Right. The KRR of 100th Bde were to push forward beyond HAZY. Zero time was fixed at 11.10 a.m. This battalion was to push forward & dig in. The 17th Divn. were to dig each strong point under cover of the barrage up to the line we were to dig into. Another still further forward for the purpose of closely reconnoitring the LE TRANSLOY CEMETERY CIRCLE. This new line was not to be occupied till dusk. At about 11.15 a.m. the Germans were seen to be issuing "D" "C" Coys moved up & placed themselves on the right of "B" Coy	

27.N
3 sheet

WAR DIARY
or
INTELLIGENCE SUMMARY.
(Erase heading not required.)

Army Form C. 2118.

Place	Date	Hour	Summary of Events and Information	Remarks and references to Appendices
	5.11.16 cont		"D" & "C" Coys then moved forward & by noon were digging in 100 yds in front of their objective & were calling out our gains. The gap between our Right Coy K.R.R. was 300 yds. During the night 5/6/16 this Coy was reduced to 100 yds & touch maintained by patrols. On this left communication was kept open with 2 W.F. on whose allegn to form up the regt were unsuccessful, but who afterwards reaching that regt to left rear of "B" Coy. The attack of the 17th Division was unsuccessful & our line was much annoyed by rifle fire from this direction.	
	6.11.16		We re-inforced and a good trench dug, taps with "T" heads now only 15 yds from our original objective. On the night of 6/7 our outposts were much improved and "C" Coy (Right Cor) had dug to gap of communication to the long dug in on Nov. 5th with D. communication trench running.	
	7.11.16		Heavy again. Batt. continued. Relieved by 1st Devons of the 4th Div. and Battalion moved to LA BRIQUETERIE - a very wet night	
BRIQUETERIE	8.11.16		Moved to MEAULTE.	
MEAULTE	9.11.16		Still at MEAULTE.	
	10.11.16		At MEAULTE - Transport moved by road to FORCEVILLE. Prince of Wales had tea and officers of the Regiment welcomed	
	11.11.16		Entrained for SERMAN COURT for AIRAINES	
	12.11.16		Arrived at AIRAINES at 3.30 am. marched to FORCEVILLE & NEUVILLE "A" & "B" quartered in FORCEVILLE. "C" & "D" quartered in NEUVILLE	
FORCEVILLE NEUVILLE	13.11.16 to		Training at FORCEVILLE & NEUVILLE.	
	30.11.16		Training at FORCEVILLE & NEUVILLE.	

Murray
Lieut-Colonel
Commanding, 2nd Bn Royal Welch Fusiliers

WAR DIARY CASUALTIES.
or
INTELLIGENCE SUMMARY.
(Erase heading not required.)

Army Form C. 2118.

Place	Date	Hour	Summary of Events and Information	Remarks and references to Appendices
BRIQETERE LES BOEUFS	2.11.16 3.11.16		One OR killed Seven ORs wounded	
	4.11.16		Four ORs — " — eight " — 3 ORs missing	
			One OR — " — five " — "	
			" — " — four " — " 3 2/Lt de Richards wounded. 61 ORs joined, and joined the 33rd Divisional Burial Party.	
Grove	5.11.16		Nineteen OR killed 54 ORs wounded 10 ORs missing 2 Lt D.M. Cohny wounded, 2 Lt T. Williams wounded.	
Grove	6.11.16		Five ORs killed 3 ORs wounded	
Grove	7.11.16		Three OR killed 7 ORs wounded 10 ORs missing 2/Lt M Leversed wounded	
Carlth	9.11.16		Forty three ORs joined the Battalion at MEAULTE	
Grove	12.11.16		Seven ORs joined the Battalion at FOREVILLE	
Grove	18.11.16		Nine ORs rejoined	— " —
Grove	19.11.16		Ten ORs joined the Battalion	— " —
Grove	20.11.16		Fifty three ORs joined the Battalion	— " —
Grove	27.11.16		Captain Foss L. Da	— " —
Grove	28.11.16		Seventeen ORs joined the Battalion	— " —
Grove	29.11.16		Ten ORs joined the Battalion	— " —

Army Form C. 2118.

WAR DIARY
INTELLIGENCE SUMMARY

December 1916

1st Bn. Royal Welch Fusiliers

Vol 29

Place	Date	Hour	Summary of Events and Information	Remarks and references to Appendices
FORCEVILLE and NEUVILLE	1.12.16	7am	Training at FORCEVILLE & NEUVILLE.	
	4.12.16	7am	C.S.M. C. DAVIES Commissioned from the Ranks.	
	6.12.16	7am	4 Other Ranks from the Base	
	7.12.16	7am	Transport moved by road to new area	
	8.12.16	7am	The Battalion entrained at AIRAINES for new area; detrained at VIGNACOURT & moved by road to VAUX sur SOMME.	
	9.12.16	7am	The Battalion with transport moved by road to Camp III N of SUZANNE. 2nd Lt CRAWSHAY of VAUX sick. 2nd Lt. E. COSTER arrived from Base.	
Camp III SUZANNE	10.12.16	7am	Camp III. N of SUZANNE.	
	11.12.16	10am	Camp III. Lt. N.H. RADFORD arrived from L.G. Course.	
	12.12.16	2pm	Camp III. 2nd Lt. JAGGER arrived from Leave. Lt. GREAVES to hospital. Lt. OWEN permitted to wear Captain's badges as acting second. Lt. RADFORD's authority to wear Capt's badges, was cancelled to date to find Capt ch MidFEMONT took over C Company. 3 other Ranks from the Base.	
	13.12.16	10am	Camp III. 2nd Lt A.T. HARRIES arrived from Leave. Lt S.B. BARNWORTH of Joined.	
	14.12.16	10am	The Battalion less L.G.A. marched to Camp 13.14.C. S.of MAUREPAS & took over the Camp from the 1st QUEEN'S Regt.	
Camp 13.14.C MAUREPAS	15.12.16	10am	The Battalion becomes Brigade reserve. 2nd Lt ROBERTSON arrived from Leave.	
	16.12.16	7am	The Drums & 14 NCO's under the R.S.M. & four syncallers left for Camp III. 2nd Lt. CRAWSHAY returned from hospital.	

Army Form C. 2118.

WAR DIARY
or
INTELLIGENCE SUMMARY
(Erase heading not required.)

Instructions regarding War Diaries and Intelligence Summaries are contained in F. S. Regs., Part II. and the Staff Manual respectively. Title Pages will be prepared in manuscript.

Place	Date	Hour	Summary of Events and Information	Remarks and references to Appendices
MAUREPAS	17.12.16.		2 Lt. T. BLOCK joined the Battalion. 2 Lt. GREAVES injured from hospital.	
	18.12.16.	2 PM	The Battalion relieved the 1/5th SCOTTISH RIFLES & night in the left sub section Hd qrs at ST PIERRE VAAST wood. Hd qrs of the Batt. was relieved during the night by B Coy. MAYNE.	
TRONCHES ST PIERRE VAAST WOOD	19.12.16.		All quiet. Snow fell.	
	20.12.16.		Fine clear day. Considerable hostile aerial activity; ineffective artillery activity to the south. Casualties killed, 1 O.R.	
	21.12.16.		A little rain fell & as the country muddy again. Enemy artillery fairly active. Casualties wounded, 2 O.R.	
	22.12.16.		The Batt. was relieved this night & the 4th Kings Regt. Guides ready 6.15 pm. Relief complete 10.40 pm. The Companies marched to MAUREPAS. HALTE & entrained for Camp 21. D1 off of 181 O.R. arrived. Casualties.	
Camp 21	23.12.16.		Cleaning up. Capt. MOODY, M.C. arrived from hos. Leave. 2nd Lt. GRIFFETHS and FARRAN'S joined the Battalion. Casualties killed 1 O.R. wounded 3 O.R.	
SUZANNE				
	25.12.16.		Christmas day. All ranks celebrated Christmas. Telegram to His Majesty The Battalion marched to Camp 13. Quiet Camp: no Rd or fire wood.	
	26.12.16.		Casualties. Died 1 O.R.	
	27.12.16.		The Battalion less transport moved to new area, entraining at EDGHILL detraining at POINT REMY, marched to billeting area at VAUCHELLS-Q-QUESNOY	

Army Form C. 2118.

WAR DIARY
or
INTELLIGENCE SUMMARY

(Erase heading not required.)

Instructions regarding War Diaries and Intelligence Summaries are contained in F. S. Regs., Part II. and the Staff Manual respectively. Title Pages will be prepared in manuscript.

Place	Date	Hour	Summary of Events and Information	Remarks and references to Appendices
VAUCHELLES & QUESNOY	28.12.16		Cleaning up.	
	29.12.16		Capt. CUTHBERT arrived from hospital. The Prince of Wales sent a letter thanking the Regiment for its Christmas Card. Draft of 120 O.R. from the Base as reinforcements.	
	31.12.16			

Cmmr
Lieut Col
C.O. 9th. Y. Divn
Comdg 9th Bn. 9. Y. Divn

WAR DIARY or INTELLIGENCE SUMMARY

Army Form C. 2118.

2nd Bn. Royal Welch Fusiliers

Vol 30   19/23

29.N.

Place	Date	Hour	Summary of Events and Information	Remarks and references to Appendices
WINCHELSEA	1-1-17		O.R. reported from base (training)	
GUESNOY	2-1-17		Training. Lieut Colonel C.H.R. Crawshay awarded the D.S.O. Commenced Baths for the Men.	
			Capt. J.C. Mann & Lieut E.R. Conning awarded Military Cross. Rev. S.P.P.B. Grundy Jr. the Battalion.	
	3-1-17		Training.	
	4-1-17		Training.	
	5-1-17		Training. = Captain W.P. Lacy, R.C. Brooke wounded. Commanding with rank of Captain seniority from October 8. 1915; 30 other rank struck off strength of Bn. having been evacuated sick. 23 O.R. rejoining from Bn. Depot. Major Geo. W. Evans from Base to Battalion 9 mos. wish.	
	6-1-17		Training. 2 Lieuts struck off strength of Bn. having been evacuated sick. Chaplain Revd. J. Fishley joined.	
	7-1-17		Training. Commenced 3 O.R. struck off strength of Bn. (sick)	
	8-1-17		Training.	
	9-1-17		Training.	
	10-1-17		Brigade "Route March".	
	11-1-17		Training. Major G.R. Rose proceeded to U.K. on duty. 4 O.R. rejoined from Base. 3 O.R.s to reinforcement.	
	12-1-17		Major G.R. Rose presented ribbon to Lieut H. Mann. C.2 Loan. General R. Hayes Comdg. 33rd Bde.	
	13-1-17		Rev. C.C.P. Bartlett S.C.F. 15.9.16.	
	14-1-17		2/Lt. H.C. June rejoined from base 3 mos. R.W. Lancashires rejoined	
	15-1-17		Lieut Colonel C.H.R. Crawshay D.S.O. proceeded from base.	
			Entrained at SENTRENG. Detrained at BRAY TOULOUBIERE & long & tedious journey at 2 am. Bray TOULOUBIERE Station to Camp 111.	
BRAY	16-1-17		Camp 111. Conf. Offices & 2 Coy. Commanders viewed the trenches at Bn. 90 R. 29.	
	17-1-17		Bn. marched to SUZANNE; 2/Lt. from billets	
SUZANNE	18-1-17		Left SUZANNE at 10 am to join 1st 13th Regt. Relief complete at 3.30 pm. marched along by in trailing before relieving 1st Bn. 10/90 Regt. French Infantry. 1st 13 Bn. relieved by Lieut Col. Grubb & Lieut Col. R.H.R. Crawshay with the Bande (?) Offrs. G2, 2 Sergt & Commander OPP visiting Dugout 20 & [?] F.S. J-8 Hill F. until Jan 22nd	
			Casualties 15 O.R. wounded.	

WAR DIARY
or
INTELLIGENCE SUMMARY.
(Erase heading not required.)

Army Form C. 2118.

Place	Date	Hour	Summary of Events and Information	Remarks and references to Appendices
CLERY	21.1.17		To the authority renewed: Bn at rest day - day spent by H.Q. Q.M. Coy & Sergts Revue of subjects. Genl Clive & officers from Bde; 2nd Lieut Bowley & Flackley of Rundle in H. Evans.	
	22.1.17		Capt Hardy Acting 2 i/c B.S. Echelon as usual, 2nd Lieut Williams relieved at Tanks on high ground No. 47 North of SOMME (Lewis & Vickers MGs). Batn joined Bn from Base 2 officers & 8 men.	
	23.1.17		Bn went from Base 2 Officers & Bn relieved Army Band.	
	24.1.17		Bn Church parade at 11am. Capt. G.B. Payne promoted Lt. Bn promoted to STAPLES as instructor for 3 months.	
	25.1.17		Paid. Quartermasters dance at SUZANNE discharged by fire; Lieut Colonel & Captn left with 5 officers of other ranks unhurt.	
	26.1.17		6 O.R. wounded. Bn left Bohain CLERY and moved into Brigade sub... relieving 5 Scottish Rifles in OLEG VILLAGE. Capt Grayill & Lieut Burkhart in temporary Command from 25.1.17.	
	27.1.17		Day and night work	
	28.1.17		Relieved 5 S.R. in left subsection (CLERY)	
	29.1.17		Day Quiet 3 n.grot & 1 wounded	
	30.1.17		Day Quiet 2 officers & 20 wounded. 10 R. Killed 5 O.R. wounded	
	31.1.17		Relieved by 4th Kings & marched by lorries to SUZANNE (Camp 9)	

M Warhurst Captain
Comdg 2 Bn Royal Welsh Fuscrs.

Army Form C. 2118.

WAR DIARY
or
INTELLIGENCE SUMMARY.
(Erase heading not required.)

2^{LA} Royal Welsh Fusiliers

Vol 31

Place	Date	Hour	Summary of Events and Information	Remarks and references to Appendices
Suzanne	1.2.17		Day quiet.	
—	2.2.17		Day quiet. 2nd Lieut A.J. Harris rejoined from Hospital. Capt Grundy (Chaplain) to Hospital.	
—	3.2.17		Day quiet. Weather very cold.	
—	4.2.17		Day quiet.	
—	5.2.17		Day quiet. 2nd Lieut Lowe returned from leave.	
—	6.2.17		Day quiet.	
—	7.2.17		Day quiet. Capt I.M. Owen returned from leave.	
—	8.2.17		Relieved 9th H.L.I. Left ½ battalion to Hospital. Capt I.M. Owen assumed command of Battalion.	
BETHUNE ROAD SECTOR	9.2.17		In the line in the BETHUNE ROAD Sector. Day quiet. 2nd Lieut W. Pugh to 1st Army H.2.	
	10.2.17		In the trenches. Quiet day. A few trench mortars & rifle grenades fell in our line. 2nd Lieut Mair accidentally wounded. V.B & L.G boys relieved by A & D Coys.	
—	11.2.17		In the trenches. Quiet day.	
—	12.2.17		Relieved by 5th S.R. After relief moved into HOWITZER WOOD men very comfortable	
HOWITZER WOOD	13.2.17		In HOWITZER WOOD. Quiet day. Very heavy convoy traffic for forthcoming operation.	
—	14.2.17		In Brigade Reserve. 2nd Lieut Lawes R.A. joined the Battalion.	
—	15.2.17		In Brigade Reserve. Capt J. Cuthbert rejoined from hospital.	
—	16.2.17		Relieved the 5th S.R. in the left of BETHUNE Sector. Relief completed by 9.30 pm.	
BETHUNE ROAD SECTOR	17.2.17		Quiet day. Lieut Orme joined Battalion.	
	18.2.17		In the Trenches. Quiet day. Preparations forthcoming operation proposed.	
—	19.2.17		In the Trenches. Lieut Lady Lipsent W.B. Bennett assumed command of the Batt.	
—	20.2.17		Quiet day. Relieved by 11th Lancashires and Battalion moved to Bde Support at P.C. MADAME	
P.C. MADAME	21.2.17		At P.C. MADAME. Very few recommendation. Good deal of archives.	
—	22.2.17		In Bde Support. Of rations again proposed. Got aimed from the 3rd Batt.	
—	23.2.17		Relieved by 4th Kings and marched to Suzanne. Relief complete at 5.30 am. Billets at Suzanne much improved.	
SUZANNE	24.2.17		In Suzanne in Divisional Support. Rain.	
—	25.2.17		At Suzanne. Day spent in cleaning up.	
—	26.2.17		At Suzanne. Training commenced. Heavy working parties.	
—	27.2.17		At Suzanne Training. Major R.S. Rome joined to Batt. as 2nd in command.	
—	28.2.17		At Suzanne Training. Heavy working parties.	

W.H. Rowe
Comdg 2 RWFus

Army Form C. 2118.

War Diary or INTELLIGENCE SUMMARY.

2 RWF March 1917 Vol 32

Place	Date	Hour	Summary of Events and Information	Remarks and references to Appendices
SUZANNE.	1/3/17.		St. Davids Day; many greetings received.	
"	2/3/17.		Training.	
"	3/3/17.		The Batt. relieved the 2nd Worcesters in the Support of the Right Sector. 1 O.R. wounded. 1 O.R. Died of Wounds.	
RIGHT SECTOR	4/3/17.		In Support. The Batt. relieved the 1st Queens in the Front Line Trenches. 1 O.R. wounded.	
"	5/3/17.		Front Line. During the day, quiet. Enemy Artillery fairly active. 20 .R.Killed. 3 O.R. wounded.	
"	6/3/17.		Front Line. Enemy quiet, during the day; in the evening intermittent shelling.	
"	7/3/17.		Front Line. Day quiet. 2 O.R. Killed. 21 O.R. wounded. Batt. from Base.	
"	8/3/17.		Front Line. Day quiet. The Batt. was relieved by 12th Batt. South Wales Borderers. "A" "B" & "C" Coys.marched to Frise Bend, "D" Coy. to the Second Line.	
FRISE BEND	9/3/17.		In Reserve. The Batt. was relieved by 18th Batt. Welch Regiment and marched to SUZANNE.	
SUZANNE	10/3/17.		The Batt. marched to Camp 13 via BRAY & Cross Roads (K 21.b.8.9.) Camp very muddy and wet. Afternoon spent in cleaning up. Lieut. J.C.Mann rejoined the Batt. from 19th Inf.Bde. and resumed duties of Adjutant.Lt-Colonel W.B. Garnett rejoined from leave.	
CAMP 13.v	11/3/17.		Training. Lieut. R.C.Shelley & Capt. R.von R.Graves to England Sick & struck off strength of Batt.	
"	12/3/17.		Training. 2nd Lieuts.Storey-Cooper, Lloyd and Sassoon joined the Batt. from Base.	
"	13/3/17.		Training.	
"	14/3/17.		Training.	
"	15/3/17.		Training.	
"	16/3/17.		Training. The Commanding Officer inspected the whole of the Battalion.	
"	17/3/17.		Training.	
"	18/3/17.		Training.	
"	19/3/17.		Training.	
"	20/3/17.		Training. 2nd Lieut. P.A.Lund to England sick and struck off strength of Batt. Lieut.J.C.Mann to England on leave.	
"	21/3/17.		Training.	
"	22/3/17.		Training.	
"	23/3/17.		Training. 1 O.R. accidentally wounded.	
"	24/3/17.		Training.	
"	25/3/17.		Training.	
"	26/3/17.		Training.	
"	27/3/17.		Brigade Route March.	
"	28/3/17.		Training.	
"	29/3/17.		Training.	
"	30/3/17.		Brigade Route March.	
"	31/3/17.		Training.	

Comdg. 2nd Battalion Royal Welch Fusiliers.
Lieut-Colonel.

Instructions regarding War Diaries and Intelligence Summaries are contained in F. S. Regs., Part II. and the Staff Manual respectively. Title pages will be prepared in manuscript.

WAR DIARY 2nd Battalion, Royal Welch Fusiliers

Army Form C. 2118.

INTELLIGENCE SUMMARY.

(Erase heading not required.)

Place	Date	Hour	Summary of Events and Information	Remarks and references to Appendices
CAMP 13.	1-4-17.		Training.	
CORBIE.	2-4-17.		Left Camp 13. and proceeded by route march to CORBIE. Comfortable billets for men. 2nd Lieuts STOREY-COOPER, LEWIS, LOWE, PHILLIPS, and T.H. DAVIES were detailed for Depot Batt.	
VILLERS-BOCAGE.	3-4-17.		Left CORBIE and marched to VILLERS-BOCAGE. Poor accommodation. Lieutenant J.C. MANN returned from leave.	
BEUVAL.	4-4-17.		Left VILLERS-BOCAGE and marched to BEUVAL. Marched past Brig-General PINNEY and Lieut-General SIR IVOR MAXSE.	
BEUVAL.	5-4-17.		Marched to LUCHEUX in the afternoon. Very crowded.	
LUCHEUX.	6-4-17.		Details left for Depot Battalion.	
SAULTY.	7-4-17.		Marched to SAULTY. Poor accommodation.	
BASSEUX.	8-4-17.		Representatives rode forward to reconnoitre line. Battalion marched to BASSEUX. Good accommodation for Officers and Men.	
BASSEUX.	9-4-17.		Baggage prepared for dumping.	
BASSEUX.	10-4-17.		Battalion at 6 hours notice to move.	
BASSEUX.	11-4-17.		Moved to M-35-C near MERCATEL. Moved at very short notice. Transport stopped at BLAIRVILLE.	
M-35-C.	12-4-17.		Battalion moved to HENIN-SUR-COJUEL. Captain J.C. DUNN returned from leave.	
HENIN.	13-4-17.		Transport moved to BOIRY-BECQUERELLE.	
HENIN.	14-4-17.		Went into trenches to relieve the 13th Northumberland Fusiliers at short notice in the HINDENBURG LINE. Relief was not complete until 4-30 a.m. 15th instant.	
HINDENBURG LINE.	15-4-17.		It may be noteworthy to record that all Battalion Headquarters were in the trench in a tunnel dugout of about 2 miles in length.	
"	16-4-17.		On morning of 16th the 19th Infantry Brigade attacked towards FONTAINE-LES-CROISILLES of which attack the CAMERONIANS were allotted the task of bombing up the HINDENBURG LINE. 4 Officers and 100 O.Rs. and 2 Lewis Guns were lent to the CAMERONIANS as support, 75 of these were actually engaged. 2nd Lieut. SASSOON and Sgt Baldwin especially distinguished themselves. 2nd Lieutenant Sassoon wounded.	
"	17-4-17.		Relieved by 4th Kings. Relief complete at 12-55 p.m. The Battalion moved to bivouac into Sunken Road at M-35-C. near MERCATEL.	
M-35-C.	18-4-17.		Representatives from Battalion reconnoitred line in front of CROISILLES.	
"	19-4-17.		Relieved 2nd WORCESTERS in front of CROISILLES. Battalion holding an outpost line. Relief complete at 9-55 p.m.	
TRENCHES.	20-4-17.		In the Line. Quiet day. 2 O.Rs. Wounded.	
"	21-4-17.		Quiet day. 2 O.Rs. killed. Relieved by 2nd WORCESTERS Relief complete at 10-45 p.m. Battalion moved to MERCATEL M-35-C. Batt reported all present at 4.0 a.m. 22nd inst.	

Army Form C. 2118.

Instructions regarding War Diaries and Intelligence Summaries are contained in F. S. Regs., Part II. and the Staff Manual respectively. Title pages will be prepared in manuscript.

INTELLIGENCE SUMMARY

2nd Battalion, Royal Welch Fusiliers.

(Erase heading not required).

Place	Date	Hour	Summary of Events and Information	Remarks and references to Appendices
MEROATEL.	22-4-17.		"A" and "C" Companies moved to HINDENBURG LINE to support the SUFFOLKS in 98th Brigade attack on 23rd. Headquarters, "B" and "D" Companies moved at 6-30 to Sunk en Road T-3-a.	
TRENCHES.	23-4-17.		The task allotted to the 4th SUFFOLKS West of the SENSEE RIVER and "A" and "C" Companies were attack with an objective about 300 yds West of the HINDENBURG Support line by a bombing detailed to picket the entrances of all dugouts. As the attack was made a party of 20 was also detailed to clear the tunnel after the objective had been gained, this party was found from "A" Company. Zero was at 4-45 a.m. and after a short but intense Artillery and Stokes Mortar bombardment the attack was launched. The SUFFOLKS advanced down the trench at great speed followed by "A" and "C" Companies, the latter Company immediately beginning to picket the dugouts At 7-30 a.m. the SUFFOLKS were within 200 yards of their Objective but held up by Machine Gun fire and lack of bombs. Every endeavour was made by the two R.W.F. Companies to get up an ample supply of bombs but the delay gave the enemy an opportunity to reorganise himself and at 10-30 a.m. he delivered a fierce counter-attack up the trench but the SUFFOLKS were forced to withdraw. "A" and "C" Companies had by this time taken from the dugouts about 400 prisoners and had removed 2 Machine Guns and one small grossdenwerfer into our original portion of trench which the enemy endevoured to rush. Capt.Owen, Lieut. Greaves of "A" Company, Capt. Radford, 2nd Lieut Jones, Sgt Williams and Sgt Hughes of "C" Coy. by throwing bombs continually held up the enemy advance. Shortly after the enemy brought a concentrated fire of rifle grenades and trench mortars on to our men by the block causing many casualties. Capt. Owen, Lieut Greaves, 2nd Lieut Jones, Sgt Williams, Sgt Hughes, L/Cpl James and Pte Bennett went over the open and bombed the enemy from a flank. This held up the enemy but when returning Sgt Hughes was killed and 2nd Lieut Jones was wounded, Sgt Williams bringing him in. Shortly after this Capt Owen was killed and 2nd Lieut Greaves wounded. 2nd Lieut Farrand and Sgt Williams organised a rifle grenade barrage and the enemy fire quietened down except for Artillery fire which was kept up pthe whole time. At 5-30 p.m. "C" Company were warned that the 5th SCOTTISH RIFLES were to attack down the HINDENBURG LINE in a similar manner to the morning. Capt Radford arranged a rifle grenade barrage and intense Lewis Gun fire was brought to bear down the trench. Zero was 6-24 p.m. but only a few 5th SCOTTISH RIFLES GOT OVER THE BARRICADE and they were immediately driven back and the enemy artillery fire increased rendering the position of men round the barricade a very trying one. 2nd Lieut Farrand was wounded and Q.S.M.Akilled about 7-30 p.m. About 7-45 p.m. the enemy made a very determined attempt to rush the barricade by a bombing attack which was driven back almost entirely by the efforts of Sgt Williams, L/Cpl James and Pte Bennett whose conduct can only be described as magnificent. From 8-0 to 10-0 p.m. Capt Radford and 6 O.Rs. held the barricade after which time the hostile shelling and bombing quietened down.	

Army Form C. 2118.

WAR DIARY 2nd Battalion, Royal Welch Fusiliers.
or INTELLIGENCE SUMMARY.
(Erase heading not required.)

Place	Date	Hour	Summary of Events and Information	Remarks and references to Appendices
TRENCHES.	25-4-17. (Contin.)		At about 4-0 a.m. on the 24th the party at the barricade was relieved by the 1st CAMERONIANS. Capt Radford took back the two Companys to a portion of the tunnel in rear of 98th Bgde.Hd.Qrs. The Battalion (Less "A" and "C" Coys.) moved to the HINDENBURG LINE at 7-45 a.m. arriving in position at 8-15 a.m. The situation at this time was not clear, the SUFFOLKS were well down the HINDENBURG LINE and portions of the ARGYLLS and MIDDLESEX had attained their objectives. The Battalion was ordered at 9-15 a.m. to occupy the jumping off trench of the 98th Brigade, and to consolidate it, futher to reconnoitre and consolidate if possible the captured German front Line. On arrival in position, consolidation was found to be practically impossible owing to the congestion and the enemy were found to be holding the trench on the ridge facing us. Batt, Hd.Qrs. was established at Hd.Qrs. of 1st MIDDLESEX. "B" and "D" Companys were warned to attack the enemys position at 2-0 p.m. this however was postponed. At 5-0 p.m. the Batt. was ordered to be prepared to attack at very short notice. At 6-0 p.m. the Batt. was ordered to attack at 6-24 p.m. Hurried preperations were made and after a short but fierce bombardment the attack was launched. The Companys advanced with great gallantry and soon all the officers and N.C.Os were seen to fall and the attack was held up owing to Maching Gun fire. Many men reached the German wire whilst the other's dropped into shell holes in "No Mans Land" A few wounded and unwounded managed to crawl in, in daylight, and a fairly large number at dusk. After night fall the majority of the wounded were brought in and evacuated to the advanced Dressing Station. Just after dawn it was discovered that the enemy had evacuated his position: patrols were immediately pushed forward and the position occupied. At 9-0 a.m. of the 25th an outpost line was established about 500 yards in front of the enemy position. The patrols which were pushed forward discovered the Companys of the ARGYLES and MIDDLESEX which had attacked in the morning. They were holding their final objective and touch was gained with them. All our officers were buried and the majority of O.Rs. The following greatly distinguished themselves :- Captain N.H.Radford, Lieut. R.C.J. Greaves, Capt.J.M. Owen,2nd Lieut. R.H.Harmer, Lt & Adjt. J.C.Mann. M.C. and Captain J. Churchill Dunn, M.C. R.A.M.C. (Attached) 10089 Sgt Jack Williams, 8675 C.S.M. William Gittins, 8510 Sgt Edwin Jones, 39572 L/Cpl Ronald Enoch James, 55169 Pte Walter Bennett, 56715 Pte William Thomas, 604 7 CSM Victor Ward, 10711 L/Cpl Henry Davies, 17202 Pte Robert Roberts, 7445 Pte Charles, White, 57134 Pte William George Taylor, 31068 L/Cpl Alan Lloyd, 5540 Pte William Davies, 33420 Pte Enoch Evans, 36505 L/Cpl Albert Perks, 54601 Pte John Owen Jones. Casualties :- Capt J.M.Owen,2nd Lieut A.Phillips, 2nd Lieut S.L.Blaxley,2nd Lieut J.B. Jackson, Killed in Action.	

Army Form C. 2118.

WAR DIARY or INTELLIGENCE SUMMARY.

2nd Battalion Royal 1 Welch Fusiliers.

(Erase heading not required.)

Instructions regarding War Diaries and Intelligence Summaries are contained in F.S. Regs., Part II. and the Staff Manual respectively. Title pages will be prepared in manuscript.

Place	Date	Hour	Summary of Events and Information	Remarks and references to Appendices
TRENCHES.	23-4-17. (Contin.)		Lieut Greaves, 2nd Lieutenants J Farrand, R.H.Hammer, R.Jones, G.W.Lowe, W.G.Lloyd and R.N.eld-Siddall, Wounded. 32 O.Rs. Killed. 70 O.Rs Wounded. 5 O.Rs Missing.	
BOIRY-BECERELLE.	24-4-17.		Battalion was relieved by the 20th ROYAL FUSILIERS. Relief complete at 1-0 p.m. The Battalion moved into bivouac at BOIRY-BECERELLE. "A" and "C" Coys had previously moved to BOIRY at 9-30 a.m.	
"	25-4-17.		Resting. Reorganisation commenced.	
BLAIRVILLE	26-4-17.		Moved to BLAIRVILLE by route march. Billets more comfortable than expected. Visited by Major-General PINNEY who complimented the men on their very fine work. Reorganisation continued. *Archer-West Lieut-General Lt D S O* *now Lieut-General.*	
BASSEUX.	27-4-17.		Moved by route march to BASSEUX.	
"	28-4-17.		Training. Draft of 136 O.Rs arrived. 2nd Lieut T.E.G.Davies returned from hospital.	
"	29-4-17.		Training.	
"	30-4-17.		Training.	

W. Ramer
Lieutenant-Colonel.,
Commanding, 2nd Battalion Royal Welch Fusiliers.

Army Form C. 2118.

WAR DIARY or INTELLIGENCE SUMMARY. =2nd BATTALION ROYAL WELCH FUSILIERS.=

(Erase heading not required.)

Instructions regarding War Diaries and Intelligence Summaries are contained in F. S. Regs., Part II. and the Staff Manual respectively. Title pages will be prepared in manuscript.

Place	Date	Hour	Summary of Events and Information	Remarks and references to Appendices
BASSEUX.	1-5-17		Training. 17 O.Rs rejoined from Base.	
"	2-5-17		Moved to bivouac near ADINFER.	
ADINFER.	3-5-17		Training. 81 O.Rs joined from Base.	
"	4-5-17		Training. Captain W.W.Kirkby proceeded to St. POL as instructor.	
"	5-5-17		Training.	
"	6-5-17		Divisional Race Meeting.	
"	7-5-17		Training.	
"	8-5-17		Training. Major R.A.Poore D.S.O. and Lieut. T.R.Conning reported off leave.	
"	9-5-17		Training.	
"	10-5-17		Training.	
"	11-5-17		Training.	
MOYENNVILLE	12-5-17		Moved to MOYENVILLE by route march. Weather very hot.	
"	13-5-17		Service at 10-30a.m. By the Rev. Aitcheson Capt. 20 R.F. Training.	
"	14-5-17		Training. Notification received that the Corps Commander had awarded the Military Medal to the following N.C.Os and men for acts of gallantry in the Field. The C.O. informed each recepient personally and congratulated him.	
			No 55169 Pte W.Bennett. 39572 L/Cpl R.E.James 4612 Sgt H.Baldwin.	
			" 10711 " R.Roberts. 5745 Pte C.White. 57134 Pte C.Taylor.	
			51068 L/Cpl A.Lloyd. 5540 Pte W.Davies. 33420 Pte E.Evans.	
			56505 L/Cpl A.Perks. 54601 Pte J.O.Jones.	
St.LEDGER	15-5-17		Battalion moved into the line, in Right Brigade Support in bivouacs in St.LEDGER-HENIN Road about one mile N.W. of St.LEDGER and relieved the 1st Queens Regt. Relief complete at 5;30 p.m.	
"	16-5-17		Battalion in same place.	
"	17-5-17		Battalion in same place.	
"	18-5-17		Battalion relieved the Cameronians in Right Sub Sector of the CROISILLES Sector in front of HINDENBURG LINE. Relief complete at 12-0midnight.	
R. SUB SECTOR	19-5-17		During the night 19/20 the Battalion was relieved by the 1st Queens The 2nd Worcesters moved up into an position in the vicinity of the quarry at T.18.b. prior to attacking the HINDENBURG LINE covering FONTAINE LES CROISILLES on the morning of the 20th. Relief complete at 12-0 midnight. The Battalion on being relieved moved into Divisional reserve in two sunken roads in squares T.30.a.T.24.c. T.29.b.T.23.d.	
T.30.a.	20-5-17		An attack by the 33rd Division was made at 5-15a.m. on the HINDENBURG RG LINE. The 5th SCOTTISH RIFLES of the 19th Infantry Brigade being on the right and forming a defensive flank on bye road Running N.and S, approx. in U.14.c. the 100th Brigade being in the centre and 98th on the Left.	

2353 Wt. W5444/1454 700,000 5/15 D. D. & L. A.D.S.S./Forms/C. 2118.

(C. SHEET No. 2.) Army Form C. 2118.

WAR DIARY 2nd Battalion, Royal Welch Fusiliers.

or

INTELLIGENCE SUMMARY.

(Erase heading not required.)

Instructions regarding War Diaries and Intelligence Summaries are contained in F. S. Regs., Part II. and the Staff Manual respectively. Title pages will be prepared in manuscript.

Place	Date	Hour	Summary of Events and Information	Remarks and references to Appendices
			The result of this attack was that the front line of the HINDENBURG LINE was captured, but not the Support Trench. Divisional Reserve were the Cameronians 2nd R.W.Fus. and 18th Middlesex and certain Engineers. During the morning "A" and "C" Companies 2nd R.W.Fus. were lent to the 100th Brigade for carrying purposes. They returned to the Battalion in the evening after carrying continually over heavily barraged ground. In the evening the Cameronians and 20th Batt. Royal Fusiliers carried out a further attack on the Support Trench of the HINDENBURG LINE between about	
T.30.a.	21-5-17		U.15.b. Central to the FONTAINE-CROISILLES Road starting 7-30 p.m. The Battalion still in Divisional reserve. During the night 21/22 the Battalion relieved the 2nd Worcesters and part of 9th Batt. H.L.I. in the HINDENBURG Front Line between the point U.14.a.10 and U.15.b.55.70. Dispositions "B" "C" and "D" Companies in front line and "A" in support in U.15.a. and T.18.b. Battalion Headquarters in the quarry at T.18.b. 72. Relief complete at 3-0 a.m. Captain P.Moody rejoined the Battalion at "B" Echelon from 1st Battalion.	
HINDENBURG FRONT LINE	22-5-17		During night 22/23rd the Battalion was relieved by the 4th Batt. Northumberland Fusiliers who took over from the 5th Scottish Rifles and 2nd R.W.Fus. The Battalion on being relieved moved N.W. of St.LEDGER to an area about the Railway Cutting in T.20.d. Relief complete at 3-35 a.m. The following decorations awarded by the Field Marshall Commanding in Chief were received this day.	
			Lieutenant (Acting Captain) N.H.Radford.	MILITARY CROSS.
			2nd Lieutenant W.Harmer.	"
			No 8675 C.S.-M. W.Giffins.	"
			10089 Sgt J. Williams.	BAR TO D.C.M.
			7626 Sgt S. Edwards.	DISTINGUISHED CONDUCT MEDAL.
			8510 Sgt E. Jones.	"
			56715 Pte W. Thomas.	MILITARY MEDAL.
T.20.d.	23-5-17		Resting.	
"	24-5-17		Resting. A few officers and O.Rs o' the Battalion were given leave to attend sports held by the 1st Battalion near ACHIET LE PETIT, these being challenged to a tug of war, improvised a team which won the pull.	
"	25-5-17		Resting. Slightly shelled.	
"	26-5-17		2nd Lieut. R.G.Shelley and 2nd Lieut. Tom Torkington joined the Batt. also from the Base, also 22 Other Ranks.	

Army Form C. 2118.

WAR DIARY
or
INTELLIGENCE SUMMARY.
(Erase heading not required.)

Instructions regarding War Diaries and Intelligence Summaries are contained in F.S. Regs., Part II. and the Staff Manual respectively. Title pages will be prepared in manuscript.

Place	Date	Hour	Summary of Events and Information	Remarks and references to Appendices
T.20.d.	21-5-17 (contin'd)		Lieutenant J.C. Mann to Hospital. "D" Company 5th Scottish Rifles attached to Battalion. Relieved 1 Coy and 2 Platoon of 6th Northumberland Fusiliers. Quiet night, relief complete at 2-30 a.m. After relief Coys were disposed as follows :- "A" and "C" Coys between PLUM LANE and Left Communication Trench. "D" Coy in PLUM LANE. "B" Coy in shell holes behind "A" and "C" Coys. "D" Coy 5th S.R. in shell holes behind "B" Coy. Casualty 1 O.R. wounded at duty.	
FRONT LINE	27-5-17		The morning was quiet and the weather very hot and sunny. On the 27th the Battalion attacked the objective being that portion of HINDENBURG Support Line between PLUM LANE and OLDENBURG LANE. The Cameronians attacked on the Left. The plan of attack was as follows ;- "A" and "C" Coys on a two Platoon front formed the first two waves. These Coys were ordered to push across the HINDENBURG LINE and establish a line of posts about a 100 yards in front. "A" Coy was also to establish a bombing block in OLDENBURG LANE in a line with these posts. Moppers up for the tunnel entrances were allotted from to "A" and "C" Coys from "B" Coy. "D" Coy was to bomb up PLUM LANE and on clearing it, turn southwards along Hindenburg Support, establish a bombing block about 80 yards down that trench. They were also ordered to attack the Hindenburg Support on right of PLUM LANE frontally by one platoon. "B" Coy formed the third wave. "D" Coy 5th S.R. were form the 4th wave. Zero was fixed at 1-55 p.m. The barrage to commence at zero and falling of barrage to be the signal for the Infantry to assault The waves advanced extremely well until the wire was reached when there was a tendency to bunch. During the advance however a gap was caused between the Cameronians and the Battalion, on the left The enemy worked round through this gap but, and this led to a retirement. A few parties reached the Hindenburg Support on the left but the right appear to have encountered an intermediate line about 50 yards in front of it. An order to retire was given to retire by someone known. and this was carried along the whole line from Left to Right and at 2-45 p.m. the whole were back in the old Hindenburg front line. Very heavy Machine Gun and rifle fire was met and casualties were heavy, only 2 2nd R.W.Fus. officers returned unwounded. Companies were quickly re-organised to meet a possible counter-attack. This appeared probable at about 7-0 p.m. but was apparently stopped by artillery fire. "D" Coy 5th S.R. was withdrawn after dark into an old assembly trench in U.13.c. The back areas were heavily shelled during the attack the hostile barrage being extremely severe between the quarry and CROIXILLES. Casualties. Captains Ormrod and Picton-Davies 2nd Lieut's Shelley and Torkington, wounded. Lieut Orme, T.R.Conning 2nd Lieut T.E.G.Davis, W.O.Lewis, T.B.Williams, J.D.M.Richards, wounded and missing.	

2353 W○ W834/1459 750000 1945 17 6. & W○ Ltd. &S./Forms/C. 2118.59 Killed, Wounded & Missing.

Army Form C. 2118.

WAR DIARY
or
INTELLIGENCE SUMMARY.
(Erase heading not required.)

Instructions regarding War Diaries and Intelligence Summaries are contained in F.S. Regs., Part II. and the Staff Manual respectively. Title pages will be prepared in manuscript.

Place	Date	Hour	Summary of Events and Information	Remarks and references to Appendices
FRONT LINE	28-5-17		Quiet day. A good deal of work was done and trench greatly improved. Relieved by 1st Queens. Before relief "B" and "C" Coys were withdrawn and moved to MOYENVILLE. Relief was complete at 1-10 p.m. Remainder of Battalion moved to bivouacs at MOYENVILLE.	
MOYENVILLE	29-5-17		Re-organisation commenced.	
"	30-5-17		Medal ribbons distributed to the above recepients by the G.O.C. 33rd Division. Battalion left MOYENVILLE at 5-0 p.m. and moved into billets at BASSEUX.	
BASSEUX.	31-5-17		Battalion left BASSEUX at 2-30 p.m. and moved into rest billets at B AILLEULVAL.	

Arthur Ames Sheene

Major, for,
Lieutenant-Colonel,
Commanding, 2nd Battalion, Royal Welch Fusiliers.

Army Form C. 2118.

WAR DIARY or INTELLIGENCE SUMMARY. 2nd Battalion, The Royal Welch Fusiliers.

(Erase heading not required.)

Place	Date	Hour	Summary of Events and Information	Remarks and references to Appendices
BAILLEULVAL	1-6-17.		Training.	
"	2-6-17.		Training.	
"	3-6-17.		Training.	
"	4-6-17.		Training. Lieutenant-Colonel W.B.GARNETT., awarded D.S.O. Lieut. & Quartermaster H.YATES, to be Captain & Quartermaster. Extracts Kings Birthday Honours London Gazette June 4th 1917.	
"	5-6-17.		Training. Captain J.C.DUNN. M.C. (M.O. R.A.M.C. Attd.) awarded a bar to his M.C.	
"	6-6-17.		Training.	
"	7-6-17.		Training.	
"	8-6-17.		Training.	
"	9-6-17.		Training.	
"	10-6-17.		Training.	
"	11-6-17.		Training.	
"	12-6-17.		Training.	
"	13-6-17.		Training.	
"	14-6-17.		Training. Lieutenants J.C.WILLIAMS., W.FARREN, and 2nd Lieuts T.H.WILLIAMSON, L.EVANS joined the Battalion. 2nd Lieut.,W.H.Fox and 2nd Lieut.,R.A.Casson, rejoined the battalion.	
"	15-6-17.		Morning, Training. Regimental Sports were held in the afternoon.	
"	16-6-17.		Morning, Training. Regimental Sports were held in the afternoon. Brigadier-General OWEN presented the prizes.	
"	17-6-17.		The Battalion marched to BASSEUX for Divine Service held under Brigade arrangements, after which the Corps Commander presented Medal Ribbons etc. to :- Captain J.C.DUNN M.C. bar to his M.C. 2nd Lieut. W.H.FOX - M.C. Sgt J.WILLIAMS - bar to D.C.M. and other recipients of 19th Inf.Bde.	
"	18-6-17.		The Battalion marched by cross country track to MOYENNEVILLE. Very hot day.	
MOYENNEVILLE TRENCHES.	19-6-17.		The Battalion relieved the 9th LEICESTERS in the right sub-sector.	
"	20-6-17.		Right sub-sector.	
"	21-6-17.		Right sub-sector. 3 other ranks wounded.	
"	22-6-17.		Right sub-sector. The Battalion was relieved by the 5th SCOTTISH RIFLES, and moved into Brigade Reserve. 5 other ranks killed. 4 other ranks wounded. No 8510 Sgt E.JONES, awarded a bar to his D.C.M. Captain L.M.ORMROD awarded Military Cross.	
"	23-6-17.		Brigade Reserve.	
"	24-6-17.		Brigade Reserve. The Battalion was relieved by the 16th Batt. K.R.R.C. and marched to Camp A. MOYENNEVILLE.	

Army Form C. 2118.

WAR DIARY / INTELLIGENCE SUMMARY

2nd Battalion, The Royal Welch Fusiliers.
(Sheet 2.)

(Erase heading not required.)

Instructions regarding War Diaries and Intelligence Summaries are contained in F.S. Regs., Part II. and the Staff Manual respectively. Title pages will be prepared in manuscript.

Place	Date	Hour	Summary of Events and Information	Remarks and references to Appendices
MOYENNEVILLE	25-6-17		Camp "A". The Battalion relieved the 16th K.R.R.C. in Brigade Reserve and became Brigade reserve to the 100th Brigade.	
TRENCHES.	26-6-17.		Brigade reserve. Very quiet day. 2nd Lieuts: (J.Sneddon, J.O.Smith, E.H.Evans, F.M.Hughes, D.Llewellyn,	
"	27-6-17.		Brigade reserve. 1 other rank killed. (W.Pilling, joined the battalion.	
"	28-6-17.		Brigade reserve. Day quiet.	
"	29-6-17.		Brigade reserve. Day quiet.	
"	30-6-17.		The Battalion was relieved by the 9th K.O.Y.L.I. and on relief marched to MONCHY-au-BOIS. Very wet day.	

1-7-1917.

W.G.Garnett.

Lieutenant-Colonel.,
Commanding, 2nd Battalion, The Royal Welch Fusiliers.

Army Form C. 2118.

WAR DIARY
or
INTELLIGENCE SUMMARY.

2nd Battalion, THE ROYAL WELCH FUSILIERS.

(Erase heading not required.)

Place	Date	Hour	Summary of Events and Information	Remarks and references to Appendices
MONCHY-AU-BOIS	1/7/17.		At MONCHY-AU-BOIS. Men only accommodated in bivouacs erected the previous day.	
ACHEUX.	2/7/17.		Marched to ACHEUX. Hot day. Men marched well. Billets poor.	
TALMAS.	3/7/17.		Marched to TALMAS. Early start. Very hot day, many men fell out. Draft of 133 O.Rs. joined the Batt.	
BELLOI-SUR-SOMME.	4/8/17.		Marched to BELLOY-SUR-SOMME. Early start, billets good.	
AIRAINES.	5/7/17.		Marched to AIRAINES. Men comfortably billetted but a little cramped.	
"	6/7/17.		Resting and cleaning up. 148 O.Rs joined the Battalion. Capt D. M¹ remont struck off on proceeding to Commanding Officers School Aldershot	
"	7/7/17.		Cleaning up and light training.	
"	8/7/17.		Church Parade on Market Square.	
"	9/7/17.		Training.	
"	10/7/17.		Brigade route March. No men fell out on line of march. 14 O.Rs joined the Battalion.	
"	11/7/17.		Training.	
"	12/7/17.		Training.	
"	13/7/17.		Battalion marched to the Brigade Training Area at RIVIERE.	
"	14/7/17.		Training. 2nd Lieut. HUGH JONES and 10 O.Rs joined the Battalion.	
"	15/7/17.		Church Parade on Market Square.	
"	16/7/17.		Training. Battalion marched to Brigade Training Area at RIVIERE.	
"	17/7/17.		Training. First day of Divisional Horse Show.	
"	18/7/17.		Brigade route March to Divisional Horse Show. 1st and 2nd prizes in Infantry Officers chargers Class won by Battalion. 2nd Lieut. E.R. STONEY-COOPER struck off the strength.	
"	19/7/17.		Training 2nd Lieut. S.I. Thomas joined the Battalion.	
"	20/7/17.		Training. 21 O.Rs. joined the Battalion.	
"	21/7/17.		Training. First day of Battalion Sports. Captain E.R. KEARSLEY D.S.O. rejoined the Battalion.	
"	22/7/17.		Church Parade on Market Square. 2nd Day of Battalion sports.	
"	23/7/17.		Training. Lieut. J.C. MANN M.O. rejoined from hospital.	
"	24/7/17.		Training at Brigade Training Area at RIVIERE.	
"	25/7/17.		Training. Lieut. M. WILLIAMS rejoined from Hospital.	
"	26/7/17.		Training.	
"	27/7/17.		Brigade Route March.	
"	28/7/17.		Divine Service on Market Square.	
"	29/7/17.		Training. Battalion less "B" Coy, marched to PONT REMY and entrained for DUNKERQUE. Left PONT REMY at 5-58 p.m. and arrived at detraining station at 5-0 a.m. on 1st August. Proceeded from DUNKERQUE	
"	30/7/17.			
"	31/7/17.		to BRAY DUNES in barges and marched from canal to Camp A, West of village. Very wet day.	

W.S. Sawell Lieut. Colonel,
Comdg., The Royal Welch Fusiliers.

Army Form C. 2118.

WAR DIARY
2nd Battalion, Royal Welch Fusiliers.

or

INTELLIGENCE SUMMARY.

(Erase heading not required.)

Place	Date	Hour	Summary of Events and Information	Remarks and references to Appendices
BRAY DUNES	1/8/17.		Battalion detrained at Dunkirk, and proceeded by barges to BRAY DUNES on the DUNKIRK-FURNESS Canal. The day was very wet and men arrived in Camp "A" on the sand dunes soaked.	
"	2/8/17.		Training commenced.	
"	3/8/17.		Training continued.	
"	4/8/17.		Training continued.	
"	5/8/17.		Church Parade at 9-30 a.m. Captain Coster to leave to U.K.	
"	6/8/17.		Training continued. The following Officers and O.Rs arrived:- Lieutenants G.E.B.Barkworth, R.Gambier-Parry., 2nd Lieuts W.J.Ramsey, T.H.Rhodes and 41 O.Rs including R.S.M. Boreham.	
"	7/8/17.		Training continued. Major R.A.Poore D.S.O. for leave to U.K..	
"	8/8/17.		Brigade route march, via sands, to ZUYDCOOTE.	
"	9/8/17.		Training continued.2nd Lieut. W.H.Fox to leave to U.K.	
"	10/8/17.		Training continued. Captain Radford M.C. to 4th Army Infantry school	
"	11/8/17.		Church Parade.conference at Brigade Headquarters for C.O. and Adjutant.	
"	12/8/17.		Battalion route march via GHYVELDE and ZUYDCOOTE.	
"	13/8/17.		Battalion tactical scheme over dunes East of camp. Warning order that 32nd Division in NIEUPORT Sector, on 17/18 August, received.	
"	14/8/17.			
OOST DUNK-ERQUE.	15/8/17.		Minimum Reserve and Drums proceeded to Depot Battalion under Captain P.Moody M.C. 2nd Lieut. E.F.C.Colquhoun from 3rd R.W.Fus. joined for duty. Battalion moved at 4-15 a.m. to OOST-DUNKERQUE and relieved 11th Borders there. The C.O. and Adjutant reconnoitred the LOMBARDZYDE Sector in the afternoon.	
"	16/8/17.		Relieved 5th West Ridings in Left subsection LOMBARDZYDE. Headquarters in redam. Ration strength 901. Numbers in line 460 and 20.Officers. 1 O.R. Killed. 2 O.R wounded.	
TRENCHES	17/8/17.		Holding left subsection. "A" & "B" Coys in the front line.	
"	18/8/17.		Holding left subsection. 1 O.R. Killed 6 O.Rs wounded.	
"	19/8/17.		Holding left subsection. Right of "D" Coy., flooded somewhat owing to a sluice being damaged by shell fire.	
"	20/8/17.		"C" & "D" relieved "A" & "B" Coys., in front line. 1 O.R. Killed 2 O.R. wounded.	
"	21/8/17.		Night disturbed, enemy fired a number of lachrymae shells around Head quarters. 3 O.Rs wounded.	
"	22/8/17.		Relieved by the Cameronians. Enemy raided our GELEIDE BROOK POST which had just be relieved by the Cameronians. He failed to get an identification. 1 O.R. Killed. 3 O.Rs wounded.	
"	23/8/17.		Relief complete at 4-0 a.m. and moved into Brigade Reserve in the South side of River YSER in NIEUPORT. The Colonel proceeded to "B" Echelon and Major R.A.Poore D.S.O. assumed temporary Command of the Battalion 1 O.R. Killed 6 O.R. Wounded.	

Army Form C. 2118.

WAR DIARY
of 2nd Battalion, Royal Welch Fusiliers.
INTELLIGENCE SUMMARY.
(Erase heading not required)

Place	Date	Hour	Summary of Events and Information	Remarks and references to Appendices
TRENCHES.	24/8/17.		Numerous working parties required in this position.	
"	25/8/17.		Day quiet. Night disturbed. "B" Coy., heavily shelled. 6 O.Rs wounded.	
"	26/8/17.		Enemy artillery very active. Brigade headquarters and two front line Battalions shelled out. Brigade moved into our Headquarters.	
"	27/8/17.		Relieved by 2nd Manchesters., 32nd Division at 10-0 p.m. and moved back to the LA PANNE area. 2nd Lieutenant W.H. Fox M.C. returned from leave and assumed command of "B" Coy.,	
LA PANNE.	28/8/17.		Battalion in LA PANNE. Cleaning up and re-equipping.	
COUDERKERKE	29/8/17.		Battalion moved at 12-0 noon to COUDEKERKE BRANCH in the SYNTHE area. by barge from ADINKERKE to DUNKIRK.	
-BRANCH.	30/8/17.		Day at COUDEKERKE BRANCH. Minimum Reserve rejoined also draft of 2nd Lieutenant A.G. Jones and 29 O.Rs. Day spent in checking deficiencies.	
MOULLE.	31/8/17.		Battalion moved by bus to MOULLE. Billets indifferent and overcrowded.	

R.K. Manon? Lieut.
Maj. for Lieutenant-Colonel.,
Commanding, 2nd Battalion, Royal Welch Fusiliers.

1/9/1917.

Army Form C. 2118.

WAR DIARY
or
INTELLIGENCE SUMMARY.

2nd Battalion, Royal Welch Fusiliers.

(Erase heading not required.)

Instructions regarding War Diaries and Intelligence Summaries are contained in F.S. Regs., Part II. and the Staff Manual respectively. Title pages will be prepared in manuscript.

Place	Date	Hour	Summary of Events and Information	Remarks and references to Appendices
HOULLE.	1-9-17		Cleaning up. A draft of 29 other ranks arrived.	
"	2-9-17		Church Parade 11-0 a.m.	
"	3-9-17		Training commenced. Battalion visited by Major-General Wood C.B.,C.M.G., commanding 33rd Division.	
"	4-9-17		Training continued. Brigade baths.	
"	5-9-17		Training continued. Training Area "A".	
"	6-9-17		Training continued. Captain Coster rejoined from leave to U.K.	
"	7-9-17		Training continued. Brigade baths, morning. Musketry "B" Range, after noon.	
"	8-9-17		Training continued.	
"	9-9-17		Church Parade.	
"	10-9-17		Training continued. 6 other ranks joined from Base.	
"	11-9-17		Brigade Route March. Transport inspected by Brigadier 19th Infantry Brigade.	
"	12-9-17		Field firing carried out at GUEMY which involved a march of 15 miles. Ration strength today is 26 officers 911 other ranks.	
"	13-9-17		Range firing for the Battalion in the morning.	
"	14-9-17		Training continued. Commanding Officers Kit Inspection of Companies and Transport.	
WULVERDINGHE	15-9-17		Marched to new area at WULVERDINGHE. arrived in billets at 2-30 p.m.	
STEENVOORDE	16-9-17		Marched to STEENVOORDE Area, via CASSEL. Started at 7-30 a.m. arrived at 5-0 p.m. Dinners on the march at OXELAERE.	
THIEUSHOUK	17-9-17		Marched to THIEUSHOUK. Started at 6-0 a.m. arrived 8-0 a.m. Billets very scattered.	
"	18-9-17		In billets. General Cleaning up. Rein. Sapping Platoon of Lieut Snedden and 30 O.Rs reformed. Captain Bles, 10th R.W.F., gave a good lecture on "Strategy of the war."	
"	19-9-17		In billets. Training continued.	
KINORA CAMP.	20-9-17		Moved at 6-0 a.m. to N.W. WELTJOUTRE area in KINORA CAMP. Captain W.W. Kirkby reformed from Depot Battalion and proceeded to Divisional Headquarters on temporary Provost duties.	(Wounded - 16.OR Sandler
"	21-9-17		Still at KINORA CAMP. General Training and preparations for proceedure to trenches.	(Gassed - 13.OR
"	22-9-17		In Camp, general training. A party of 100 other ranks proceeded by lorry to trenches for Digging. Casualties :- Nil.	(Killed - 1 OR
"	23-9-17		Church Parade 10-0 a.m. 300 other ranks proceeded to the trenches for digging. Casualties :-	
"	24-9-17		Still in Camp. 2nd Lieut. I.Williams and 6 other ranks joined from the Base.	
TRENCHES	25-9-17		Moved up to Railway embankment, and thence to the support line, in readyness for the attack.	
"	26-9-17		Received orders at 8-15 a.m. from B.G.C. 98th Brigade to attack and consolidate a line from CALEDON HOUSE to REUTELBEEK by passing through the Australian lines West of Polygon Wood. Moved off from STIRLING CASTLE Area at 10-5 a.m. one ~~two companies~~ moved and proceeded to BLACK WATCH CORNER passing round the Northern side of GLENCORSE WOOD - Casualties caused by shell fire, from 12 to 15 O.Rs.	

2353 Wt: W-3141/1454 700,000 5/15 D. D. & L. A.D.S.S./Forms/C. 2118.

Army Form C. 2118.

WAR DIARY
of 2nd Battalion, Royal Welch Fusiliers
INTELLIGENCE SUMMARY.
(Erase heading not required.)

Sheet (2)

Place	Date	Hour	Summary of Events and Information	Remarks and references to Appendices
TRENCHES (continued.)	26-9-17		Formed up on line shown in GREEN on accompanying map, by 11-45 on a two Company frontage, with one company in Support and one company in reserve. Casualties by M.G. and shell fire - slight. Zero 12-0 noon. Front line moved off followed by support company. Two Companies failed to keep connection owing to left front company pivotting too quickly for the right. The support company reinforced the left front company and extended in front of CARLISLE FARM. Two Reserve Platoons of reserve company were in rear and occupied gun emplacements and pill-boxes. Casualties about 120 including Major R.A.Poore D.S.O., Adjutant, three Company Commanders and three subalterns. Approximate positions shown in RED on accompanying map. Companies were reorganised in those positions by Captain N.H.Radford M.C. on whom the command had devolved. At dusk the front companies fell back in conjunction with the Australians, who likewise had exhausted all their S.A.A. on to the line shown BLUE. This necessitated a second reorganisation. Twice before midnight an S.O.S. barrage was put down but no Infantry attack developed on this Battalion front. A patrol was sent out in the early hours of the morning but only a hostile listening post was once entered. Casualties :- Killed.- Major R.A.Poore D.S.O.(Royal Wilts Yeomanry attached 2nd R.W.F.) A/Captain and Adjutant J.C.Mann M.C., A/Captain E.Coster M.C., 2nd Lieut. R.A.Casson. 2nd Lieut. E.F.C.Colquhoun., 2nd Lieut. H.Ll Evans, 2nd Lieut. I.Williams. Wounded :- Captain N.H.Radford D.S.O., Lieu.M.Williams., Wounded (at duty) 2nd Lieut. E.H.Evans. Killed :- 31 other ranks. Wounded :- 121 other ranks. Wounded (at duty) 1 other rank. Wounded and Missing :- 1 other rank. Missing :- 36 other ranks. on 26th & 27th.	
TRENCHES	27-9-17		Captain E.R.Kearsley D.S.O. sent up from "B" Echelon and took over command of Battalion. Orders were received to again attack and mop up the CAMERON HOUSE and JUT FARM area., in conjunction with the Australians on the left. This attack was carried out without Artillery preparation, after careful reconnaissance, by means of filtering men through in small numbers. CAMERON HOUSE was found to be occupied by the Australians and JUT FARM was then rushed and 14 prisoners taken. The final approximate positions were as shown in BLACK. For the purpose of this second attack a company of the 5th Scottish Rifles was attached and formed part of the right of the advance. During the attack casualties were slight but when going out to inspect the line Captain E.R.Kearsley D.S.O. was wounded and Captain N.H.Radford M.C. again assumed command. At 6-0 p.m. a taking-over party of the 8th Yorks Regt. came up to arrange relief. The relief was slightly delayed by an S.O.S. barrage from 7-0 - 8-0 p.m. but on arrival of incoming troops a quick relief took place and was completed at 10-15 p.m.	

Army Form C. 2118.

WAR DIARY
or
INTELLIGENCE SUMMARY.

(Erase heading not required.)

2nd Battalion, Royal Welch Fusiliers.

Instructions regarding War Diaries and Intelligence Summaries are contained in F.S. Regs., Part II. and the Staff Manual respectively. Title pages will be prepared in manuscript.

Place	Date	Hour	Summary of Events and Information	Remarks and references to Appendices
DICKEBUSCH	28-9-17		Transport left DICKEBUSCH for BLARINGHEM Area at 7-30 a.m. Battalion embussed just East of DICKEBUSCH at 6-0 p.m. and arrived in billets at BLARINGHEM Area about 2-0 a.m. 29-9-17.	
BLARINGHEM AREA.	29-9-17		Minimum Reserve rejoined the Battalion. Captain J.Cuthbert takes over duties of senior major, temporarily. Lieut. R.Gambier-Parry takes over duties of A/Adjutant. No parades. General rest and cleaning up for everybody.	
"	30-9-17		Church Parade at Battalion Headquarters. Service taken by Senior Chaplain. 2nd Lieut. J.R.Williams joined the Battalion, from Base. Draft of 12 other ranks arrive.	

W.B. Farrer.
Lieutenant-Colonel,
Commanding, 2nd Battalion, Royal Welch Fusiliers.

1-10-1917.

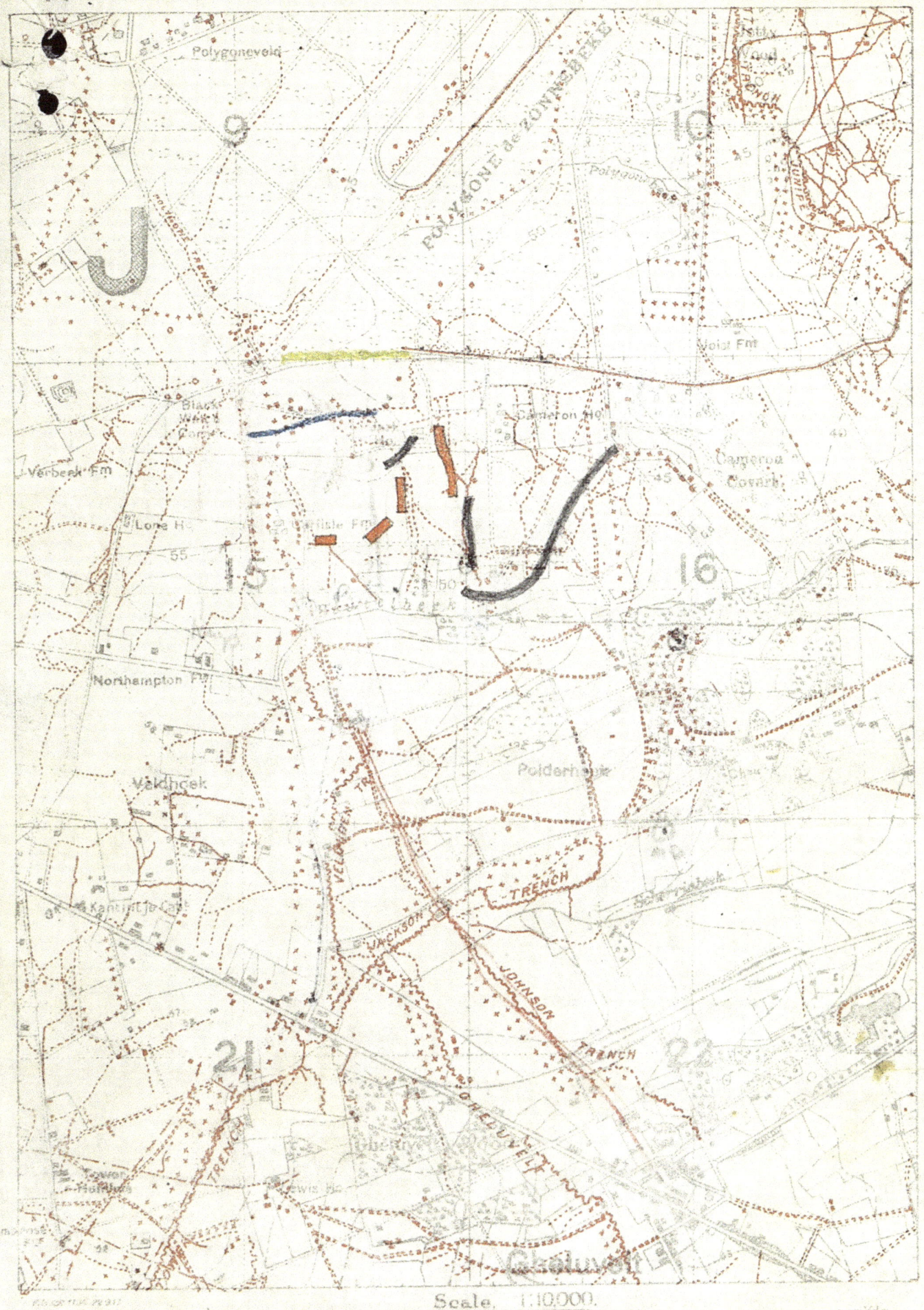

MESSAGE FORM.

To:—   No.

1. I am at........................ { Note:—Either give Map Reference or mark your position by a X on the Map on back.

2. I have reached limits of my Objective.

3. My Platoon / Company is at........................ and is consolidating.

4. My Platoon / Company is at........................ and has consolidated.

5. Am held up by (a) M.G. (b) Wire at........................(Place where you are).

6. Enemy holding strong point........................

7. I am in touch with........................on Right / Left at........................

8. I am not in touch with........................on Right / Left.

9. Am shelled from........................

10. Am in need of —

11. Counter Attack forming at........................

12. Hostile (a) Battery
    (b) Machine Gun   active at........................
    (c) Trench Mortar

13. Reinforcements wanted at........................

14. I estimate my present strength at........................rifles.

15. Add any other useful information here:—

Name........................
Platoon........................
Time............in.   Company........................
Date............1917.   Battalion........................

(A). Carry no maps or papers which may be of value to the Enemy.

(B). Give no information if captured, except the following, which you are bound to give:—

Name and Rank.

(C). Collect all captured maps and papers and send them in at once.

Army Form C. 2118.

WAR DIARY
or
INTELLIGENCE SUMMARY.
(Erase heading not required.) 2nd Battalion, Royal Welch Fusiliers.

OCTOBER 1917.

Vol 39

Place	Date	Hour	Summary of Events and Information	Remarks and references to Appendices
BLARINGHE.	1/10/17		2nd Lieut J.A.Williams, joined from base, Captain G.E.R. de Miremont, rejoined from Senior Officers Course ALDERSHOT; training under Company arrangements.	
-:-	2/10/17		Practice parade for Field Marshal C,in, O's inspection; Lieut., W.R.Smith, 2nd Lieut., W.R.C.Koepfer, and 2nd Lieut., D.A.Jones, joined from base.	
-:-	3/10/17		The Brigade was inspected by Field Marshal SIR DOUGLAS HAIG who expressed entire satisfaction with appearance and turnout of battalion; Captain Radford N.H. MC. lectured all officers on the recent operations.	
-:-	4/10/17		Parades under Company's arrangements.	
-:-	5/10/17		Battalion moved by road to A_QUIN a 10 mile march; only 2 men fell out.	
ACQUIN	6/10/17		Moved by road to WIZERNES, entrained and went to BAILLEUL, detrained and marched to KORTEPYP CAMP very cold night.	
KORTEPYP	7/10/17		All watches put back one hour for "WINTER TIME"; rained all day.	
CAMP.				
MESSINES	8/10/17		Relieved the 5th S.R. in SUPPORT LINE; MESSINES LEFT SUB-SECTOR; very bad night for relief; very dark and wet.	
-:-	9/10/17		Enemy shelled a little in the early morning; "B" Company carried R. E. Stores after dark.	
-:-	10/10/17		All companies employed in carring from "BELLE FARM DUMP" to "SWAINE'S FARM DUMP" and from there after dark to front line.	
-:-	11/10/17		Carrying again as yesterday, also sent up a working party to front line.	
-:-	12/10/17		Relieved the 5th S.R. in the front line; "D" Company got caught in a barrage on "FANN" O.T. 2nd Lieut., ELLIS and 5 other ranks killed, 2nd Lieut., Hammes RHODES and 7 other ranks wounded.	
FRONT LINE	13/10/17.		Battalion Headquarters shelled with 5-9 Howitzers from 9-0 a.m. til 11 dark; several direct hits; a new Headquarters was established in the support company Headquarters.	
-:-	14/10/17		Relieved by the 15th Battalion K.L.R. a very quick relief; "D" Comp any had 3 other ranks wounded coming out; marched back to billets in NEUVE EGLISE.	
NEUVE EGLISE.	15/10/17.		Resting and cleaning up.	
-:-	16/10/17.		Company training in the morning; baths in the afternoon; sent three working parties (total 100 men) for work up the line under R.E's.	
-:-	17/10/17.		Company training; same working parties as yesterday; Commanding Officers conference for all officers at 12-30 p.m.	
-:-	18/10/17		Moved by bus to MENIN Gate YPRES and took over a camp from the 4th Kings Liverpool Regiment; attached for work to 1st ANZAC CORPS.	

Army Form C. 2118.

WAR DIARY
or
INTELLIGENCE SUMMARY.
(Erase heading not required.)

Instructions regarding War Diaries and Intelligence Summaries are contained in F. S. Regs. Part II. and the Staff Manual respectively. Title pages will be prepared in manuscript.

Place	Date	Hour	Summary of Events and Information	Remarks and references to Appendices
YPRES.	19/10/17		Found 400 men for road making and timber carrying in forward area; "B" Company got heavily shelled; 3 other ranks killed and 4 wounded and 4 missing; believed to have been blown up by a shell.	
-:-	20/10/17		Same working parties as yesterday; no casualties except:- 3 men of "A" Company knocked down and bruised.	
-:-	21/10/17		Same working parties as yesterday; 2 other ranks killed and wounded; 2nd Lieut's. C.C.Davies, E.F.Gorney, O.T.Ricketts, C.F.Larson, J.Aubrey, T.Smith joined from base.	
-:-	22/10/17		Same working parties; 2nd Lieuts. W.J.Ramsay, D.J.Hugh-Jones, A.G.J ones left to join the R.F.C. Military Medals awarded by Corps Commander to the following:- No.1 0740 Sgt. Griffiths,J. MXXXX 9045 Cpl,A/Sgt Poole, C. 353* Pte Richards F. 40038 Pte Jones W.T. 9826 Cpl,Troman, E. 24405 Pte Walters J. 57755 Pte Morgan, T. 55359 Pte Kempster, H. 1 5751 Pte Prandle,O. 55265 Pte Lewis, T. 5160 Pte Brogan, J. 57158 Pte Guest, I. 40308 Pte Williams F. 40490 Pte Humphreys, R. 5592 Pte Pago, J. Bar to Military Medal to :- 5745 L/Cpl White, C. Same working parties, less 50 men not required; Lieut Gentry in charge of the work speaks very highly of the way the men are working.	
-:-	23/10/17			
-:-	24/10/17		Same working parties; no casualties.	
-:-	25/10/17		Same working parties in the morning; Relieved by 2nd Battalion EWorcestershire Regiment at 3-0 p.m. and embussed at 4-0 p.m.; went back to NEUVE EGLISE and occupied BULFORD CAMP.	
BULFORD CAMP.	26/10/17		Cleaning up and resting; PALMER BATHS at the disposal of the battalion; Captain MOODY,P. MC. Regimental	
-:-	27/10/17		Parades under company arrangement for trainings;- M.O., arrived from base and takes over duties	
-:-	28/10/17		Church Parade in Y.M.C.A. Tent.; 2nd Lieut., J.P. Jones, of Bombing Officer.	
-:-	29/10/17		Parades under Company arrangements for training; Captain J.C.DUNN,M.C. (RAMC) Attached 2nd R.W.Fus. awarded the D.S.O.	
-:-	30/10/17		Relieved the 1st Battalion Argyle and Sutherland Highlanders in MES SINES LEFT SUB-Sector SUPPORT LINE; night very cold and wet; Casualties:- 1 other rank killed 2 other ranks wounded; 2nd Lieut., T.Towcher, joined from base and posted to "A"Company.	
SUPPORT TRENCHES LEFT SUB-SECTOR	31/10/17		Captain N.H.Radford MC. awarded the D.S.O. 2nd Lieut.,R.Nield-Siddall, awarded the M.C. Captain E.R.Kearsley, D.SO. awarded bar to D.S.O. No.6047 C.S.M. V. Ward, "B" Coy. No.25020 Sgt. E.Morgan, "C"Company, No.4549 L/Sgt G.Moon, "B" Coy. awarded Distinguished Conduct Medals. Lieutenant General W.BIRDWOOD, Commanding 1st ANZAC CORPS expressed his appreciation and entire satisfaction for the good work done by the battalion whilst attached to the CORPS under his Command. This message together with the congratulations of the GOC PS, Divisional and Brigade Commanders, were expressed to the officers and other ranks of the battalion.	

NHRadford
Captain
Acting Commander Battalion

Army Form C. 2118.

WAR DIARY
OF
INTELLIGENCE SUMMARY.
(Erase heading not required)

Place	Date	Hour	Summary of Events and Information	Remarks and references to Appendices
Support Trenches	1/11/17.		Left Sub Sector. .... On carrying duties by day and at night. Major de Miremont continued work with similar party to previous night.	
–do–	2/11/17.		Left Sub Section. .... Carrying and work on support trench as previous day.	
Front Line	3/11/17.		Relieved 5th Scottish Rifles in front Line. "A" "B" "C" from right to left. "D" Coy in support. During relief "A" Coy had 2 men wounded by our own shell fire, which fell short, and had a Lewis Gun knocked out. 2nd Lieut BOWMAN, United States Rifles, was attached for instruction, and did duty with "B" Coy.	
Front Line	4/11/17.		Left of Battalion Trenches very wet. Otherwise trenches in very fair condition.	
Front Line	5/11/17.		Quiet day, 168 Other ranks joined from Base.	
Front Line	6/11/17.		2 Other ranks wounded by Rifle Grenade. Lieut W.R. SMITH admitted to Hospital.	
Front Line	7/11/17.		Relieved by 9th H.L.I. and marched to billets in BULFORD CAMP. (Extract from Battalion Orders dated 7/11/17. Capt C.E.R. de Miremont to be Acting Major on Head Quarters. 11/11/17. Ty/Lieut J.L.C. WILLIAMS to be Acting Captain 11/10/17. Lieut C.E.B. BARKWORTH to be Acting Captain 11/10/17. T/Capt N.H. RADFORD M.C. to be Adjutant vice Lt (Act Capt J.C. MANN M.C. killed 20/9/17.	
BULFORD CAMP	8/11/17.		Cleaning up and checking deficiencies.	
–do–	9/11/17.		Baths allotted to Battalion, from 8.0am to 12 Noon. Small working parties.	
–do–	10/11/17.		"A" Coy on Range, Rained nearly all day. Small working parties.	
–do–	11/11/17.		Church Parade 10.45am. Small working parties. (Extract from London Gazette. 2nd Lt A.T. HARRIES to be Lieutenant. July 1st 1917.	
–do–	12/11/17.		Training in Camp Area.	
–do–	13/11/17.		Training continued. 2nd Lieut LLEWELLAN admitted to hospital.	
Line of march	14/11/17.		Marched by route march to STRAZELLE, via BAILLUEL.	
STRAZELLE	15/11/17.		At STRAZELLE.	
–do–	16/11/17.		At STRAZELLE.	
Line of march	17/11/17.		Moved by Bus from STRAZELLE area to WHITE CHATEAU area at 1PM ES.	
WHITE CHATEAU	18/11/17.		In WHITE CHATEAU area. Camp shelled by German long range gun.	
POTIJZE	19/11/17.		Moved to Camp in POTIJZE area.	
–do–	20/11/17.		In POTIJZE area. reconnoitred the PASCHENDAEL Sector. Working parties.	
–do–	21/11/17.		Working parties.	
–do–	22/11/17.		Working parties. Captain P. WOOD. M.C. takes over command of "C" Coy. Sub.	
–do–	23/11/17.		Working parties.	
PASCHENDAEL	24/11/17.		Relieved the Cameronians in Support Left Sector, PASCHENDAEL Sector. "A" "C" Coys heavily shelle	

War Diary

Summary

Place	Date	Summary
Passchendaele (continued)	24-11-17	During the night at ABRAHAM HEIGHTS. B and D Companies at HAMBURG
" "	25-11-17	(Still in support) Shelling intermittent
" "	26-11-17	(Still in support) Shelling intermittent. "B" Co. relieved the forward companies of the CAMERONIANS at CREST FARM
" "	27-11-17	Relieved the CAMERONIANS in the front line. Left subsector PASCHENDAELE sector "D" Co. Right front Company "A" Company left front Company "C" Co. Battalion Reserve "B" Co. at CREST FARM. Very heavy shelling during the night
" "	28-11-17	Still in front line. Shelling continues in spurts
" "	29-11-17	" "
" "	30-11-17	Relieved by the 16th K.R.R. A good relief and a quiet journey down to POTIZZE where the Battalion spent the night. (Total Casualties for period 24-11-17 to 1-12-17 — KILLED 49 OR WOUNDED — 47 OR WOUNDED AT DUTY — 23 OR MISSING — 3 OR

M Raafrey
Captain
Adjutant 8th A. Royal Welch Fusiliers

Army Form C. 2118.

WAR DIARY
2nd Battalion, ROYAL WELCH FUSILIERS.
INTELLIGENCE SUMMARY.
(Erase heading not required.)

Instructions regarding War Diaries and Intelligence Summaries are contained in F.S. Regs. Part II. and the Staff Manual respectively. Title pages will be prepared in manuscript.

Vol 41

40. W.
6 sheet

Place	Date	Hour	Summary of Events and Information	Remarks and references to Appendices
BRANDHOEK	1/12/17		Training.	
- do -	2/12/17		Training.	
- do -	3/12/17		Training.	
- do -	4/12/17		Training.	
- do -	5/12/17		Training.	
- do -	6/12/17		Training.	
MENIN GATE	7/12/17		Moved to MENIN GATE, YPRES, by road.	
- do -	8/12/17		In camp at MENIN GATE. The Battalion was employed on Working Parties.	
- do -	9/12/17		Battalion employed on Working Parties.	
- do -	10/12/17		Battalion employed on Working Parties.	
WATOU AREA	11/12/17		Moved from MENIN GATE and proceeded by train to the WATOU AREA.	
- do -	12/12/17		Billeted in WATOU AREA - Cleaning up - Billets very scattered, but good.	
- do -	13/12/17		Cleaning up etc.	
- do -	14/12/17		Training.	
- do -	15/12/17		Training.	
- do -	16/12/17		Training. Major Kearsley D.S.O., Lieuts Charlton & Evans J.T.S. joined the Battalion	

Army Form C. 2118.

WAR DIARY
of 2nd Battalion, Royal Welch Fusiliers.
INTELLIGENCE SUMMARY. - (2) -

(Erase heading not required.)

Place	Date	Hour	Summary of Events and Information	Remarks and references to Appendices
WATOU AREA	16/12/17 (continued)		The Corps Commander awarded the MILITARY MEDAL to the following N.C.Os and men :- No.60257 Pte Blomley J. "C" Coy. No.7936 Pte Lee G. "C" Coy. No.13183 L/Cpl Evans W. "D"	
- do -	17/12/17		Training. MILITARY MEDAL awarded to the following men :- No.55034 Pte T.Lewis "D" Coy attached M.G.Corps and No.70235 Pte J. Hill "A" Coy.	
- do -	18/12/17		Training. Mentioned in despatches, London Gazette dated 18/12/17 :- Lt-Col W.B.Garnett D.S.O., A/Major E.R.Kearsley D.S.O., A/Capt. N.H. Radford D.S.O., M.C., A/Capt J.C.Mann M.C. Lieut. A.T.Harries., No.8232 Sgt.J.Meredith.	
- do -	19/12/17		Training.	
- do -	20/12/17		Training.	
- do -	21/12/17		Training. Left WATOU AREA and proceeded by road to POPERINGHE. Transport and Classes under instruction left in WATOU AREA.	
POPERINGHE	22/12/17		Billeted at POPERINGHE. On Working Parties.	
- do -	23/12/17		Employed on Working Parties. D.C.M. awarded to No. 8773 C.S.M. Cumberland A.H.	
- do -	24/12/17		Working Parties. M.C. awarded to Captain J. Cuthbert.	
- do -	25/12/17		Christmas Day. Whole Holiday. Divisional Commander visited the Battalion to convey his good wishes.	
- do -	26/12/17		Working Parties.	
- do -	27/12/17		Working Parties.	

Army Form C. 2118.

WAR DIARY
or
INTELLIGENCE SUMMARY. - (3) -

(Erase heading not required.)

Instructions regarding War Diaries and Intelligence Summaries are contained in F. S. Regs., Part II. and the Staff Manual respectively. Title pages will be prepared in manuscript.

Place	Date	Hour	Summary of Events and Information	Remarks and references to Appendices
POPERINGHE	28/12/17		Working Parties. Corps Commander awarded the MILITARY MEDAL to No. 55577 Pte W.Jones.	
- do -	29/12/17		Moved by march route to WATOU Area and occupied billets vacated on 21st.	
WATOU.	30/12/17		Church Parade at Headquarters.	
- do -	31/12/17		Baths allotted to Battalion at WATOU. All officers except 2 Company Commanders and Adjutant, attended lecture by Sir Aylmer Hunter-Weston, The Corps Commander, on training etc. This was followed by lecture and Demonstration by Lieut-Colonel DEVT DWS.O. VIII Corps School, on Platoon work.	

[signature], Captain,
Commanding, 2nd Battalion, Royal Welch Fusiliers.

1/1/18.

Army Form C. 2118.

WAR DIARY
2nd Battalion. ROYAL WELCH FUSILIERS.
INTELLIGENCE SUMMARY
(Erase heading not required.)

Instructions regarding War Diaries and Intelligence Summaries are contained in F. S. Regs., Part II. and the Staff Manual respectively. Title pages will be prepared in manuscript.

Place	Date	Hour	Summary of Events and Information	Remarks and references to Appendices
WATOU AREA.	1/1/18.		Holiday. Lieut. C. JONES and Lieut. E.T.E.GWALCHMAI reported from the Base.	
- do -	2/1/18.		All men of the Battalion passed through the Gas Hut, STEENVOORDE.	
BRANDHOEK.	3/1/18.		Moved by rail to TORONTO CAMP, BRANDHOEK.	
- do -	4/1/18.		Moved by bus to YPRES, thence to ALNWICK CAMP, moved to HAMBURG in evening and relieved 7th D.L.I. (Support Battalion).	
HAMBURG.	5/1/18.		Relieved 5th BORDER REGT., in left Sub-sector, PASSCHENDAELE. "B" Coy. Left Front Coy. "C" Coy. Right Front Coy. "A" Coy (Support Coy) CREST FARM., and "D" Coy (Reserve) HAALEN SUPPORT.	
PASSCHENDAELE	6/1/18		Enemy quiet. Hard Frost.	
- do -	7/1/18.		Enemy quiet. Snow and Frost. "A" Coy relieved "B" Coy in the Left Front Coy. "D" Coy relieved "C" Coy in the Right Front Coy.	
- do -	8/1/18.		Enemy quiet. Snowed all day.	
- do -	9/1/18.		Enemy heavily shelled Batt. H.Q. and working parties in rear from 10=0 a.m. to 1=0 p.m. Relieved by 9th H.L.I. at 5=0 p.m. Relief complete 1=30a.m. Moved to billets in YPRES.	
YPRES	10/1/18.		Moved by Light Railway to BRANDHOEK.(St LAWRENCE CAMP)Remainder of day spent in cleaning up.	
BRANDHOEK.	11/1/18.		Whole Battalion bathed at BRANDHOEK.	

Army Form C. 2118.

WAR DIARY
or
INTELLIGENCE SUMMARY.
(Erase heading not required.)

Instructions regarding War Diaries and Intelligence
Summaries are contained in F. S. Regs., Part II.
and the Staff Manual respectively. Title pages
will be prepared in manuscript.

- (2) -

Place	Date	Hour	Summary of Events and Information	Remarks and references to Appendices
BRANDHOEK.	12/1/18.		Cleaning up and booking deficiences.	
- do -	13/1/18.		Moved to WHITBY CAMP by Light Railway.	
WHITBY CAMP	14/1/18.		Working Parties of 1 senior Officer, 2 Subs. per Coy and 3 Coys, commencing at 5-0 a.m. at HANNIXS JUNCTION and returning at 11-30 a.m. (Work between HAMBURG & ABRAHAM HEIGHTS making Light Railways.)	
- do -	15/1/18.		Above Working Parties. Very wet.	
- do -	16/1/18.		- do - cancelled owing to floods.	
- do -	17/1/18.		- do - , snow and rain.	
- do -	18/1/18.		- do -	
- do -	19/1/18.		- do - Major E.R.KEARSLEY D.S.O., to hospital with broken leg.	
- do -	20/1/18.		- do -	
- do -	21/1/18.		- do -	
- do -	22/1/18.		- do - Baths at YPRES. "A" Coy.	
- do -	23/1/18.		- do - Baths at YPRES. "B" Coy. Lieut. C.JONES and Lieut. R.D.BRIERCLIFFE reported from the Base.	

Army Form C. 2118.

WAR DIARY
or
INTELLIGENCE SUMMARY.
(Erase heading not required).

Place	Date	Hour	Summary of Events and Information	Remarks and references to Appendices
			- (3) -	
WHITBY CAMP	24/1/18		Working Parties. Baths at YPRES. "C" Coy. Lt.Col. W.B.Garnett returned from leave to U.K.	
- do -	25/1/18		- do - Baths at YPRES. "D" Coy.	
- do -	27/1/18		Battalion moved to LONGUENESSE (St OMER) by train from St JEAN Station at 4-20 p.m. arriving at St OMER Station at 8-20 p.m. Cookers, watercarts and mess cart entrained at VLAMERTINGHE and detrained at WIZERNES. Remainder of Transport by road.	
LONGUENESSE	28/1/18		Billeted in LONGUENESSE. Billets good and clean. Companies cleaned up.	
- do -	29/1/18		Continued cleaning up and 2 hours training. Capt. J.E.GREAVES reported from the 10th R.W.F.	
- do -	30/1/18		Training near Billets.	
- do -	31/1/18		Specailist classes and training near billets.	

W.Garnett

Lieutenant-Colonel.,
Commanding, 2nd Battalion, Royal Welch Fusiliers.

33RD DIVISION
19TH INFY BDE

18TH BN ROYAL FUSILIERS
NOV 1915 – FEB 1916

TO L of C FEB 1916

DISBANDED APRIL 1916

(NO DIARIES FOR MAR OR APL)

98th Brigade
33rd Division.

Disembarked Calais 14.11.15

Battalion transferred to 19th Infantry Brigade 27.11.15

~~98th Battalion~~

18th BATTALION

ROYAL FUSILIERS

NOVEMBER 1915.

18th Royal Fusiliers.

WAR DIARY
or
INTELLIGENCE SUMMARY.
(Erase heading not required.)

Army Form C. 2118.

Instructions regarding War Diaries and Intelligence Summaries are contained in F. S. Regs., Part II. and the Staff Manual respectively. Title pages will be prepared in manuscript.

Place	Date	Hour	Summary of Events and Information	Remarks and references to Appendices
Tidworth	Nov. 1st	Mon.	Various parades & classes of instruction in Entrenching, Scouting, revetments, Bayonet Fighting, Judging Distance, Rapid loading, Wire entanglement, Bomb throwing, Machine Gun, Range Finding etc. Arrival of new equipment. Machine Gun Sections fire on BULFORD Ranges. 2/Lt. WESTOVER appointed Brigade M.G. Officer. 2/Lt. DAWSON appointed Battn. M.G. officer - 2/Lt. KNIGHT, 2nd M.G. Officer.	
do.	Nov. 2nd	Tues.	Mobilisation Parade - Inspection by G.O.C. 98th Brigade at 9.30 a.m. Machine Gun Sections continue practice on Ranges after above parade. Draft of 30 men arrive from 28th Reserve Battn: from EPSOM. Range finders do revolver practice.	
do.	Nov. 3rd	Wed.	Lecture on care & use of telescopic sights on rifles by Lt: LATTEY of the BISLEY School of Musketry, & officers to attend. Lecture on the use of Machine Gun in the Field by Major MAKIN, D.S.O. to M.G. officers & NCOs. Class of instruction in bombing for officers commences - Inspection by C.O. of each company in new equipment - Range takers revolver practice. Snipers fire on BULFORD "F" Range. Machine Gun practice on BULFORD "G" Range. Tattoo in future to be at 9.30. Lights out 9.45 p.m. All leave stopped. Arrival of blankets for overseas.	
do.	Nov. 4th	Thurs.	New draft & casuals fire Parts I & II on "F" Range BULFORD. Machine Gun practice continued on "G" Range. Grenadier, Range Taking etc. classes as usual. Remainder of Battn: Trench Warfare at HARE WARREN.	

Army Form C. 2118.

18th Royal Fusiliers.

WAR DIARY
or
INTELLIGENCE SUMMARY.
(Erase heading not required.)

Instructions regarding War Diaries and Intelligence Summaries are contained in F.S. Regs., Part II. and the Staff Manual respectively. Title pages will be prepared in manuscript.

Place	Date	Hour	Summary of Events and Information	Remarks and references to Appendices
Tidworth	Nov. 5th Fri.		Divisional operations in BEDLAM TRENCHES. 18th Battn. Div. Reserve Troops. Reserve Machine Gun detachments fire on "G" range. Battn. Snipers practise Field Firing at BEECHES BARN. New draft & camels fire Part III on "H" range. Inspection of 1st line transport horses & mules. JW	
"	Nov. 6th Sat.		Barrack inspection by C.O. Various instructional parades in & near barracks, including wire entanglement making, sand bag revetments, incinerators, bayonet fighting etc. Officers complete revolver shooting. JW	
"	Nov. 7th Sun.		Church parade. 11.30 am parade at SEVEN BARROWS to practice March past.	
"	Nov. 8th Mon.		Inspection by H.M. the Queen on SALISBURY PLAIN. 33rd Division inspected in line of masses, followed by March past in column of double platoons. Instructional parades in barracks 2.45 pm to 4.45 pm. JW	
"	Nov. 9th Tues.		Parades cancelled owing to rain. Company mobilization inspections - Transport mobilization. Machine Gun Detachments fire on Range. JW	
"	Nov. 10th Wed.		Morning devoted to completing Companies' clothing & equipment. Afternoon Company route marches & grenadiers practice throwing real bombs at HARE WARREN. ·303 service ammunition drawn & served out to NCOs & men. JW	

T2134. Wt. W708—776. 500000. 4/15. Sir J. C. & S.

1st B" Royal Fusiliers

Army Form C. 2118.

WAR DIARY
OF
INTELLIGENCE SUMMARY.
(Erase heading not required.)

Instructions regarding War Diaries and Intelligence Summaries are contained in F.S. Regs., Part II. and the Staff Manual respectively. Title pages will be prepared in manuscript.

Place	Date	Hour	Summary of Events and Information	Remarks and references to Appendices
TIDWORTH	Nov.11th Thurs.		8 a.m. to 9 a.m. Bayonet Fighting & Physical Drill. 9 a.m. onwards Mobilization Inspection of Companies by C.O. Inspection of Transport Workmen & details to proceed with Transport by Adjutant, in all 4 off's & 1222 NCOs & men plus all animals. Afternoon - Grenade throwing by Grenadiers. Company parades.	
do.	Nov.12th Fri.		7.30 a.m. Transport & Machine Gun Section & details parade for overseas. Leave TIDWORTH station at 9.15 a.m. General Fatigue in barracks or lines. Inspection by C.O. Instructions received at 4 p.m. that departure of Battn., which was to have been at 9.15 a.m. on 13th, is postponed for 24 hours, presumably on account of bad weather in the channel.	
do.	Nov.13th Sat.		Company parades. Half holiday.	
BOULOGNE	Nov.14th Sun.		Battn. left TIDWORTH station by ½ Battalions 2.30 & 2.50 a.m. Arrived FOLKESTONE 7.45 a.m. & 8.15 a.m. Embarked on "Princess Victoria". Good crossing. Arrived CALAIS 11.15 a.m. owing to floating mines could not enter BOULOGNE harbour. Entrained for BOULOGNE. Arrived there 3 p.m.	
do.	Nov.15th Mon.		Day spent in rest camp. Company parades & route marches.	
THIENNES	Nov.16th Tues.		Entrained at PONT DE BRIQUES at 10.15 a.m. Travelled via CALAIS & ST.OMER route to THIENNES. Arrived 6.30 p.m. Marched into billets at TANNAY.	

18th Royal Fusiliers

Army Form C. 2118.

WAR DIARY
or
INTELLIGENCE SUMMARY.
(Erase heading not required.)

Instructions regarding War Diaries and Intelligence Summaries are contained in F. S. Regs., Part II. and the Staff Manual respectively. Title pages will be prepared in manuscript.

Place	Date	Hour	Summary of Events and Information	Remarks and references to Appendices
TANNAY	Nov 17th Wed.		Spent at TANNAY – Company parades – visited by new Brigadier-General STRICKLAND, C.M.G., D.S.O.	
do	Nov 18th Thurs.		Spent at TANNAY.	
ROBECQ	Nov 19th Fri.		Battn. left TANNAY district 9.30 a.m. Marched via ST VENANT & billeted South of LA BASSEE Canal at ROBECQ. Bad billets.	
BETHUNE	Nov 20th Sat.		Brigade left ROBECQ district 9.30 a.m. Marched via CHOCQUES to BETHUNE. Arrived 1 p.m. Billeted (battalion) at Tobacco factory – 6 officers under Major HARTLEY & 16 NCOs went into 6th Brigade trenches for instruction, returning to billets that night.	
VERMELLES	Nov 21st Sun.		Battn: went into trenches by companies for instruction, attached to 1st Herts, 1st Kings Liverpool & 2 Coys: with 'K.R.R.' Headquarters at Brigade Advance HQrs: at BARTS ALLEY – No casualties – Details (about 200 men) left at BETHUNE under Major HARTLEY.	
	Nov 22nd Mon.		Battn: remained in trenches – B Coy. exchanging with C., & D with A Coy. No casualties.	
ANNEQUIN SOUTH	Nov 23rd Tues.		Companies relieved from trenches 10.30 a.m. Marched to billets at ANNEQUIN-SOUTH, where joined by details from BETHUNE – Transport remained at BEUVRY.	
ANNEQUIN SOUTH	Nov 24th Wd.		Battn: returned to trenches for instruction – D Coy. relieved Coy. of 5th Kings Liverpool T. M.G. Section split up into 3 parties of Royal Berks – A Coy, Coy of S. Staffs – B & C Coys, 2 Coys for instruction – 1 casualty (Pte: CLARKE of B Coy.) HQrs: at ANNEQUIN.	

Army Form C. 2118.

18th Royal Fusiliers.
WAR DIARY
of
INTELLIGENCE SUMMARY.
(Erase heading not required.)

Instructions regarding War Diaries and Intelligence Summaries are contained in F. S. Regs., Part II. and the Staff Manual respectively. Title pages will be prepared in manuscript.

Place	Date	Hour	Summary of Events and Information	Remarks and references to Appendices
ANNEQUIN SOUTH	Nov 25 Thurs.		Remained in trenches. Pte. HERRMANN (B.Coy.) killed & buried at CAMBRIN Churchyard. Pte. METCALF of C.Coy. badly wounded, a few minor wounds. Pte. MCMICHAEL died in Bethune	
BETHUNE	Nov 26 Fri.		Relieved from trenches about 11.30 a.m. & marched to BETHUNE, billeted at L'Ecole de Jeunes Filles. - Capt. MAYOR, acting Sgt. cook died of pneumonia, buried at BETHUNE in churchyard.	
do	Nov 27 Sat.		Billets moved to Tobacco factory & L'Ecole Michelet. B.attn. transferred to 19th Brigade, command taken by Gen. ROBERTSON C.M.G. from todays date. Sgt. REISS promoted C.S.M. A Coy in place of C. Sgt. Major TANCRED, resigned & reverted to Sgt. at own request dated 24th inst. Sgt. TANCRED takes charge of cooks temporarily. Lts: JENSEN & HAZELDINE detached for course of instruction in Trench Mortars.	
BETHUNE	Nov 28 Sun.		Services. Holy Communion 7a.m & 8a.m. Upper room BETHUNE New Theatre, Rue Victor Hugo. Ch. of Engl. 12 midday. Unfinished Church. Farewell address by Rev. R.H. ELLISON (98th Bde.) Commanding Officer & Adjt. reported about 9.30 a.m 21st Inf. Brigade H.Q. on LA BASSEE Canal E. of LE QUESNOY, & were conducted round section of GIVENCHY Lines to be taken over by Battn. on 30th inst. Major HAMILTON, 1st Cameronians, attached to give instruction. Hard frost.	
BETHUNE	Nov 29 Mon.		Inspection of billets, clothing & equipment. Practice in putting on gas helmets (D.P.) Wet day.	
do	Nov 30 Tues.		Relief to-morrow cancelled for 24 hours. 2/Lt: BACON detached for instruction in listening posts. Company paraded & route marched to BEUVRY.	

P. Allen Vaughan, Major R.W.
for Colonel 18th R.F.

20

18th Reg: Inos:
Vol 2

12/
7910

33/40/573

19th Bde. from 98th

Dec "15
Sep "16

Army Form C. 2118.

WAR DIARY
or
INTELLIGENCE SUMMARY.
(Erase heading not required.)

18th R.W.F.

Place	Date	Hour	Summary of Events and Information	Remarks and references to Appendices
BETHUNE	Wed. Dec 1	12.30 pm	Marched from BETHUNE, via LE QUESNOY to LE PLANTIN, N.W. of GIVENCHY. Took over trenches from Junction of SCOTTISH and NEW TRENCHES to FIFE ROAD on left. A Coy took over from 1st Yorkshire Regt. B, C, D Coys from 1/4th Camerons at lines (i) Firing line, (ii) GEORGE STREET, (iii) GROUSE BUTTS and O.B.L., (iv) LE PLANTIN Village. Relief completed by about 11 p.m.	
GIVENCHY Section	Dec 2		Found trenches very wet, badly drained, parapets old & broken, most of the shelters unsafe. No communication trench between support line and firing line. Relief at night only and most difficult - men lost boots, equipment, + some rifles in trenches - LE PLANTIN and YELLOW ROADS shelled with shrapnel by the Enemy about 5.30 p.m. Pte. BLACK A Coy killed.	
do	Dec 3rd		Situation normal except for occasional bursts of fire on both sides from Artillery & Machine Guns.	
do	Dec 4th		Collapse of shelter in GEORGE STREET causing deaths of Ptes THOMAS and HYATT. Great artillery bombardment in afternoon - took with some damage communication trench and repairing parapet.	
do	Dec 5th		Quiet day except for bombardment by our guns at 11.30 a.m. followed by Enemy retaliation. Ptes GORE and 2 men wounded by shell in LE PLANTIN. Relieved by 20th Bn Battn. Camerons. 7 killed Corp. Evans + Pte Reason wounded in GEORGE STREET.	

Army Form C. 2118.

WAR DIARY
or
INTELLIGENCE SUMMARY.

(Erase heading not required.)

1st R.F.

Instructions regarding War Diaries and Intelligence Summaries are contained in F. S. Regs., Part II. and the Staff Manual respectively. Title pages will be prepared in manuscript.

Place	Date	Hour	Summary of Events and Information	Remarks and references to Appendices
ESSARS	Tues. Nov 7	3 a.m.	Relief completed. A/D Coys billeted Rue du Roi - C Coy in ESSARS - BETHUNE ROAD. B Coy 1st mn GIVENCHY REDOUBTS from 20th R.F. General cleaning up - Baths &c.	
do.	Nov 8th		Cleaning equipment - 18 grenadiers per pltn to GIVENCHY & attached to 5th Scottish Rifles for instruction in trench throwing &c. - C Coy relieves B Coy in redoubts.	
do.	Nov 9th		Inspection by A/Adjt of Platoons - 18 grenadiers from D Coy relieved those of C Coy & attached to 5th Scottish Rifles for 24 hrs bomb instruction.	
do.	Nov 10th		Company parades - C Coy relieved at GIVENCHY Redoubts by C Coy Queens and return to billets at ESSARS. Transport men from LE QUESNOY to ESSARS. 19th Brigade relieved in GIVENCHY section by 37th Inf. Brigade.	
FONTES	Nov 11th	9 a.m.	Marched from ESSARS via BETHUNE, CHOCQUES & ILLERS - arrived 2 p.m. Billets good in village street. Wet march.	
do.	Nov 12th		General cleaning up.	
do.	Nov 13th	12	Inspected by Brigadier General Robertson.	
do.	Nov 14th		Company parades - Regiment Drill, Bayonet Exercises, Nipping, Sandbag & wire work. Staff of subalterns etc.	
do.	Nov 15th		Construction of Range (100 yards) in chalk pit 600 yards N.W. of FONTES. Company parades. Practice in use of Semaphores by Seniors.	

WAR DIARY
or
INTELLIGENCE SUMMARY.

Army Form C. 2118.

1st P.F.

Place	Date	Hour	Summary of Events and Information	Remarks and references to Appendices
FONTES	Dec 16	9.30	Brigade Route march. Station point Welcomring E.O.J HAM - EN - ARTO 13 - Australia. 9 range preceded with ad Company parades in afternoon -	
do	Dec 17th		Brigadier General inspect range work - Company rifle marches & founders -	
do	Dec 18th	10.20	Inspection of billets by Brigadier General - Company with ranches & ponders - A Company firing on range.	
do	Dec 19th		D Coy provide fatigue party of 100 NCO & men with 2 officers to neighbouring aerodrome to dig drains & lay cables - Church parade -	
do	Dec 20th		Musketry on range and Company musketeers & parades. Instruction in entrenching and wiring & revetting. Bombing machine guns, and Sniping Classes as usual - 2.30 p.m. Lectures on Sanitation in trenches - Parades by Companies as above and musketry -	
do	Dec 21st		Ditto -	
do	Dec 22nd		Instruction at steam 12 noon by 1st Army Div 2/wk in wearing Brakehelts in barn full of gas -	
do	Dec 23rd		Company parades & musketry (Rapid firing) - "C" Coy firsts fold of field of fire & officers + 100 NCO & men at aerodrome -	
do	Dec 24th		Company parades as above - "C" Coy musketry (Rapid firing) - Canada firing on range -	

18th R.F.

Army Form C. 2118.

WAR DIARY
or
INTELLIGENCE SUMMARY.
(Erase heading not required.)

Place	Date	Hour	Summary of Events and Information	Remarks and references to Appendices
FONTES	Dec 25th		Church parades Holy Communion at 7 and 8 a.m. Church of England (Voluntary) 9.30 a.m. Roman Catholic Mass 10 a.m. Company football competition. Section Competition - Musketry, loading & firing 5 rounds at disappearing head & shoulder target.	
do	Dec 26th	11.30 a.m.	Sunday - Church Parade 11.30 a.m.	
do	Dec 27	8.30 a.m.	March via BUSNES, GONNEHEM, ROBECQ to BETHUNE - to train 99th Infantry Brigade - Order of march Batt. Signallers, A.B.C.D. Coys. 1st Gun Section, Stretcher bearers, Transport - Road blocked in parts - Total march about 16 miles. Billeted at MONTMORENCY BARRACKS.	
BETHUNE	Dec 28	8 a.m.	Marched via BEUVRY to ANNEQUIN FOSSE, about 5 miles - Billeted in dilapidated miners' cottages - C.O., Adj, Coy. Commanders, Bombing and Signalling officers went to 2nd Section of CAMBRIN Trenches to look over line to be taken over next day - Heavy shelling about ANNEQUIN and LA BASSEE Road -	
ANNEQUIN FOSSE	Dec 29		Terrific bombardment of enemy line immediately South of LA BASSEE Road all night.	
		1.30 p.m.	Marched to 2 Section of Trench line E. of CAMBRIN + South of LA BASSEE Road (a way of WILSONS WAY and BURBURE ALLEY. Advanced by ½ sections at interval of 100 x from ANNEQUIN FOSSE to trenches - Front of line BOYAU 14 on right to GUNSTREET on left. D. C. B. Coys in front and support lines - A Coy in reserve at end of MAISON ROUGE Trench about 40 yards through Section of LA BASSEE ROAD. Relief WINPOLE STREET - Cookers & Waterarts at HARLEY STREET on LA BASSEE ROAD. Trenches taken over from 23rd Sir J.C. Campbell 4.45 p.m.	[signature]

Army Form C. 2118.

18th R.F.

WAR DIARY
or
INTELLIGENCE SUMMARY.
(Erase heading not required.)

Instructions regarding War Diaries and Intelligence Summaries are contained in F. S. Regs., Part II. and the Staff Manual respectively. Title pages will be prepared in manuscript.

Place	Date	Hour	Summary of Events and Information	Remarks and references to Appendices
Trenches Z3	Dec 30th		Royal Fusiliers (Col. Lord MAITLAND) - 19th Royal Fusiliers on left. Pte. PATTISON shot in head at water cart at HARLEY ST. Infantile & Periph Gen Patterson of those trenches left of us both fallen with in week of repairs. Garrison (few of us in right flank, used queries, followed by bombardment in late afternoon.	2nd Roy Welsh Fusiliers on right —
do	Dec 31st		Work on repairing parapets and fire steps and communication trenches —	

Roy Scott Farrel
Comdr 18 Royal Fus —

T2134. Wt. W708—776. 500000. 4/16. Sir J. C. & S.

Army Form C. 2118.

18th Royal Fusiliers.

WAR DIARY
or
INTELLIGENCE SUMMARY.
(Erase heading not required.)

Instructions regarding War Diaries and Intelligence Summaries are contained in F. S. Regs., Part II. and the Staff Manual respectively. Title pages will be prepared in manuscript.

Place	Date	Hour	Summary of Events and Information	Remarks and references to Appendices
CAMBRIN TRENCHES Z₂ Subsection	Jan 1st		Situation normal, except for artillery activity on both sides. Parapet, firesteps, and communication trenches repaired, revetted, and mud pumped out. Old gascylinders removed from parapet of firing line and carried to CAMBRIN SUPPORT POINT.	
do	Jan 2nd	11 a.m.	Intense bombardment of CAMBRIN and Brigade office. Brigadier and staff compelled to retire to cellar for 2 hours, about 8 men killed round Brigade Office, which was set afire. Brigade HQrs moved to end of MAISON ROUGE and WIMPOLE STREET, and took over Batt: 14th or 15th R.F.	
do	Jan 3rd	4 p.m.	Batt: HQrs moved up to Sidcup 6 out of WILSONS WAY. Enemy blew up mine behind firing line on left of St Section Z₂. Enemy bombarded with High Explosive and Shrapnel 16th R.R.R's on immediate left of Z₂ Subsection, wire cut, and trenches much knocked about. Continuous activity of artillery on both sides. 2/Lt HAMILTON shot in thigh getting over parapet with party proceeding by night to repair wire entanglements.	
do	Jan 4th		Relieved (ABC Coys) by 20 R.F. D Coy remain in WIMPOLE STREET as Reserve Company, also D Coy 20 R.F. find Guard at G.H.Q. Relief commenced 8.30 am., completed at 10.45 a.m. Batt: withdrew to billets in ANNEQUIN SOUTH. Transport remains at BEUVRY. Shower baths by Companies. One Company to Sulroy Acquick and ready to march.	My Coth Colonel Commdg

T2134. Wt. W708—776. 500000. 4/15. Sir J. C. & S.

18th R.F.

WAR DIARY
or
INTELLIGENCE SUMMARY.

Army Form C. 2118.

Place	Date	Hour	Summary of Events and Information	Remarks and references to Appendices
ANNEQUIN SOUTH	Jan 5th		at four minutes white Monaning Companies in 1/4 hour. Quiet night, little shelling - Cellars cleared. Dugouts strewn and trenches consolidated on BETHUNE side of houses as shelter from GERMAN Shell fire from direction of LA BASSEE. Fatigue parties sent to look under REs in trenches and carrying parties to RUSSELL-SKEEP to carry out Gas Cylinders.	
do	Jan 6th		Normal situation. Some fatigues as above. Lt ANDERSON, RAMC, battn doctor admitted hospital with Influenza (5th inst) - Lt Hicks RAMC (from Toronto, Canada) detailed to take his place. Inspection of C.O. of C Company in marching order.	
do	Jan 7th		Inspection of C.O. of B Company and Machine Gun Detachmt in marching order. Fatigues in trenches carrying gas cylinders as before.	
do	Jan 8th	10.30 a.m.	A.B. Coys marched via BEUVRY, BETHUNE to billets in FOUQUEREUIL (Refs. Cart. Sheet BETHUNE 36 A r.36B) E.1H.e.3 arrived 1.15 p.m. - Relieved in ANNEQUIN SOUTH by 21st R.F.	
FOUQUEREUIL	Jan 9th		Church of England parade service 10.30 am - Holy Communion in Village School 11.15 am. Billets cleaned and inspected.	
do	Jan 10		Inspection of "A" Company by C.O. in marching order. Baths for 3 Companies at L'ecole des Jeunes Filles, BETHUNE - Both in billets.	

Aug Noth [signature] Lt Colonel
Comdg 18th R.F.

Army Form C. 2118.

18th R.F.

WAR DIARY
or
INTELLIGENCE SUMMARY.
(Erase heading not required.)

Instructions regarding War Diaries and Intelligence Summaries are contained in F. S. Regs., Part II, and the Staff Manual respectively. Title pages will be prepared in manuscript.

Place	Date	Hour	Summary of Events and Information	Remarks and references to Appendices
FOUQUEREUIL	Jan 11th		Inspection of "D" Company by C.O. Physical Drill, Bayonet Exercise, Platoon Drill, Musketry parades - Bombing instruction - 2/Lt BACON left Battn. for work as Intelligence Officer at Pontoise Area - Received news of Evacuation of GALLIPOLI. Battn. in readiness from 5 pm to 10 pm until 5 am tonight, ready to move at shortest notice.	
do	Jan 12th		Company parades as above. C.O. and Adjutant go to lecture from BETHUNE to AIRE for lecture on "Cooperation of Artillery with Infantry".	
do	Jan 13th		C.O. Adjutant and O.C. Companies visit A1 Section of trenches, immediately north of LA BASSÉE Road at CAMBRIN SUPPORT POINT. Company parades in morning - Staff holiday and Company football matches in afternoon.	
do	Jan 14th	9am	March via BETHUNE and BEUVRY to ANNEQUIN NORTH. Exchanging billets with 16th K.R.R.	
ANNEQUIN NORTH	Jan 15th	7pm	Reliev'd "A"Queens & "A"Inskillin HARLEY STREET. Major Douglas proceeded Brigade at Tmp. S.C.	
& A.1. Sect	16th		A Coy left at Finz Linz R on night C in Cuinchy and Braddell Rafre D Cadn. Support point - Braddell point is regularly shelled and for a short period each day, and the front line suffers from "Minnies" - German aeroplane persisted over Annequin whilst march out of line. Similar state of affairs. Gen. Landon went round the line.	
do	17th			
do	18th			

T2134. Wt. W708—776. 500000. 4/15. Sir J. C. & S.

Army Form C. 2118.

18 R Fus.
WAR DIARY
or
INTELLIGENCE SUMMARY.
(Erase heading not required.)

Instructions regarding War Diaries and Intelligence Summaries are contained in F. S. Regs., Part II. and the Staff Manual respectively. Title pages will be prepared in manuscript.

Place	Date	Hour	Summary of Events and Information	Remarks and references to Appendices
At Sloodi	19 Jan	2 pm	Firing line Coys relieved by C (A) and D (B) in the afternoon. German artillery and aeroplane are very active. We have casualties in our line but so far Minni has held to today and our Howitzers have been very energetic.	
do	20 Jan		Quiet day first. 1 Platoon Cyclist Company came to instruction. Placed half with C & half with D. Artillery wolf pounding. Attempts for support to D Co in reply to bombard. Trench mortar was erratic - partly behind own lines - reported to Brigade. Death of 2Lt D.M.H Jewell - in mine shaft.	
do	21 Jan		Jewell buried at Windy Corner - chief things trying to renew a heavy fire to prevent his funeral after German bombarded a mine near own & provoked & blocking ours. Quite day that his. We are keeping him in quite with good artillery assistance - activity mainly against D Coy on river. No casualties.	
do	22 Jan		Quiet day, no casualties - Incoming trails. 20 WRF	
	23 Jan		Relieved after dark by 20 W RF found trenches (Col & Coy's officers) and marched to BEUVRY NORTH. We arrived 1 o'c mass and time late to fallen out.	
BEUVRY NORD	24 Jan		Reveille 7.0 am - days rest. One half of 50 men sent to Annequin. Concert at 6.0 pm - anxious by Shay - "Bath" ready to have at 1/2 hour after arrived. 1 hour day. Whd at Bewry.	
	25 Jan		1st Parade 9.30 . Heavy fatigue Cloth trenches. B & C Coys. Capt Gosson returned from hospital.	Ly Scott below 18 R Hfd

Burroway 18 R Hf

18th Rs.

Army Form C. 2118.

WAR DIARY
or
INTELLIGENCE SUMMARY.
(Erase heading not required.)

Place	Date	Hour	Summary of Events and Information	Remarks and references to Appendices
do	26 Jan		Saw stretchers. D + A Coys. otherwise easy day.	
do	27 Jan		Kaisers birthday. had Test mobilisation during afternoon.	
do	28 Jan		Bath. Relieved 6th Seaf. Rfls. in B.1. section. A + B Coys firing line and redoubt C+D Coys in support at Pont fixe.	
B1 section	29 Jan		Quiet day. C Coy & pioneers worked all night clearing communicn trenches damaged by shelling yesterday. Snipers are inclined to be troublesome to B Coy on right – but only 3 slight casualties so far.	
do	30 Jan		A + B Coys patrolled ground in front during night. Night was quiet on our front. Frosty.	
BETHUNE	31 Jan		Relieved bef. on evening of 30th by 2nd R Fus and marched back carrying packs to Rue d'AIRE. Last party (machine guns) arrived about 4.0 a.m. Two Lewis guns teams were left in trenches to be relieved today by 98th Brigade – but attend gun had to be left as one officer & two Keldon in trenches by 2nd RFus was out of order. Billets here are scattered & not comfortable. Bath is under Brigade Scheme, under 2 hours notice. Leave has been limited in consequence.	

WAR DIARY or INTELLIGENCE SUMMARY.
(Erase heading not required.)

Army Form C. 2118.

Hour, Date, Place	Summary of Events and Information	Remarks and references to Appendices
Feb 1st 1916. Rue d'AIRE BETHUNE	Morning parades. Inspection of coys by C.O.	
„ 2nd „ „	do. Battn. in waiting from 5 p.m.	
„ 3rd „ „	Morning parade. Battn. in waiting till 5 p.m.	
„ 4th „ „	do. Afternoon football match v 20th R Fus. in field off Rue de Lille — drew 1 – 1.	
„ 5th „ „	Battn. paid to move to ANNEQUIN SOUTH. Order cancelled and battn. to stand fast.	
„ 6th „ „	Battn. moved to ANNEQUIN STH. BILLETS. hand occupied by 16th KRR and mixture of many units were in a very bad condition. and some buildings having been converted to serve as habitats. This is hopeless enough accommodation. Transport remains one day at BETHUNE.	
„ 7th „ ANNEQUIN S.	Spent in cleaning billets, repairing dugouts and furnishing watering parties. C.O. left to attend Conval at AIRE. Fatigue party carrying material wood. Cuthell (?) invisible to other Cancelled ditto. nothing to record.	
„ 8th „ „		
„ 9th „ „	ditto. Cal Baly came round & complimented Battn. Had not seen better billet & would return so to the General. ADMS	
„ 10th „ „	ditto. nothing to record.	
„ 11th „ „	Battn. relieved 2 R.W.F. in Z.O. in the evening. A, C & D coys in the firing line – B in RAILWAY TR. RLWY KEEP AND FACTORY TR. Relief complete at 9.30 p.m.	

WAR DIARY
or
INTELLIGENCE SUMMARY.
(Erase heading not required.)

Army Form C. 2118.

Instructions regarding War Diaries and Intelligence Summaries are contained in F.S. Regs., Part II. and the Staff Manual respectively. Title pages will be prepared in manuscript.

Hour, Date, Place		Summary of Events and Information	Remarks and references to Appendices
12th Feb.	Z.O.	Line heavily shelled 2.15 - 4.30 pm. Communication trenches knocked about, only B Casualties. Line otherwise fairly quiet and trenches better than any others we have been in.	
13th Feb.	Z.O.	Quieter. 7th LEINSTER Officers visited trenches.	
14th Feb.	Z.O.	Batt. relieved by 7th LEINSTERS & marched to BETHUNE - HdQrs A + C Coys ECOLE JEUNES FILLES B & D Coys FERME DU ROI. Last man in about 2.30 a.m.	
15th Feb.	BETHUNE	Baths all day at ECOLE des JEUNES FILLES.	
16th Feb.	"	In billets, nothing to report.	
17th Feb.	Z.O.	Batt. relieved 7th LEINSTERS in Z.O. D.C & B Coys in firing line A Coy in support. Relief complete 9.15 p.m.	
18th Feb.	"	Day quiet with exception of some activity on part & forefront of enemy snipers.	
19 Feb.	"	Quiet day. 1 Coy. Munster Regt. relieved C Coy - cadre part. to 3 dug in trenches.	
20th Feb.	"	Quiet day - one of our planes brought down near La Serre Rd.	
21st Feb.	"	Quiet day. Wind Easterly. Usual precautions observed - had coys had test gas alarms by night.	
22nd Feb.	"	Relief by 1st Middlesex. Relief complete 8.40pm. Battn marched to billets in RUE D'AIRE BETHUNE.	

Army Form C. 2118.

WAR DIARY
or
INTELLIGENCE SUMMARY.
(Erase heading not required.)

Instructions regarding War Diaries and Intelligence Summaries are contained in F.S. Regs., Part II. and the Staff Manual respectively. Title pages will be prepared in manuscript.

Hour, Date, Place	Summary of Events and Information	Remarks and references to Appendices
23rd Feb BÉTHUNE	Inspection of New draft of 25 men by Comm'g Officer.	
24th "	Day spent by Batt'n in having baths at ECOLE DES JEUNES FILLES.	
25th "	Inspection & farewell speech by Brigadier General Robertson. CMG.	
26th "	Batt'n moved by train to St OMER. Great difficulty experienced in getting Transport to BETHUNE station owing to roads being frozen. From S'd OMER station Batt'n marched to Billets in CAMPAGNE. Billets found in bad condition.	
27th Feb CAMPAGNE	Day spent in cleaning and improving billets.	
28th "	Company parades morning and afternoon. Owing to heavy fall of snow parade grounds are very wet.	
29th "	Nothing fresh to report. Company parades and route marches in morning and afternoon.	

Huy Scott Clerk
Cap'n 1st Royal Fusiliers

(73989) W. 4141—463. 400,000. 9/14. H.&J.Ltd. Forms/C. 2118/10.

18th Royal Duo:
Vol: 3

30

33RD DIVISION
19TH INFY BDE

20TH BN ROYAL FUSILIERS
NOV 1915 – FEB 1918

DISBANDED 15.2.18

Box 2423

98th Brigade
33rd Division.

Battalion disembarked Calais 14.11.15.

Battalion transferred to 19th Brigade 27.11.15

"

20th BATTALION

ROYAL FUSILIERS

NOVEMBER 1 9 1 5

Original

Army Form C. 2118.

2⁰ᵈ U.S. Batt⁰ ROYAL FUSILIERS

WAR DIARY
or
INTELLIGENCE SUMMARY.

For month of November 1915 from date of Disembarkation

(Erase heading not required.)

Instructions regarding War Diaries and Intelligence Summaries are contained in F.S. Regs., Part II. and the Staff Manual respectively. Title pages will be prepared in manuscript.

Place	Date	Hour	Summary of Events and Information	Remarks and references to Appendices
BOULOGNE	14.11.15	6.0 p.m.	Batt⁰ reached OSTROHOVE camp, nr CALAIS, L⁰ D C	
"	18.11.15	12.00 m.n.	Batt⁰ proceeded by rail to THIENNES. Quartered in billets, L.D.C.	
THIENNES	19.11.15	9.0 a.m.	Batt⁰ marched to LECLEME. Quartered in billets, L.D.C.	
LECLEME	20.11.15	9.30 a.m.	Batt⁰ marched to BETHUNE. Quartered in MONTMORENCY Barracks, L.D.C.	
"	"	7.30 p.m.	6 Officers and 18 N.C.O's units trenches, L.D.C.	
BETHUNE	21.11.15	6.30 a.m.	A & B Coys attached to 19th Brigade for instruction and visited trenches Z1 and Z2, east of CAMBRIN. Units to which attached Argyll-Sutherland Highlanders & Scottish Rifles south of La BASSEE canal, L.D.C.	
CAMBRIN	22.11.15	6.45 a.m.	C & D Coys relieved A & B Coys. A & B billets with H.Q. at S⁺ ANNEQUIN. Transport and other detail remained at BEURRY. Casualties; 3rd L.D.C. wounded, wounded, L.D.C.	
S. ANNEQUIN	23.11.15	9.0 a.m.	Batt⁰ moved from S⁺ ANNEQUIN to N. ANNEQUIN C & D Coys left trenches. Batt⁰ attached to 5⁺⁺ Brigade, L.D.C. Units to which attached 2ⁿᵈ Oxford Light Infty and 9⁺⁺ Highland L⁺ Infty.	
N. ANNEQUIN	24.11.15	9.0 a.m.	A & B Coys occupied trenches A1 and A2, relieving Coys of OXFORD & BUCKS L.I. and HIGHLAND L⁺ Inf⁺ respectively, L.D.C.	
"	25.11.15	9.0 p.m.	C & D Coys relieved A & B Coys, L.D.C.	
"	26.11.15	10.0 a.m.	Batt⁰ moved from N. ANNEQUIN to billets in RUE D'AIRE BETHUNE, L.D.C. BETHUNE.	
BETHUNE	27.11.15	12.0 noon	Batt⁰ transferred to 19⁺⁺ Brigade and moved to barracks at Tobacco factory, BETHUNE, L.D.C.	

C. A. Dunnett
Lt Col Commdg
20.ᵗʰ S. Batt⁰ R. Fus⁺

Original

20th S. BATTN
ROYAL FUSILIERS
WAR DIARY
or
INTELLIGENCE SUMMARY. For month of December 1915

Army Form C. 2118.

Instructions regarding War Diaries and Intelligence Summaries are contained in F. S. Regs., Part II. and the Staff Manual respectively. Title pages will be prepared in manuscript.

(Erase heading not required.)

Place	Date	Hour	Summary of Events and Information	Remarks and references to Appendices
BETHUNE	1.12.15	9.11 a.m	Battn (less A Coy) moved to billets at E, G, & C (map reference Carvin sheet 46 SW BETHUNE) on relieving 1st Battn of 19th Brigade in trenches. A Coy occupied GIVENCHY KEEP, HILDER REDOUBT, MOAT HOUSE REDOUBT, HERTI REDOUBT, WINDY CORNER KEEP, MARAIS E, MARAIS S. J.D.C.	
E.G. & C	4.12.15	3.0 p.m	A Coy relieved A Coy J.D.C.	
E.G. & C A2	6.12.15	5.0 p.m	Battn relieved 18th S. A. R. in trenches E of LE PLANTIN. B Coy and 2 platoons of D Coy left at LE PLANTIN. C Coy 2 platoons in left section of front line, 2 platoons in GEORGE STREET, A Coy 2 platoons in GROUSE BUTTS, 2 in OLD BRITISH LINE, H.Q. in GROUSE BUTTS, 1 Platoon of D in right of front line (in touch with left of section held by 2nd R. WELSH FUSILIERS), 1 platoon in GROUSE BUTTS. 1 Sergt wounded in LE PLANTIN. Platoon on left 7.14 2nd Mx. Queens 22nd Div R.W. Fus 22nd R.W. Fus 22nd Div	
A2	7.12.15	a.m	7 wounded in LE PLANTIN. Snipers active. Our snipers behind our front line say 20 y⁰ to left of our left flank. Work carried out on parapet, shelters, drainage and lateral flooring J.D.C.	
		6 p.m	Platoons in fire trenches relieved J.D.C.	
	8.12.15		Slight sniping on part of enemy. Work as before.	
		6 p.m	Platoons in fire trenches relieved J.D.C.	
	9.12.15	6 p.m	Situation unchanged. Work as before. Platoons in fire trenches relieved J.D.C.	
	10.12.15	3.0-10 p.m	Situation unchanged. Work as before. Battn relieved by 7th E. SURREY Regt. marched by platoons to billets at THE ORPHANAGE, BETHUNE J.D.C.	
BETHUNE	11.12.15			
	12.12.15	9.0 a.m	Battn marched to billets at HAM-EN-ARTOIS. J.D.C.	
HAM-EN-ARTOIS	13.12.15 14.12.15	11.0 a.m	Battn inspected by G.O.C. 19th Inf. Brigade. J.D.C.	

20th S. Battn. R. Fus.

WAR DIARY
or
INTELLIGENCE SUMMARY.

Army Form C. 2118.

(Erase heading not required.)

Hour, Date, Place	Summary of Events and Information	Remarks and references to Appendices
1AM EN ARTOIS 15. 12. 15	Company and Platoon Training P.C	
16 " "	Route March " "	
17 " "	Company and Platoon Training P.C	
18 " "	" " " "	
19 " "	Church Parade P.C	
20 " "	Company and Platoon Training P.C	
21 " "	" " " "	
22 " "	" " " " P.C	
23 " "	" " " " P.C	
24 " "	" " " " P.C	
25 " "	" " " " P.C	
26 " "	Battn training Baths in and R.E Stores collected P.C	
27 " "	Battn moved to BETHUNE. Billets at THE ORPHANAGE L.P.C	
BETHUNE 11.30 28 " "	D Coy moved to CHOQUES attached for duty with 1st Corps H.Q. L.P.C	
PM " "	Battn moved to billets at S. ANNEQUIN, F 30 At map reference	
30 " "	36a BETHUNE (40,000) as reserve Battn of 19th Brigade being L.P.C	
	Tactics S.O.S. Alarm signal	

M Cornell Lt Col Commg
20th S Br R Fus.
31. 12. 15

Army Form C. 2118.

20th BATTN ROYAL FUSILIERS
WAR DIARY
or
INTELLIGENCE SUMMARY.
(Erase heading not required.)

Place	Date	Hour	Summary of Events and Information	Remarks and references to Appendices
S.ANNEQUIN F.2.9.6.	January 1		Battn in billets in reserve	Map reference BETHUNE Sectional Sheet 40,000
"	2	11.0 a.m.	LA NASSEE Road east of billet area bombarded. 1 man slightly wounded	
"	4	8.30 a.m.	Battn relieved 3 coys of 18th R.Fus in Scotch Trench, BOYAU 14 — GUN STREET (exclusive). A Coy right, C coy centre and RUSSELL'S KEEP, B Coy left. 2nd R. WELSH FUSILIERS on right flank, 16th K.R.R. (100th Brigade) on left. 1 Coy 18th R.FUS in reserve line of trenches.	
"	5		Work on trenches. Wire parties out 5 - 8 p.m. 1 wounded	
LA NASSEE BOYAU 14 — GUN STREET				
"	7		Increased sniping and machine gun activity. 2nd Lt C.A. STUART and 8 other ranks wounded (Shrapnel and Rifle Grenade) Draft of 27 men received and posted with Transport at BEUVRY	
"	8	9.0 a.m.	Bombardment of ground between Reserve line of trenches and CAMBRIN SUPPORT POINT. 1 man wounded (billet).	
"	9	3.0 a.m.	Battn relieved by 20th R.FUS. Relief complete by 7.30 a.m. In billets at S. ANNEQUIN till 10.0 a.m. Battn moved to BETHUNE & quartered in MONTMORENCY BARRACKS.	
BETHUNE	10 and following days		Training in Grenade throwing, Bayonet fighting, Rapid loading	
"	14th	4.30 p.m.	Battn relieved 16th MIDDLESEX Regt in trenches B1 and B2 whence A1 & b. 1st Bn CAMERONIANS on right flank across canal. 2nd SUFFOLK REGT on left. 2 Coys in front line and Redoubt, 1 Coy + 1 Coy 5th SCOTTISH RIFLES in billets at PONT FIXE	
A 14.b	15		Drainage work commenced and carried out during period of occupation. Intermittent shelling of PONT FIXE for three and subsequent days.	
"	16		No change in situation. One man wounded 7.0 p.m. while on wiring duty.	
"	17		Two wounded by shrapnel in support billets at PONT FIXE	
"	18	5.0 - 11.0 p.m.	Coy in left sub-section relieved by Coy in support billets	

Situation unchanged

Army Form C. 2118.

2nd Bn. ROYAL FUSILIERS

WAR DIARY
or
INTELLIGENCE SUMMARY.
(Erase heading not required.)

Place	Date	Hour	Summary of Events and Information	Remarks and references to Appendices
A 1 & 2	24/9		One man wounded (Shrapnel) in trenches held by Batt. relieved by 5th Scottish Rifles, and moved to billets at BEUVRY	
BEUVRY (a)	25th Sept	5.0 PM – 10.0 PM	Batt. in billets.	
		8.0 PM – 8.0 PM	Batt. relieved 1st Royal Fusiliers in trenches A 1. Map reference A 21. to extend to & extend 2nd R.W.F. on left.	
A 21 x 22			100th Brigade on right. A Coy on left flank, D Coy on right flank. C Coy in support at CUINCHY SUPPORT POINT and BRADDELL POINT. B Coy of 1st CAMERONIANS in reserve at CAMBRIN SUPPORT POINT, Rely complete 8 P.M.	
	26th	9.30 AM	CAPTAIN v ADJUTANT L.D CANE killed by sniper (firing his.) Buried in evening at CAMBRIN CHURCH. One man killed & two wounded by rifle & ltr. (unchanged).	
	26th		Situation unchanged	
	26th		Situation unchanged. Two men wounded.	
	27th		Situation unchanged. Two men killed. Three wounded	
	28th		One man killed. Heavy bombard next all day. Batteries supporting our immediate front being our stay in the sector 70th R.F.A. 062 and D 64. 56 Howitzer battery allotted to A 1.	
	29th	4.30 PM –10 PM	Batt. relieved by 19th Royal Fusiliers of 98th Brigade. Relieve complete 10. P.M. Batt. marches to billets at Ecole MICHELET, BETHUNE	
BETHUNE	30th		Training in billets.	
	31st	noon	Training in billets.	

W. Rosevelt Lt. Col.
O.C. 20th Royal Fusiliers

Army Form C. 2118.

WAR DIARY
INTELLIGENCE SUMMARY
(Erase heading not required)

1916 FEB — 1916 JUNE

Place	Date	Hour	Summary of Events and Information	Remarks and references to Appendices
BETHUNE (Essars area)	February 1916 1st to 6th		Training in billeting area.	FM
do	7th	2.30 PM to 5.15 PM	Moved into billets at ANNEQUIN FOSSE F.29.d. (Bethune reduced sheet 1:40000 J.6.4. Edition). The battalion relieved the 2nd Royal Welsh Fusiliers. D company moved to 1/5th Scottish Rifles in Z. Sector.	FM
ANNEQUIN FOSSE				FM
F.29.d.	8th to 12th		Training in billeting area. Reserve 1/3. Z. Sector.	FM
do	12th to 13th	5.15 PM to 9.30 PM	Relieved 1/5th Scottish Rifles in Z2. BOYAU 15 (A.27.6.4.4.) to BOYAU 27 (A.21.d.6.7.) B.C.D. Coys. in firing line & supports. A coy in reserve. 1 Platoon 1/5th Scottish Rifles in RUSSELS KEEP, 1 Platoon in LEWIS KEEP. D coy relieved 7th LEINSTER'S company. We were Masters & Scottish Rifles for instruction. Relief complete 9.30 PM. Battalion on left 100th Brigade Batteries on right 1st Cameronians on left Centre coy. D/63 Supp. coy. C/63. RIGHT coy. A/63. Hostile comm: post B/65 Bombard much in afternoon. Trench damages. 2 men killed & 8 wounded (3 returned to duty).	FM
Z2.	13th		Casualties 6 killed. 9 wounded.	FM
do	14th		Casualties 2 wounded. One of these returned to duty.	FM
do	15th			FM
do	16th	6.0 PM	Relieved by 1/5th SCOTTISH RIFLES and moved to billets at ANNEQUIN FOSSE. Left A company & Lewis in reserve to 1/5 S.R. Relief complete 9.30 PM.	FM
ANNEQUIN FOSSE F.29.d.	17th		Working parties. Training in billets. Reserve Battn. Z. Sector	FM
do	18th			FM

… **WAR DIARY** or **INTELLIGENCE SUMMARY.**
(Erase heading not required.)

Army Form C. 2118.

Hour, Date, Place	Summary of Events and Information	Remarks and references to Appendices
ANNEQUIN FOSSE F.29.d Z.2	19th February 1916. Working parties.	
5.0 P.M. to 10.20 P.M.	Relieved 1/5th SCOTTISH RIFLES in Z.2 Area. Area reconnoitred Relief taken over on 12/2/16. B. & D. companies attracting training for instruction with C. Company of Royal Munster Fusiliers 6th Battn. These three companies held firing & support lines. Our C. Coy in RUSSELL's and LEWIS KEEPS. A Coy in reserve. Relief complete 10.20 P.M. Battalion reporting as on 12/2/16. 100th Brigade on LEFT, 2nd Royal Welsh Fusiliers on RIGHT.	7 PM
20th	1 Rifle & 2 O.R. wounded. Wet. Hazy at intervals.	7 PM
21st	1 trench mortar 1 O.R. killed 3 O.R. wounded.	7 PM
22nd	Relieved by 2nd Argyll and Sutherland Highlanders & handed to BEUVRY. Relief complete at 9.30 p.m. Bullet at BEUVRY NORTH H.Q. at F.14.a.8.2	7 PM
5.30 P.M. to 9.30 P.M.	Attached in case of attack to 100th Brigade.	
BEUVRY NORTH F.14.a.8.2 23rd to 29th	Training in Billeting area. Reserve Battalion stationed 100th Brigade in sector A and B.1.	7 PM
4.45 P.M. to 10.20 P.M.	Relieved 16th KINGS ROYAL RIFLES in B.1. Area. A.16.c.o.6. to A.15.&.9 LA BASSEE CANAL on right. 2nd WORCESTERS on right. 13th Royal WELSH FUSILIERS on left. Battalion in many A.156 ("14 pounder) 4.2" Howitzers.	7 PM
A.15 a.b.	Relief complete 10.20 P.M.	7 PM

J. Ashbey Major
O.C. 20th Battn Royal Fusiliers.

Army Form C. 2118.

WAR DIARY
or
INTELLIGENCE SUMMARY.
(Erase heading not required.)

Instructions regarding War Diaries and Intelligence Summaries are contained in F.S. Regs., Part II. and the Staff Manual respectively. Title pages will be prepared in manuscript.

Hour, Date, Place	Summary of Events and Information	Remarks and references to Appendices
BETHUNE (Billet Area 2)		
March 10th 1915 1st	1 O.R. killed. 2 O.R. wounded. one of latter returned to duty.	
2nd	1 O.R. killed. 3 O.R. wounded. one of latter returned to duty.	
4th	1 O.R. died of wounds. 3 O.R. wounded.	
5th 5.15 & 6th	Captain J.D. Henniker shot by own side too hour later.	
7th	Relieved 1/10th Welch Regiment of 114th Brigade. Relief complete 8.35 AM.	
6.0 PM	Moved to billets in LE QUESNOY. BHQ 7 & 6 b ii.	
LE QUESNOY Feb 7 8.30 PM	Batt. in Reserve. D company as Reserve company at CAMBRIN SUPPORT POINT CUINCHY section to 5th SCOTTISH RIFLES.	
Do. 9th 10th 11th 12th	Relieved the 5th SCOTTISH RIFLES in CUINCHY SECTION (Trojan 20 to Trojan 32 A.21.d.55.0 to A.21.b.7.2) On our right 1st Queens. on left 2nd R.W.F. Battalion supporting D.166 for right flank. C.162 for centre.	
A.21.b.d. 5.0 PM to 11.30 PM	B.162 for left flank. Hartlepos A.167 for whole front. B. Coy 5th S.R. attached in reserve at Coulson Buttock Point & Braddell Point. Relief complete 11.35 PM.	
Do. 13th	Fire opened by enemy at A.21.d 7.5.25. At 6.15 AM Crater blown between our G.3 points: no casualties. Point sheltered by enemy's a county: repeated. Captain E.T. Brught killed 3 rifle grenades. 2nd Lieut T.S. Page wounded. 4 O.R. killed. 8 O.R. wounded. (one in rear of).	
	Remains of 2nd Lieut we left near top of crater.	
14th	1 O.R. killed. 6 O.R. wounded.	
9.0 PM	Small attack by enemy on Bosch repulsed.	

Army Form C. 2118.

WAR DIARY
or
INTELLIGENCE SUMMARY.
(Erase heading not required.)

Instructions regarding War Diaries and Intelligence Summaries are contained in F.S. Regs., Part II and the Staff Manual respectively. Title pages will be prepared in manuscript.

Hour, Date, Place		Summary of Events and Information	Remarks and references to Appendices
A.21.d.v.d.	14th / 15th / 16th	7 O.R. wounded 7 sho wounded remaining of M.T. Quiet day.	
	17th / 17th / 6.0 PM	Relieved by 1st H. Beaon Regt s marches to BETHUNE. Whole Bn BETHUNE billets pte B340 9 Rue d'Eglise Huymalt. Brigade in reserve.	
BETHUNE	16th 8.15 PM		
Do	18th to 20th		
Do	21st	Inspection by G.O.C. 11th Army Corps.	
Do	22nd to 25th	Brigade in Reserve.	
Do	25th 26th & 27th 28th	Battalion in Reserve	
ANNEQUIN (SOUTH)	11.30 AM 2.0 PM	Relieved 2nd Borderers at ANNEQUIN SOUTH. B&Q F29 L9.8. The new Brigade relief 19th relieving 100th to date	
Do			
G.4 a.w Azyd	29th	Relieves 1/5th Scottish Rifles in Archy right subsection. Began 1 to 8 (9.12th Division) (Ref. reference G.4.a.75.75 to A.27.d.87) 1st Coldson an on relv. 7th Suffolks for night A,B,D Coys form Bn. C. Coy in Reserve. Batteries supporting Left B.166 Centre B.156 Right D.169 Thunder evening made post B.167. Relief complete 8.52 PM	
Do	29th	A & B Coys 162 Nth & Derby shared an A & D Coys who returned to Annequin Sth. Relief complete 10.30 PM 3 O.R. wounded (remaining of draft)	M Burnett Lt. Col. Comdg 20. Royal Fusiliers
Do	30th	Notes. Daily sketches for information	
Do	31st	E & D companies at 162 Nth & Derby relieved A & B coys of that regiment. Relief complete 10.50 PM Our A & D companies relieved C & D companies of 118 Nth Derby. Relief complete 9.40 PM	

"D" Wells 7.0.
Army Form C. 2118.

Vol 5

WAR DIARY
or
INTELLIGENCE SUMMARY. 10th R Fus.

(Erase heading not required.)

Hour, Date, Place	Summary of Events and Information	Remarks and references to Appendices
April 1916.		
AUCHY right subsection 1st		
G.4.b and A.27.d 7.15pm BETHUNE 10.50pm	Relieved by 16th Battalion Notts and Derby 117th Brigade 39th Division. Relief complete 10.50 p.m. Marched to BETHUNE. Billets in École de Jeunes filles.	7pm
Do 2nd 3rd		
Do 3rd 4th		
Do 4th		
ANNEQUIN SOUTH 5pm to 7/15pm	Relieved 5th Scottish Rifles in ANNEQUIN SOUTH. Battalion in reserve.	7pm
Do 5th 6th 7th	Working parties. Battalion in reserve.	7pm
AUCHY right subsection 7.0 PM to	17th Notts and Derby attached to battalion for company training. A+B	7pm
G.4.b and A.27.d 10.20pm	companies of our battalion with A+B coys of 17th Notts. Derby relieved 5th Scottish Rifles in AUCHY right subsection. On left 2nd Royal Welsh Fusiliers on right 8. Sussex of 12th Division. Battalions reporting right Coy D 162, left + centre coy B.168. Hostile batterys hot shells from D.167. B + C coys relieved A + B companies of ANNEQUIN. Relief complete 10.20 pm	
Do 8th	Two companies (C+D) 4 + 7 Notts - Derby relieved A+D coys of Bn. Relief complete 9.40 pm. 1 O.R. wounded	7pm
Do 9th	Our B + C companies relieved C+D coys of 17th Notts v Derby. Relief complete 9.15 pm	7pm
Do 10th		7pm
BETHUNE 8.0 pm to 10.40pm	Relieved by 17th Notts v Derby. Battalion marched to BETHUNE Billeted at Trinity Orphey Barracks. 17th Notts/ Derby and 39th Division training battalion v special class Brigade in Reserve	7pm
Do 11th to 17th		
Do 17th 18th		
LE QUESNOY 2 pm - 3pm	Relieved 16th Kings Royal Rifles at LESBOEUFNOY Battalion in reserve.	7pm

WAR DIARY
or
INTELLIGENCE SUMMARY.
(Erase heading not required.)

Army Form C. 2118.

Hour, Date, Place	Summary of Events and Information	Remarks and references to Appendices
April 1916 LE QUESNOY 10th to 21st (F&6.6.1)	LE QUESNOY billets: latter in reserve	FM
CUINCHY left subsection 6.0 PM 22nd (BRICK STACKS) BOYAU 32 to LA BASSEE CANAL A.21.b.8.a. to A.16.c.o.6.	Relieved 1st Battalion CAMERONIANS in CUINCHY left subsection. On left by 2nd R.W.Fus. with north side of LA BASSEE canal 1st Royal SUSSEX of 39th Division. On right 2nd ROYAL WELSH FUSILIERS. Batteries supporting Left & centre B.156, centre and right C.156. Howitzer battery for all front A.167. Relief complete 8.57. P.M.	FM
Do 23rd		FM
Do 24th	2 O.R. wounded	FM
Do 25th	1 O.R. killed	FM
Do 26th	1 O.R. wounded. Battalion relieved by 1st Batt. CAMERONIANS. Battalion marched to LE QUESNOY. Battalion in reserve. Relief complete	FM
LE QUESNOY 7PM – 9.45AM F.9.2.2.6		
Do 27th	Gas was reported as having been discharged South: lehwih we put on at both times gas was experienced though to lorry in having been discharged by the enemy near HULLUCH + having travelled 7 miles in two hours. No casualties.	FM
Do 6.15AM – 8.30AM		
Do 28th, 29th	Battalion in reserve. 1 O.R. wounded one of whom remains at duty	FM
Do 30th	Relieved 1st Batt. CAMERONIANS in CUINCHY left subsection. On left that is north side of LA BASSEE canal 11th Royal Sussex of 39th Division. On right 2nd Royal Welsh Fusiliers. Batteries supporting Left & centre B.156 centre & right C.156. Howitzer battery for whole front A.167. Relief complete 9.15 PM. 1.O.R. wounded)	FM
CUINCHY left subsection 6.15PM – 9.15PM (Brickstacks) BOYAU 032 to LA BASSEE CANAL A.21 b.8.2. to A.16.c.0.6.		FM

M.Sinnett Lt-Col
Comdg 2nd Royal Fusiliers

Army Form C. 2118.

20 R Fus
XXXIII Vol 7
6.H.
(2 sheets)

WAR DIARY
or
INTELLIGENCE SUMMARY.
(Erase heading not required.)

Instructions regarding War Diaries and Intelligence Summaries are contained in F.S. Regs., Part II. and the Staff Manual respectively. Title pages will be prepared in manuscript.

Hour, Date, Place	Summary of Events and Information	Remarks and references to Appendices
May 1916		
CUINCHY Left Subsection (Brickstacks) 1st	1. O.R wounded recovered at My	F91
Boyan 32 to LA BASSÉE CANAL A21 d 6.2 to A 15. c.0.6.		
2nd		F91
Do 3.4.	1. O.R wounded.	F91
	1. O.R killed 1 O.R bombed, recovered at My. Two small raids by patrols in conjunction with Tank mortar Battery. Planned to attack enemy saps & posts. On last, got into our post on A.8. & trenches but found it unoccupied. Other ½ of force being still in occupation & after finding trench retired. Casualties – 1 O.R wounded and 1 died of wounds at My.	F91
Do 4th	1 O.R wounded at My.	F91
8.0PM—9.40PM	Relieved by 4th King's Liverpool Regiment. Marched to BETHUNE West of RUE D'AIRE. Relief complete 9.40 P.M.	F91
BETHUNE (RUE D'AIRE) 5th to 15th	Training in Corps area. Brigade in reserve.	F91
16th	Relieved 1st Royal Berks (request'd) – Auchy left subsection. On right 3rd Royal Berks Fusiliers: on left 1st Queens Victoria Regt. Battalion supporting, 16 howitzer, A27 d 9 to A22 d 55.00	F91
Do 17th to 20th	Left coy A.166 Centre coy A.166 × A.162 Right company A.162. Head qrs White Hart D.16.J. Relief complete 10.15 P.M. Casualties, 3 O.R killed, 1 O.R died of wounds. 17 O.R wounded of which number 11 remained at duty.	F91
Do 22nd		F91
ANNEQUIN SOUTH 9.30PM to 11.30PM	Relieved by 1st Cameronians. Marched to ANNEQUIN SOUTH; Battalion in Divisional reserve. Relief complete 11.30 P.M.	F91
Do 23rd to 28th	Battalion in reserve. Working parties.	F91

WAR DIARY
or
INTELLIGENCE SUMMARY.
(Erase heading not required.)

Army Form C. 2118.

Hour, Date, Place	Summary of Events and Information	Remarks and references to Appendices
ANNEQUIN SOUTH F.30.c.3.8. AULCHY Redoubt Bogan 26 A.27.d.5.7.6 A.21.d 55.06.		
29/: 8.30 PM to 10.15 PM	Relieved 1st Camerouins in Auchy left subsection. On right 5th Scottish Rifles, on left 1/4th Suffolks. Battalion disposing 1st howitzer left coy A.166 Centre company A.166 - A.162. Right company A.162. Frontage taken from post D.166 (old D.167). Relief complete — 10.15 PM. Casualties 3 O.R. wounded.	J.S.M.
30:		
29: A.27 & 6.9 to midnight	4. O.R. wounded midway 2 at 9.15. at 12 midnight we threw a mine at S.E. corner of midwall crater. Built to strengthen midnight crater live 3. Right centre. Have command of new L.L. retaining ports. retaliation slight. Position A.27 & 6.9.	J.S.M.
30/: 3.AM	A company 2/5th borewick attacked for instruction. Two platoon attacked on C coy Relief complete 145 AM. only two platoons were in trenches. Relief to Kingsman and OLD BOOTS TRENCH.	J.S.M.
30:	4. O.R. wounded midway on all duty.	J.S.M.

C. Yerston
Captain
a/O.C. 20th Royal Fusiliers.

20. R. Fus
Army Form C. 2118.
Vol 8
of June

XXXIII

7.H.
(3 sheets)

WAR DIARY or INTELLIGENCE SUMMARY.
(Erase heading not required.)

Instructions regarding War Diaries and Intelligence Summaries are contained in F.S. Regs., Part II. and the Staff Manual respectively. Title pages will be prepared in manuscript.

Hour, Date, Place	Summary of Events and Information	Remarks and references to Appendices
June 1916 1st		
AUCHY LEFT SUBSECTION. Bryan 8.5	In the line with 2/5th Warwicks. A company attached to our C and D companies. 1 O.R. Died of wounds.	7.9.M.
7pm A2·7·0·7 & A2·d·55·0·0.		
BEUVRY (NORTH) 6.30 P.M.-11.3 P.M.	Relieved by 1/5th CAMERONIANS. A company 2/5th Warwicks attached to 'B' company of that regiment. Relief complete 11.3 P.M. Thanks to whole Battalion in reserve in BEUVRY.	7.9.M.
3rd to 7th	Battalion in reserve.	7.9.M.
OBLINGHEM 4.0 P.M. W.20.c and 26.a.	Relieved by 16th K. KINGS ROYAL RIFLES. Marched to OBLINGHEM billets in Divisional reserve.	7.9.M.
8th to 17th	Brigade in reserve. Training. Information received that 5969 Private WOOLFENDEN. R. had been awarded Military Medal attached 251st Company R.E.	7.9.M.
17. 6.30 P.M.	Relieved 16th KINGS ROYAL RIFLES in BEUVRY NORTH. Relief complete 6.30 P.M.	
BEUVRY (NORTH) 6.30 P.M. to 18th & 20th	Brigade in reserve.	7.9.M.
20th 9.30 P.M.	Relieved 4th KINGS ROYAL LIVERPOOL REGIMENT in GIVENCHY right subsection	
GIVENCHY RIGHT SUBSECTION. Bryan 36 to Bryan 53 inclusive. A.22 ⦿ A.0.6.6. to A.15.6.8.9.	16th KRR on right, 2nd RWF on left. Batteries in support B.156 Bryan 36 to Bryan 46 A.16 Bryan 46 to Bryan 53. C.156 in charge of guns in VER MELLES sector. Latrol explodes trackertacks about Bryan 36 to Bryan 38.	7.9.M.
22nd	D156 Howitzer north of canal.	7.9.M.
	Casualties Captain COCKELL wounded. 4.OR Killed 22. O.R. wounded mostly &	
	remained on duty. All casualties caused by artillery barrage of enemy previous to and following enemy experience. Enemy came over them at 1.55 a.m. and red flares on parts of right company of 2nd R.W.F. battalion immediately on our left enemy entered trench but were driven out and over by A.& W.F. coyees	

WAR DIARY
or
INTELLIGENCE SUMMARY.
(Erase heading not required.)

Army Form C. 2118.

Place	Date	Hour	Summary of Events and Information	Remarks and references to Appendices
Givenchy Rspt outside Village A.22.c.6.6 A.15.b.6.5	June 1916 22nd		A. D. R. reported of Num 3 remained at Dug	AppM
Do	24th		2nd Lt. Brown F.H. wounded 2.0.R wounded	AppM
Do	26th	10.0pm	Relieved 1st Cameronians. Battalion in Village Line Disposed as follows A Company Givenchy Keep. Heat farm	AppM
VILLAGE LINE A.8.9.14.15		11.30pm	H. Sec. RednM. Herk RedvM. C Cy Pont Fixe south W. D.y Conners, de Plantin South. B Cy	AppM
Do	27, 28, 29, 30	July 1	PONT FIXE. NORTH. D Coy reserve company Battalion in support.	AppM

M Merriott Lt Col
Comdg 2nd Battalion Royal Fusiliers

19th Inf.Bde.
33rd Div.

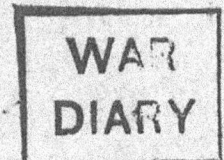

20th BATTN. THE ROYAL FUSILIERS.

J U L Y

1 9 1 6

33 July
20th & 2nd Royal Fusiliers
Army Form C. 2118.
1/33 VOL 9

S.H.
(3 sheets)

WAR DIARY
INTELLIGENCE SUMMARY.

Place	Date	Hour	Summary of Events and Information	Remarks and references to Appendices
Village Line	July 1916			
	1st	1 pm	Battalion in support occupying Gruntz Keep, Hinders redoubt, Moat Farm, Herts Redoubt, Windy Corner Keep, Le Plantin South Keep, Post Five North & Post Five South.	7 pm
Givenchy right	2nd	11 noon 8 pm	Relieved 1st Cameronians in Givenchy Right subsection. On night 16th KRRC on left 5th Scottish Rifles Battn on right B/156. These companies in reserve. 2 Company in reserve.	7 pm
sub sector A 1 to 6 & A 9 & c 9.		9 pm	Left A 16 7 - 18 June 9m Thos. Fr. D/156. Relief complete 9.10 pm.	7 pm
do	3rd to 6th		Casualties 5 others O.R. killed 15 O.R. wounded of which 3 remain at duty.	7 pm
	8th	9.30 pm 11.30 pm	Relieved by 1st Herts. Battn marched to Annezin.	7 pm
Annezin	9th		Billets at Annezin	7 pm
do	10th	3 am	Left by train for Longpré (Athies) arrived 11.0 am. Marched to Poulainville Brigade Billets Area	7 pm
Poulainville	11th	2.0 pm	Marched to Vecquemont. Billets Area	7 pm
Vecquemont	12th	2 pm	Left Vecquemont having been back there & marched to Buire on L'Ancre arriving	7 pm
Buire on L'Ancre			at about 6.0 pm.	7 pm
do	13th		Company rest.	7 pm
do	14th	11.0 am	Marched on to Méaulte. Battn Hd Qr moved on 9pm to have billets to bivouac.	7 pm

Army Form C. 2118.

WAR DIARY
or
INTELLIGENCE SUMMARY.
(Erase heading not required.)

Instructions regarding War Diaries and Intelligence Summaries are contained in F. S. Regs., Part II. and the Staff Manual respectively. Title pages will be prepared in manuscript.

Place	Date	Hour	Summary of Events and Information	Remarks and references to Appendices
MEAULTE	July 14.	6 p.m.	Ground between MEAULTE and BÉCORDEL BÉCOURT. Brigade bivouacked there.	701.
MAMETZ WOOD	15th	7 a.m.	Left bivouacy found at 4.20 a.m. & marched & bivouacked on ground below MAMETZ WOOD: arrived there 7.0 a.m. stayed there all day & bivouacked there at night	701.
"	16th		Left at 3.0 a.m. to relieve 16th K.R.R. in support. S.g.d. 9.0. to S.g.d. 8.0. & back on road S.g.d. 5.5. Left drawn again at 10.0 p.m. to support advance of MAMETZ WOOD. Casualties 4 = O.R.	701.
BAZENTIN				
MAMETZ WOOD	17th		to support advance of MAMETZ WOOD. Casualties 16. O.R.	701.
Do	18th			701.
BAZENTIN	18th	5 p.m.	Move up to relieve 5th SCOTTISH RIFLES front line from QUARRY to WINDMILL. Relieved by 4th KINGS about 9.0 p.m. & then to bivouac huts below BAZENTIN-LE-PETIT WOOD preparatory to attack. Lt Ziegler, Lt Pleasure & 2nd Lt Evans wounded 28 O.R. casualties.	701.
Do	19th			
HIGH WOOD	20th		19th Brigade attack at 3.25. a.m. on HIGH WOOD. Attack by 1st CAMERONIANS and 5th SCOTTISH RIFLES. 20th Royal FUSILIERS in support 2nd ROYAL WELSH FUSILIERS in reserve. North corner & North with corner of WOOD not taken. rest taken & consolidated. 2nd ROYAL WELSH FUSILIERS came up about 12 noon. A front & support line consolidated	701.
(Map reference MARTINPUICH AREA)			across WOOD from East to West about with a strong point about S.4.d.2.8. in support line.	

Army Form C. 2118.

WAR DIARY
or
INTELLIGENCE SUMMARY.
(Erase heading not required.)

Place	Date	Hour	Summary of Events and Information	Remarks and references to Appendices
(Map MARTINPUICH AREA) HIGH WOOD	July 20th		Held on to it, position until relieved by 100th Brigade at midnight the. with drew to old bivouac lines around MAMETZ WOOD. Casualties. Lt Col Bennett wounded, Lt Rannie, Lt Palmer, 2nd Lt Pierce 2nd Lt Coulter, missing, 2nd Lt Haire, missing, believed killed, Capt Tolle, 2nd Lt Bullock, Lt Evans, wounded, Capt Hollingworth, 2nd Lt Bell, 2nd Lt Cooke, 2nd Lt Brooke, 2nd Lt Fabrius, 2nd Lt Ives, 2nd Lt Heeles O.R. rank killed, wounded & missing 375.	RM FM
MAMETZ WOOD	21st			FM
do	22nd	4.0pm	Withdrew to BUIRE au L'ANCRE.	FM
BUIRE au L'ANCRE	23rd		} Reorganising	
do	24th			
do	16 31st		Reinforcements recvd 2 officers 701. Also under Reorganising & training in arms & Wiletony area. Military Medals awarded to 7053 Pte T.B. Ashworth, 4655 Pte S. Clayton, 5268 Pte C.C. Macintyre, 5598 Pte F.G. Scott and 8735 Pte F.S. Snow.	

V. M Kirk Major
Commanding 20th Royal Fusiliers

19th Brigade.
33rd Division.

20th BATTALION

ROYAL FUSILIERS

AUGUST 1 9 1 6

Army Form C. 2118.

20th Royal Fusiliers

Vol 10

WAR DIARY
INTELLIGENCE SUMMARY.
(Erase heading not required.)

Place	Date	Hour	Summary of Events and Information	Remarks and references to Appendices
	August 1916			
BOURE sur L'ANCRE	1st to 4th		Training division out of the line	
"	5th			7PM
"	6th	10.0 AM to 12 Noon	Marched to E 12.a. (Sheet FRANCE 62.D.(N.E.) to bivouac was occupied and	7PM
HEAULTE E.12.a.	7th to 12th		HEAULTE. Brigade in Divisional reserve.	
"	12th		The Brigade in Divisional reserve. Major W. B. Garnett from 1st R.W. Fus. assumed command of the battalion	7PM
MAMETZ WOOD S.9.b.55	13th	4.0 PM	Brigade moved into support. Battalion relieved 2nd Argyll and Sutherland Highlanders in MAMETZ WOOD. Sig b.55. relief complete 4.0 AM	7PM
"	14th 15th 16th		Brigade in support, working parties. Brigade relieved 96th Brigade.	7PM
S.9.c.g.o.	16th	5.0 AM		
S.10.b.60.75 to S.10.b.85		2.45 PM 4.20 PM 5.20 PM	War order 92nd Brigade attacks WOOD LANE at 2.45 PM. Battalion cover S.9.c.g.o. to Crucifix companies in support of 1/1st Suffolks, and 4th Kings. Ordered to move up. Rest of battalion at 5.20 PM took over with companies from 4th Kings. The front company supporting 1/1st Suffolks.	7PM
S.9.c.g.o.	19th	4.0 AM	Relieved by 1st Cameronians & went to Craonne Comm S.9.c.g.o. having been relieved	7PM
S.19.b.55	20 & 21	6.0 PM	Day and returned to MAMETZ WOOD in Brigade reserve. Reported 19th Brigade and became battalion in reserve to front brigade.	7PM
"	21st	10.0 PM	Moved into companies forward to trenches to support if necessary attack by 2nd Brigade. Went to companies took over night of 22nd of King of 5th Scottish rifles. Attack so not succeed. Companies left trenches upon	9.H. (20th etc) 7PM

2353 Wt. W2514/1454 700,000 5/15 D.D.&L. A.D.S.S./Forms/C. 2118.

Army Form C. 2118.

20th Royal Fusiliers

WAR DIARY
INTELLIGENCE SUMMARY.
(Erase heading not required.)

Instructions regarding War Diaries and Intelligence Summaries are contained in F. S. Regs., Part II. and the Staff Manual respectively. Title pages will be prepared in manuscript.

Hour, Date, Place	Summary of Events and Information	Remarks and references to Appendices
August 1916		
Fraffue 22nd 8.0 AM S4 c.05.50 to S.10 d.9.9.	Remaining Companies came up + battalion took over from 5th Scottish Rifles holding from right edge of HIGHWOOD to S.10 d.9.9. Each A. E. WALKER killed. Relief complete 10.0 AM	JM
Do 23rd		
Do 24th 6.0 AM	Two Companies 5th Scottish Rifles attached to battalion in order to relieve two companies to mount an attack at 100' Brigade on NEW GERMAN TRENCH. Attack at 5.45 PM. Called on to send two platoons to take over part of line taken by 1st QUEENS. Took over trench Last of the coys at S.11.a.3.3 and started to connect S.11.a.3.3 with say A S.10 d.9.5.	JM
Do 25th/26th	Finished trench connecting S.11.a.3.3 with S.10.d.9.5. 2/Lt HUMPHRYS killed.	JM
26th 5.0 AM	Relieved by 5th Scottish Rifles and returned to MAMETZ WOOD. Relief complete 7.0 AM	JM
MAMETZ WOOD S.19 6.55.		
27th 7.30 AM	Move to MONTAUBAN ALLEY. Brigade becoming Reserve Brigade in region 1st battalion being sections together with 1st Camerons to 98th Brigade.	JM
MONTAUBAN ALLEY A.1.6.75 & S.26.c.9.4		
Do 28th	Working parties.	JM
FRICOURT WOOD 29th 7.30 AM	Relieved by 2nd Royal Welsh Fusiliers : moved to FRICOURT WOOD.	JM
Do 30th		
Do 31st	33rd Division relieved by 1st Division Brigade marched back to RIDGEMONT Billeted there. Casualties whilst Division was in the line :— from 6.8.16 to 31.8 :— 2 officers killed 23 O.R. killed 137 wounded (18 at duty 11. O.R. missing	JM
RIDGEMONT		

W.B. Barnett Lt Colonel
Commg 20th R. Fus.

(73989) W4141–463. 400,000. 9/14. H.&J.Ltd. Forms/C. 2118/10.

WAR DIARY / INTELLIGENCE SUMMARY

Army Form C.2118

1916 SEPT — 1916 DEC
Vol. 1
20th Royal Dublin [Fusiliers] September 1916

Place	Date	Hour	Summary of Events and Information	Remarks and references to Appendices
	September 1916			
RIBEMONT	1st		Brigade marched to MOLLIENS-AU-BOIS billeting area for battalion	7pm
MOLLIENS AUBOIS	2nd		" " BERNAVILLE billeting area for battalion	7pm
BERNAVILLE	3rd		Rested at BERNAVILLE	7pm
"	4th		Brigade march to BONNIÈRES billeting area for battalion	7pm
BONNIÈRES	5th		" " ŒUF billeting area for battalion	7pm
ŒUF	6th		Battalion marched to CROISETTE and billeted	7pm
CROISETTE	7th		Rested at CROISETTE	7pm
"	8th		Brigade marched SIBIVILLE billeting area for battalion	7pm
SIBIVILLE	9th		" " LE SOUICH billeting area for battalion	7pm
LE SOUICH	10th		" " BIENVILLERS-AU-BOIS and POMMIERS billeting area for battalion	7pm
BIENVILLERS AUBOIS and POMMIERS	11th 12th	12.10am	Battalion relieved 8th South Staffords of 51st Brigade 17th Division in the line. Z section (HANNESCAMPS) relief completed on night of 12/13. Took over line	7pm
HANNESCAMPS Z section etc. Z section	13th 14th 15th		From F.11.b.o.6. to E.17.c.1.4. Trenches Z62 to Z75. Three companies in line + one in reserve. Relief complete 9.45 P.M. 1st Cameronians on right, 46th Division on left.	3pm
BIENVILLERS AU BOIS	16th	10.0pm	Relieved by 2nd Royal Welsh Fusiliers as well as BIENVILLERS AU-BOIS two platoons in FONQUE- VILLERS and M. Rel. complete 10.0. P.M.	7pm

10.H (2 wheelers)

Army Form C. 2118.

WAR DIARY
or
INTELLIGENCE SUMMARY.
(Erase heading not required.)

Instructions regarding War Diaries and Intelligence Summaries are contained in F.S. Regs., Part II. and the Staff Manual respectively. Title pages will be prepared in manuscript.

Place	Date	Hour	Summary of Events and Information	Remarks and references to Appendices
	September 1916			
BIENVILLERS AU-BOIS	19th to 21st		Battalion in BIENVILLERS-AU-BOIS with 2 platoons in FONQUEVILLERS REDOUBT. Infantry batties.	7 PM
HANNESCAMP	21st	10.10 PM	Relieved 2nd Royal Welsh Fusiliers in HANNESCAMPS. 2 section left under Lieutenant Rose late. 1st Camerons on right, 1/Leicester 147th Division on left.	7 PM
Position left unknown	22nd to 23rd		As before. Relief complete 10.10 PM	7 PM
BIENVILLERS AU-BOIS	24th	9.55 PM	Relieved by 2nd Royal Welsh Fusiliers and sent to BIENVILLERS-AU-BOIS. Two platoons in FONQUEVILLERS REDOUBT. Relief complete 9.55 PM. Total casualties 10 O.R. to 24th but 2 Officers wounded. 10 R. killed 11. O.R. wounded (Officers 2nd Lt F.E. Cornwell, 2nd Lt P.L. Stocker)	7 PM
do	30th	12 Noon	Relieved by 1/4th West Riding Regiment and marches to HUMBER CAMP. Buttetes Res.	7 PM
HUMBERCAMP	29th			7 PM
do	30th	6.40 AM	Marched to DOULLENS. Brigade went Battalion billets in DOULLENS.	7 PM

B. Barnett Lieut. Col.
Commanding 2nd Royal Fusiliers

Army Form C. 2118.

WAR DIARY
or
INTELLIGENCE SUMMARY.
(Erase heading not required.)

Vol 72

11.H.
(6 sheets)

Place	Date	Hour	Summary of Events and Information	Remarks and references to Appendices
OCTOBER 1916				
JOULLES	8		B Echo - JOULLES. 2nd Lieut J.O. Smyth posted to & joined the Battalion.	
"	9		Transport in field. Lieut A.O. Coggan accidently wounded 9-10-16	
LUCHEUX	11		Move to LUCHEUX as reserve to 12 CATERHAMS. Lt MOYLE rejoins the Battalion	
"	12		Bivvo - LUCHEUX. Lieut A.O. Coggan returns from hospital 12.10.16. 2nd Lieut O Thomas	
"	"		accidently wounded 16.10.16	
NEUVILLETTE	18		Transport left to road for VILLE-SUR-L'ANCRE	
"	19		Battalion left by busses for VILLE SUR L'ANCRE	
"	24		Billets at VILLE-SUR-L'ANCRE. Captain MAXWELL left on attachment to 24th Royal Fusiliers posting	
CHATEAU DE VERT			Marches to the fitted F.21.b. (ALBERT continued sheet). Bivouaces in tents and huts. Heavy	
(ALBERT continued sheet)			relieves on the pm of WEST YORKS regiment	
BERNAFAY WOOD	22		Battalion marches again by the by way to BERNAFAY wood and took over bivouacs from Bart King's	
(continued of F.21.d)			own shot L.O.I.H.. Battle of the transport stage behind was bivouaced at F.24.93 (ALBERT	
F.24.99 (ALBERT			Lt Hugh Holden in command.	
continued sheet)				
SEPT BAY	23	2.30 am	Battalion moved to SERAFBAY (French mile of GINCHY). O'Keith to "Divisional reserve to	
"	"		H. Brigade. 5529 Sgt F.Roberts struck off the strength on appointment to commission posted to 2nd Lieut 6th D.F.	
"	25	4 pm	To-day returns 1st Royal Warwicks and 2nd Royal Dublin Fusiliers left intrate of F.E.	

Army Form C. 2118.

WAR DIARY
or
INTELLIGENCE SUMMARY.
(Erase heading not required.)

Instructions regarding War Diaries and Intelligence Summaries are contained in F. S. Regs., Part II. and the Staff Manual respectively. Title pages will be prepared in manuscript.

Place	Date	Hour	Summary of Events and Information	Remarks and references to Appendices
October 1915 Trench MAP 57.c.5w T5 a&c to T5 a&c.77	25th		Right brigade. Two companies in front line in support in OX trench SHAMROCK trench and FOGGY trench. 2nd RWF on the right. 12th MIDDLESEX on the left.	
	26th	9.0 a.m.	B echelon transport moved A & c.o.o. (ALBERT continues rest). Lt E. R. WILLIS HURST wounded.	
	27th		Lt A. O. COGGIN and 2nd Lt HENLEY killed. Major A. H. T. HICKLEY resumed his duties and took command of A company. 2nd Lt F. ROBERTS killed.	
T9	28th	4.0 a.m.	Relieved by 5th SCOTTISH RIFLES and became battalion in support in HOGS BACK TRENCH	
Attacked Attacked continued about A.2. d 4.0.	30th	2.0 p.m.	Relieved by 16th KRRC and marched to A.2 d 4.0 huts (ALBERT continues rest). Lt HAIR wounded	
	31st		Throughout the period 22nd to 31st very heavy rains fell and the roads were rendered very muddy, and movement was necessarily very slow. Total Casualties during the period 3 Officers killed, 2 Officers wounded shown above, 4 missing. Other Ranks 18 killed 48 wounded including 4 on duty. W. B. Sarnwell Lt. Col. Commanding 20th Royal Fusiliers	

20th (S) Battn Royal Fusiliers.

WAR DIARY or INTELLIGENCE SUMMARY.

Army Form C. 2118.

19/33

12.11
(2 sheets)

Place	Date	Hour	Summary of Events and Information	Remarks and references to Appendices
	NOVEMBER 1916.			
ALBERT combined sheet A2d40. CARNOY	1st		Battalion in huts at CARNOY A2d4.0. echelon B transport at CARNOY A.13.6.9.3.	
"	2d		2nd Lieut MOYLE wounded on visiting trenches.	
LES BOEUFS	3d		Battalion proceeds to Trenches NE of LES BOEUFS relieving 4th West Kent Regt during night of 3/4th Novr. Left Brigade — Two Companies in front line, one in support (THISTLE, WINDY + LEMON STREET TRENCHES) (ALBERT- combined Sheet)	
			One in reserve (COY TRENCH) — Battn H.Q. at T4.a.2.2. (Albert- combined Sheet). —	
			On right 2 R.Welsh Fus, on left 7th East Yorks.	
"	4th		Capt YORSTON wounded — at duty.	
"	5th		Lieut BUTCHARD killed at commencement of advance of Sunken Road from front line (STORMY v. SUMMER TRENCH).	
			to establish a Bombing Post at N.35.c.1.9. (ALBERT combined Sheet)	
"	6th		Lieut BULBECK killed during third and successful attempt at establishing Bombing Post at N.35.c.1.9. (ALBERT- combined Sheet)	
"	7th		On night of 7th/8th Battalion was relieved by 2nd Middlesex Regt	
BRIQUETERIE CAMP A.16.b.3.7.	8th		Battalion arrived at BRIQUETERIE Camp A.16.b.3.7. (ALBERT- combined sheet) near BERNAFAY WOOD, on night of 8th.	
MÉAULTE	9th		Battalion proceeded to MÉAULTE, where it was billeted till midday 11th.	
"	10th		Capt YORSTON evacuated to Hospital — sick.	
"	11th		Battalion left MÉAULTE for Rest Billets, entrained at EDGEHILL STATION for AIRAINES at 4 p.m.	over.

Army Form C. 2118.

WAR DIARY
or
INTELLIGENCE SUMMARY. (2)

(Erase heading not required.)

Instructions regarding War Diaries and Intelligence Summaries are contained in F. S. Regs., Part II. and the Staff Manual respectively. Title pages will be prepared in manuscript.

Place	Date	Hour	Summary of Events and Information	Remarks and references to Appendices
1916. November. ALBERT - Combined Sheet 57d.D.G.				
HERELESSART	12th		Battalion detrained at AIRAINES at 5 am, marched to Rest Billets at HERELESSART where it arrived at 7.30 am.	
"	1/4/30		Battalion at HERELESSART.  2/Lt. CLAUGHTON and 2/Lt. CLARK joined 1st Battalion.	
	23rd		Owing to heavy rains that had fallen roads were found very muddy and movement was very slow - during period 3/8 Nov. Total Casualties during the period 2 Officers killed and 2 Officers wounded including one at duty including Klein abri. Other Ranks 22 Killed 68 wounded including 8 at duty. 14 Missing.	

WBRawnsley
Commanding 2/5th Rev at Dun (ers)

T.J.134. Wt. W708—776. 500000. 4/15. Sir J. C. & S.

SECRET.

Army Form C. 2118.

WS/14

20th (S) Battalion Royal Fusiliers.
WAR DIARY
or
INTELLIGENCE SUMMARY.
(Erase heading not required.)

13.H
(2 sheets)

Place	Date	Hour	Summary of Events and Information	Remarks and references to Appendices
MERELESSART	December 1916 Dec/1		Battalion in Rest-Billets.	Map References throughout are to ALBERT – centre sheet 1/40000
	,, 2		No 4882 Pte PRESCOTT. T. awarded Military Medal.} Recommended for work done during period 3rd – 6th November 1916	
	,, 4		No 536. Sgt MURGATROYD A. awarded D.C.M. }	
	,, 6		Lt Col C.H. BENNETT D.S.O. rejoined the Battalion from England.	
ALBERT entrained ,, 8		4 a.m.	Battalion left MERELESSART at 4 a.m., entrained at AIRAINES Station, detrained at EDGEHILL Station and marched to MORLANCOURT arriving at 2 p.m.	
put up pos at MORLANCOURT			(Transport left on 7th at 7 a.m. & marched with Brigade Transport to ARGOEUVRES – Left there on 8th & arrived at MORLANCOURT at 5 p.m.)	
			Lt Col W.R. GARNETT proceeded on leave to England.	
Camp III L.2.a.9.9.	,, 9	9.30 a.m.	Battalion left MORLANCOURT at 12-noon marched to Camp 112 at L.2.a.9.9.	
Camp III L.2.b.	,, 10/,,		Battalion remained at Camp 112 on 10th Bn moved across to Camp III at L.2.b. remaining there the	
PRIEZ FARM B.14.4.4.	,, 11/14		11th Battalion marched at 8 p.m. to PRIEZ FARM via BRAY – MARICOURT – HARDECOURT – MAUREPAS – COMBLES. 14th Bn	
			Transport left at 9.30 a.m. & proceeded to MAUREPAS RAVINE – B.14 Central.	
	,, 14/,,		Battalion in Support at PRIEZ-FARM.	
Se RANCOURT C.2.d.5.b.9.C.9.5.	,, 15		The Battalion moved into the right sub-sector SE of RANCOURT – officer's S.P. RANCOURT – opposite St PIERRE VAAST WOOD, relieving the 13th Cameronians. The 3rd Royal Welsh Fusiliers were on the left and the 9th H.L.I. on the right. Disposition of Battalion – Front Line – C.2.d.7.5. to C.3.c.9.5. – A Company on left, B Company on right, C Coy in Support & D Coy in Reserve – Bn H.Q. at C.8.B.6.6.	

SECRET.

20(S) Battalion Royal Fusiliers (2)

Army Form C. 2118.

WAR DIARY
or
INTELLIGENCE SUMMARY.
(Erase heading not required.)

Place	Date	Hour	Summary of Events and Information	Remarks and references to Appendices
December 1916	(continued)			
SEQRANCOURT (3d.7.5h.C3.c9.5)	Dec 18 (cont)		During the relief Capt J.H. WYLIE commanding C Coy and 2Lt C. NORREY commanding A Coy were both wounded by shrapnel fire. They had reached the Regina Trench. Lt & t/Capt C.H. BENNETT left the Battalion on appointment to the command of the 33 Div. "B" Battalion (He went sick the same day and moved transports to B. April) on 22 Dec." The front line companies were relieved nightly from Suffolk & Reserve Companies.	
—	— 19/20		1st Col W.B. Garnett returned from leave.	
—	— 20			
Camp 21. L3c3.4.	— 22/3		The Battalion was relieved by 2 A. & S.H. & proceeded to HAMECAMPS HALTE B13.b.5.2. from which place it was conveyed by lorries to Camp 21 at [crossed out] L3C34, where it remained till 26th Dec".	
—	— 26		The Battalion moved to Camp 13 - K22.c.5.8. arriving there at 5pm	
—	— 27		Battalion marched to EDGEHILL Station & entrained for PONT REMY (5 miles SE of ABBEVILLE). From here it marched to YAUCOURT (3½ miles E of ABBEVILLE). (The Transport left Camp 13 at 6am & marched to ARGŒUVRES on 26th "but on 27th marched from ARGŒUVRES to YAUCOURT) Battalion in Rest Billets at YAUCOURT and (BUSSUS.)	
	20/30		During the time the Battalion was in the line - 18th & 22nd Dec - a bad front was succeeded by a thaw which made that had been marched became impassable in places. as a consequence movement was very slow and the relief of the Companies in the front line, carried out nightly, occupied the greater part of each night. — Casualties during December. 2 Officers wounded. Other Ranks. 1 Killed. 14 wounded (including 1 at duty) 2 missing. W.B. Garnett. Lt Col Commdg 20th Royal Fusiliers	

T.2134. Wt. W708—776. 500000. 4/15. Sir J. C. & S.

20th Royal Fusiliers.   1917 JAN – 1917 JUNE

Army Form C. 2118.

WAR DIARY
or
INTELLIGENCE SUMMARY.
(Erase heading not required.)

Vol 15

14.H. (Bahute)

Place	Date	Hour	Summary of Events and Information	Remarks and references to Appendices
January 1917				
YAUCOURT-BUSSUS. (Sheet 14. ABBEVILLE 1/100,000)	1st		Battalion in billets at YAUCOURT-BUSSUS near ABBEVILLE. (Rest Area) Training in area till 19-1-17. London Gazette 1st January: For distinguished service in the Field. (a) To be granted next higher rate of pay under Article 241 of Royal Warrant Quartermaster and Hon Lieut C.L.A. Calch. As Awards the Military Cross Temy. Captain and Adjutant F.G. Modera.	79A
	4.		London Gazette dated 4th January:- For gallant service and devotion to duty mentions in dispatches. Temy. Lt Col W.B. Garnett, 1st Batt. Royal Welsh Fusiliers attached 20th Royal Fusrs. Temy Captain & F.A. Templer Temy 2nd Lieut S.F. Humphreys (killed)	79A
	6th	12 noon	Captain F.A. Templer returned from hospital and reported to the Adjt. & pass to offr. Messages received by GOC 39th division of msgs to Master of A. Hungerton? McHam? & 99078? Pte? Tweed. R. Dem? to ? A. Hungerton? HL?am? & 9802? Pte? Tweed 19 Infantry Brigade. Coy 20 Royal Fusrs. left rest area and kits over M.G.O.C. 99th Brigade. Battalion came under	79A 73? 79A
	18.	6.30 AM	Battalion transport left by road in advance of battalion for Camp 12 near BRAY sur SOMME.	79A
	19.	4.0 AM	Battalion left YAUCOURT and entrained at LONGPRÉ Detrained at EDGEHILL near MERICOURT	79A

T2134. Wt. W708-776. 500,000. 4/15. Sir J.C. & S.

2nd Royal Fusiliers

Army Form C. 2118.

WAR DIARY
or
INTELLIGENCE SUMMARY.
(Erase heading not required.)

Instructions regarding War Diaries and Intelligence Summaries are contained in F.S. Regs., Part II. and the Staff Manual respectively. Title pages will be prepared in manuscript.

Place	Date	Hour	Summary of Events and Information	Remarks and references to Appendices
	January (continued)			
Camp 12 (R32d)	19"	2.0 PM	and marched to Camp 12 near BRAY. (R29d ALBERT coming Road & 4 coys) Arrived there 2.0 PM. Transport having travelled by road arrived about 4.30 PM.	J.M.
[ALBERT cooking Road R.14.4.000.0] Camp. 13. (K.22.c)	20"	2.0 PM	Battalion moved to Camp 13. K.22.C. Major R.H. GOLDTHORP (4th Bn. Duke of Wellington Regiment) reports for instructions.	J.M.
do	21st		At Camp 13. 2nd Lieut E.L.POWELL joined battalion for duty.	J.M.
do	22nd		At Camp 13. 2nd Lieut T.B.WHITER and 2nd Lieut U.P. DAVIS joined the Bn for duty.	J.M.
Camp 18 (G.18.d)	22nd	2.30 PM	Battalion moved via BRAY and SUZANNE to Camp 18 (G.10.d.) arriving there 2.0 PM. 2nd Lieut T.H. HARRISON joined the battalion for duty.	J.M.
Map 62c NW Edition 4. Howitzer Wood (H.3.6.5.1) Reserve Battn. Right Brigade	23rd	4.30 PM	Battalion moved to HOWITZER WOOD (H.3.6.5.1) where they relieved 1/4th SUFFOLKS and became under orders of G.O.C. 19" Brigade as Reserve battalion of RIGHT BRIGADE of the Division. Transport returned to FRISE BEND about 66.a central. O.R. less at VAUX and surplus personnel at Camp 19. (K.22.c) under 2nd Lt T.H. HARRISON.	J.M.
Right Sector (Right subsec) H.16.6.5 & H.7.6.0.0	24"	4.30 PM to 6.30 PM	Battalion moved to relieve the CAMERONIANS in front system. RIGHT subsector of RIGHT Brigade sector. Three Companies in front line and 1 company on island OMMIECOURT for CLERY; 1 coy in reserve FRENCH on its right. 3rd R.W.F. on left. Relief complete 6.30 PM. Line left from H.18.a.6.5 & T.4.b.8.9. Battn HQ.	J.M.
Bn HQ H.12.6.9.2			B.HQ H.12.4.9.2. 32nd Div. Artillery – 162 Brigade – supports battalion for front line and left July.	J.M.
do	25"		Supplies personnel moved to line under 2nd Lt T.H. HARRISON.	
do	26"		Transport and quartermasters stores under Major MODERA concentrated at FRISE BEND G.12.b. central	J.M.

T2134. Wt. W708–776. 500000. 4/15. Sir J.C. & S.

20th Royal Fusiliers

WAR DIARY
or
INTELLIGENCE SUMMARY.
(Erase heading not required.)

Army Form C. 2118.

Place	Date	Hour	Summary of Events and Information	Remarks and references to Appendices
January (continued)				
Mon 61 on B4				
RIGHT SECTOR	29.	1 AM	2" Lieut B H WHITER killed	JM
Right Section H18 b 65 b Z7 6 50 B HQ H18 b 93	28.	6.30 PM	Battalion relieved by CAMERONIANS with the exception of the whole post until relieved over by half company 20: Royal Fusiliers. Relief complete 6.30 am. Disposition after relief: 3 companies BHQ trenches and BHQ also at FRISE BEND G.18.b cental, 1 company at HOWITZER WOOD and ½ company at OMNIECOURT-LES-CLERY	
RIGHT BRIGADE RESERVE				
FRISE BEND G.18.b central HOWITZER WOOD OMNIECOURT	29. 30.		Relief of right brigade. Casualties during Jan. 2 officer killed, 1 officer wounded, 3 O.R killed, 10 O.R died of wounds, 10 O.R wounded, 2nd Duty. 2nd R.HOME attached R.F.C. as observer on probation.	JM JM JM
	31.	6 PM	Remained RIGHT BRIGADE reserve. All coms made orders of G.O.C. 98th Ld Brigade.	7 J17

W.S.James Lt Col
Comdg. 20th Royal Fusiliers.

SECRET.

Army Form C. 2118.

20th Battalion Royal Fusiliers.

WAR DIARY

INTELLIGENCE SUMMARY.

(Erase heading not required.)

15.H.
(3 sheets)

Vol 16

Instructions regarding War Diaries and Intelligence Summaries are contained in F. S. Regs., Part II. and the Staff Manual respectively. Title pages will be prepared in manuscript.

Place	Date	Hour	Summary of Events and Information	Remarks and references to Appendices
Fetenburg Map 62cNW 1/20000 Edition 4.	1st		Battalion disposed as follows:- 2 Companies, H.Q + "B" Echelon at FRISE BEND (G.18.b central); 1½ Companies at HOWITZER WOOD (H.3.b.5.2); ½ Company at OMIECOURT Island: - acting as Battalion in Reserve to Right Brigade. (98th Infantry Brigade).	Yes
FRISE BEND 2nd - 3rd (G.18.b central)	2nd 3rd		-as above-	Yes Yes
Camp 19 (G.16.a.5.6)	4th	3.0pm	Whole Battalion moved to Camp 19 (G.16.a.8.8) on relief by 5th Scottish Rifles, & came then under the orders of G.O.C. 19th Infantry Brigade as a Battalion of Brigade in divisional reserve.	Yes
"	5th-7th		Training in Camp 19.	Yes
Left Brigade Sector Right subsection (C.26.b.17 to I.2.a.4.6.)	8th	4.45pm to 11.15pm	Battalion relieved 1st Queens in right subsection of left Brigade Sector. Three Companies + one platoon in front & support lines, 3 platoons in Support. Line held from Sap 5 (exclusive) to Sap 2, inclusive. B.H.R. at C.25.c.3.5.— On night 2 A + S.H. of 98th Brigade, in left of 2nd R.W.Fus., Batteries supporting:- Field Guns A,B + C 156 and Howitzer D 156. Relief completed 11.15 p.m. "B" Echelon under 2nd Lt W.B. Garnett remained at FRISE BEND (G.6.c. central). Major F.S. Nathan M.C.	Yes
"	9th-10th		proceeded up the line with the Battalion.— Battalion disposed as adm— 2/Lt E.F. Chapman + 2/Cpl HOWIES complimented by Brigadier General on Patrol work carried out during the night of 9th/10th — 2/Lt T. Robinson accidentally wounded when firing a rifle grenade.	Yes Yes
"	11th			Yes
Support Battalion of Left Brigade ROAD WOOD (C.25.A + C.)	12th	10.20pm	On relief by 1st Cameronians the Battalion became Support Battalion to the Brigade in the line. Three Companies in Trenches in ROAD WOOD (C 25 A + C) One Company in MAIN + MERLIN Trenches (C 25 c + d). B.H.R at C.25.b.47.—	Yes
"	13/15		Battalion in Brigade Support.	Yes
LeftBrigade Right subsection	16th	10.35pm	Battalion relieved 1st Cameronians in Right subsection of left Brigade. Two Companies in front line - each night One Company in Support. One Company remained as part of Support Battalion (5th Sco Rif)	Yes (2)

2353 Wt. W2544/1454 700,000 5/15 D.D.& L. A.D.S.S./Forms/C. 2118.

20th Battn Royal Fusiliers.
WAR DIARY (continued).
(2).
INTELLIGENCE SUMMARY.

Army Form C. 2118.

Place	Date	Hour	Summary of Events and Information	Remarks and references to Appendices
Map 62 C NW Bouzincourt Edition 4. Left (Brigade) Sector Right Sub-section	16th (cont)	10.35pm	relieved the Company of 1st Cameronians in left of front line. BHQ at C.2.S.C.3.5. Relief complete 10.35pm. On the night the 16th KRR, 100th Brigade, & on left 2nd R. Irish Fus. 19th Brigade. Supporting Artillery became on during period 8/11. The disposition of Companies was arranged in preparation for an attack by 2nd R.I.Fus & 20th R.Fus. This attack was known halted & subsequently cancelled.	Yes M.
	17/19		Battalion in the line. On the 17th the hard frost that had held since the beginning of the month gave place to a thaw. The ground became very soft & movement in consequence very slow & difficult.	Yes M.
	21st 19th	2.6am	Lieut Col: W.R. Garnett assumed temporary command of 2nd R.W.Fus Major F.R. Moore M.C. " " " 20th R.Fus.	Yes M.
Howitzer Wood (H.3.b.)	21st	2.5am	Battalion relieved by 5th Scottish Rifles from ROAD WOOD (Support Battalion). The relief was considerably delayed owing to the heavy state of the ground. Relief complete 2.5am. On relief the Battalion marched to HOWITZER WOOD (H.3.b.) where it remained as Reserve Battalion to the Brigade till 23rd 8.10pm.	Yes M.
Suzanne (G.8.C.)	23rd	8.10pm	On relief of 79th Brigade by 100th Brigade, the 2nd A. & S.H. became reserve battalion to 100th Brigade & the relief of 20th R.Fus Battalion, including the Bechlin, moved to SUZANNE (G.8.C.) where it remained in Camp under canvas until the end of the month. The 19th Brigade was in Divisional Reserve. Lt Col D.W. Figg. D.S.O. was attached to the command of the 20th Battn R.Fus. Casualties during the month – Officers – One accidentally wounded. Other Ranks – 18 wounded, 2 missing, 3 died of wounds.	Yes M.

mmf Lt Col.
Comdg 20th R.Fus. —

SECRET.

Army Form C. 2118.

Vol 17

20th (S) Battn Royal Fusiliers.

WAR DIARY
or
INTELLIGENCE SUMMARY.
(Erase heading not required.)

Instructions regarding War Diaries and Intelligence Summaries are contained in F. S. Regs., Part II. and the Staff Manual respectively. Title pages will be prepared in manuscript.

Place	Date	Hour	Summary of Events and Information	Remarks and references to Appendices
March 1917.				
Map 62cNW 1/20,000 SUZANNE	1/2		Battalion in Camp under Canvas.	Yes
FRISE BEND	3		A. Battalion, including "B" Echelon, marched to FRISE BEND and disposed as follows. Reserve Battalion to 100th Infy Brigade. 2½ Companies at FRISE BEND, 1 Coy at HOWITZER WOOD and ½ Coy at OMMIECOURT (H.12.c+d). BHQ at G.18.a.1.2.	Yes
CLERY SECTOR BHQ at H.2.69.3	4		A. Battalion moved into the Right (CLERY) Subsection of Right Brigade Front. Brigadier 3 Companies in front line, one in Support - BHQ at H.12.B.83. Supporting Artillery 156th +162nd Brigade +55" Howrs. Lt Col D.W. FIGG D.S.O., temporarily commanding the Battalion, was sniped at Hotpoint I.7.c.5.44. with front line at 12.30pm. He died at 5.30pm at Battn Aid Post. Capt D.W. Hollingsworth assumed temporary command of the Battalion.	Yes
	5			Yes
	6/7		Battalion in the line.	Yes
A. SECTOR K CLERY SECTOR	8	9.5pm	Battalion relieved by 17th Welch Regt of 119th Brigade, 40th Divn - relief completed at 9.5pm.	Yes
BHQ at H.6.c.t.6.			On relief Battalion became Brigade Support to 119th Brigade & were disposed as follows:- One Coy at H.Q. of 17th Sherp Battn (I.1.B.7.3). ½ Coy at CLERY Chateau. ½ Coy at OMMIECOURT (H.12.c+d) detachment + 2 Companies in WURZEL+MAUD Avenue Trenches (just north of CLERY) - BHQ at PEMBERTON (H.6.a.7.6)	Yes
	9	8.50pm	On relief in Support by 19th R.Fus of 119th Brigade, the Battn marched to SUZANNE where it was accomodated under canvas for the night, moving on next day to Camp 12 (K.33.B.5.5).	Yes 16.H. (2 phros) (2)

20th Batt" Royal Fusiliers

Army Form C. 2118.

SECRET.

WAR DIARY
or
INTELLIGENCE SUMMARY.

(2)

(Erase heading not required.)

Instructions regarding War Diaries and Intelligence Summaries are contained in F. S. Regs., Part II. and the Staff Manual respectively. Title pages will be prepared in manuscript.

Place	Date	Hour	Summary of Events and Information	Remarks and references to Appendices
	March 1917			
Pt 40f 62c NW 1/40,000 10/31			Battalion in training at Camp 12.	
Camp 12 K.33.B.5.5.	14		Special training for open warfare. Major L.F. Leader, The King's (Liverpool Reg.) appointed temporary command of Battalion.	
	19		2nd Lt. 9 J.C. Badcock, Bombing Officer, accidentally killed whilst superintending bombing practice. Casualties during the month.	
			Officers One died of wounds received in action (Lt. Col. Figg). One died of wounds received accidentally (2/Lt Badcock).	
			Other Ranks 2 Killed	
			11 Wounded (one at duty)	
			2 Wounded - accidentally	
			2 Missing - believed prisoners of war	

L.F. Leader Lt.Col.
Comdg 20th Batt" Royal Fusiliers

31.3.17.

2nd Bn Royal Fusiliers

19/33

SECRET

Army Form C. 2118.

17.H.
(4 sheets)

WAR DIARY
or
INTELLIGENCE SUMMARY.
(Erase heading not required.)

Instructions regarding War Diaries and Intelligence Summaries are contained in F. S. Regs., Part II. and the Staff Manual respectively. Title pages will be prepared in manuscript.

Place	Date	Hour	Summary of Events and Information	Remarks and references to Appendices
April 1917 MAP AMIENS 1/100,000				
Bufire Humbercamp	1		Battalion in training at Coy & Bn Special Training for open Warfare.	CRC
	2		Battalion moved at 10.15am to Billets at CORBIE marching via the	CRC
CORBIE	3		BRAY. CORBIE road. 2/Lt. R.O. GREENWOOD joined the Battalion. The Battalion moved via QUERRIEU – ALLONVILLE – COISY – & Billets at BERTANGLES.	CRC CRC
BERTANGLES	4		at 11.30am via VILLERS-BOCAGE–TALMAS–LA VICOGNE to	CRC
MOVING to BEAUVAL	5		Billets at BEAUVAL. Battalion moved via DOULLENS & BROUCHES to LUCHEUX. H Companies were in	CRC CRC
LUCHEUX	6		Huts – H.Q. & Stab + B.H.Q. in Billets. Battalion rested for the day.	CRC CRC
	7		moved via WOMECOURT – GAUDIEMPRE to HUMBERCAMP. A+B Coys in Huts & Dets.H.Q. & other Coys in Huts at BAILLEUVAL.	CRC
HUMBERCAMP	8		C+D Coys in billets at BAILLEULMONT, also B.H.Q.	CRC
			La CAUCHIE to BAILLEUMONT – BAILLEUVAL. A+B Coys Billets at BAILLEUVAL.	CRC
BAILLEULMONT BAILLEULMONT	9/10		Battalion disposed as above. Training for open Warfare carried on.	CRC
	11		Battalion moved at 10 minutes notice at 4pm via BASSEUX – BELLACOURT – BRETENCOURT – BLAIREVILLE – FICHEUX to Bivouacs at BOISLEUX-au-MONT.	CRC

T2134. Wt. W708–776. 500000. 4/15. Sir J. C. & S.

Army Form C. 2118.

SECRET

WAR DIARY
or
INTELLIGENCE SUMMARY (2)

(Erase heading not required.)

Instructions regarding War Diaries and Intelligence Summaries are contained in F. S. Regs., Part II. and the Staff Manual respectively. Title pages will be prepared in manuscript.

Place	Date	Hour	Summary of Events and Information	Remarks and references to Appendices
BOISLEUX au MONT	April 12	3 pm	Moved across country from BOISLEUX au MONT to N 27 a 7.7. and took over from 18th Manchester Regt. in the front line. Relieved 89th Infy. Bde. 62nd Infy. Bde. on our right. 56th Div on our left. The trenches had been taken this day from the enemy. Trenches not badly damaged but Gluant dugouts badly smashed.	CRC
In the line	13	7 am	Moved from above position and occupied a line from N 35.c.2.7. to T 16.f.8.0. Left Bttn Support to 19th Infy. Bde. 2/Lt. A.S. MURGATROYD wounded. Killed 5 men wounded 21 O.R.	CRC
	"	11 am	Withdrew and occupied HINDENBURG SUPPORT line from N 35.c.2.7. to N 28.d.4.0. BHQ N 28d 4.0	CRC
	14	3.30 am	Moved to HINDENBURG front line & occupied line from N 35.a.8.1. to T.16.f.8.a. R.H. Q T 32.32 The Battalion was in Bttn.Support.	CRC
	15	7 am	2 Companies moved to N 35.t. + H.Q. + 2 Coys to HINDENBURG SUPPORT line N 36.	CRC
	16	1.30 am	H.Q. + 2 Companies to N 35.f. to reinforce 2 Companies already there. Night march successfully carried out and arrived at place of assembly at 2.45 am. Attacked enemy position in N 36 d. with Battalion A + D Coys in front line. B Coy in second + C Coy in third. A + D + B Companies formed up + proceeded about 100 yds when heavy machine gun fire was opened from front + flanks. Progress than was slight and the attack was inclining too much to the right. The advance was stopped + "C" Coy entered the Trenches the attack would have been successful but M.G. fire	CRC

Army Form C. 2118.

SECRET (4)

WAR DIARY
or
INTELLIGENCE SUMMARY.
(Erase heading not required.)

Instructions regarding War Diaries and Intelligence Summaries are contained in F. S. Regs., Part II. and the Staff Manual respectively. Title pages will be prepared in manuscript.

Place	Date	Hour	Summary of Events and Information	Remarks and references to Appendices
	April 1917			
BOYELLES.	22		In bivouac at BOYELLES.	CBC
	23		General attack by 1st & 3rd Armies. The Battalion was in Divisional reserve and under orders to move at 10 minutes notice.	CBC
		10pm	Battalion moved into shelters in sunken road running from T.3.a.24 to T.3.c.7.9. BHQ at T.3.a.7.9.	CBC
Ed. Hindenburg	24	9.30am	Moved into front line facing FONTAINE-LES-CROISILLES. A Coy on right + D Coy on left on a line running from the HINDENBURG SUPPORT Trench at T.6.a.5.7 to Sunken road at N.36.d.9.9. The enemy had just retired and the advanced line was held by a series of 10 strong posts. Patrols were pushed out as far as the river SENSEE. B + C Coys were in support.	CBC
	25	11pm	Battalion relieved by 10 K.O.Y.L.I. and moved to Bivouacs at BOIRY-BECQUERELLE.	CBC
BOIRY BECQUERELLE	26	5pm	Moved to BOYELLES and took over Posts of 18th MIDDLESEX (Pioneers)	CBC
BOYELLES.	27	11.30am	Battalion moved via BOISLEUX au MONT - FICHEUX - BRETENCOURT - BELLACOURT - BASSEUX to BAILLEULVAL.	CBC
BAILLEULVAL	28/30		Battalion billeted at BAILLEULVAL. Training for open warfare.	CBC
			Total Casualties for the month. 71 killed; 111 wounded; 18 missing; 3 wounded and at duty.	CBC

T.A. Deacon Lt Col
Comdg 20th (S) Bn Royal Fusiliers

Army Form C. 2118.

WAR DIARY
or
INTELLIGENCE SUMMARY.
(Erase heading not required.)

SECRET

Instructions regarding War Diaries and Intelligence Summaries are contained in F. S. Regs., Part II. and the Staff Manual respectively. Title pages will be prepared in manuscript.

(3)

Place	Date	Hour	Summary of Events and Information	Remarks and references to Appendices
April 1917				
In the line	16	1.30am	was too late to retrieve & the attack failed.	
			2/Lts UP DAVIS, K.S.C. RO, R.Q. SCOTT & E. POWELL killed. Lt & Adjt T. MILLARD severely wounded. 2nd Lt LF LEADER & 2/Lt AC GRAHAM slightly wounded but remained at duty.	CBC
		7.30pm	HQ + 2 Companies withdrawn to HINDENBURG SUPPORT line thus 2 Companies then marched to N.26.C.O.8. arriving at 5am 17th	
	17.	4pm	The 2 Companies covering the left flank at N.35.b. relieved by 2 Companies 1st Manchester Regt. then 2 Coys BHQ then moved to N.26.C.O.8. near NEUVILLE VITASSE arriving 5am 18th	CBC
NEUVILLE VITASSE	18.		BHQ in dugout, Battalion in shelters near NEUVILLE VITASSE BHQ N.26.C.O.8. Coys in Divisional Reserve.	CBC
	19.		As above. Weather wet + cold.	CBC
	20		Battalion moved into the line + relieved 4th Suffolks. C Coy in HINDENBURG front line from T.5.b.4.3. to T.5.b.1.7.3 + holding a block at T.5.b.7.3. D Coy in HINDENBURG support line from T.5.b.5.7. to T.5.b.8.8. holding a block at T.5.b.8.8. B Coy holding a trench from T.5.b.5.7. to T.5.b.5.9. A Coy in HINDENBURG support line. BHQ at T.5.A.4.7.	CBC
In the line	21.		Dispositions as above. At 6pm Battalion was relieved by the 4th Suffolks + moved to bivouacs at BOYELLES. BHQ at S.18.b.4.5.2/Lt @ABERDEIN wounded on his way down.	CBC

SECRET.

WAR DIARY 20th (S.) Bn. Royal Fusiliers Army Form C. 2118.

or

INTELLIGENCE SUMMARY.

(Erase heading not required.)

Vol 19

18 H
(5 sheets)

Place	Date	Hour	Summary of Events and Information	Remarks and references to Appendices
BAILLEUVAL	1.5.17		The battalion was billeted in BAILLEUVAL, the training of open warfare being continued and special classes held for Scouts, Signallers, N.C.O's map reading &c.	01H
	2 "	2.20pm	From BAILLEUVAL the battalion marched via BERLES-au-BOIS - BIENVILLERS - MONCHY-au-BOIS to bivouac at ADINFER.	02H
ADINFER	3 "		Open Warfare training continued and special classes under officers. A General attack by the 3rd, 1st and 5th Armies, the 33rd Division being in CORPS Reserve.	03H
ADINFER	4/5.		Companies were trained in Trench attack and exercised in Bombing communication Trenches. Five officers and five N.C.O's per Company were taken in night marching by compass.	45H
ADINFER	6/7		Training continued. The battalion being moved in artillery formations and exercised in deployment.	67H
ADINFER	8.		Divisional sports were held on ground 2 miles NE of DOUCHY 45s. A.7 & 7.7.	8H

SECRET.

WAR DIARY 20TH (S) BN ROYAL FUSILIERS. Army Form C. 2118.

N°. 2 INTELLIGENCE SUMMARY.

Place	Date	Hour	Summary of Events and Information	Remarks and references to Appendices
	MAY.			
ADINFER	9th		The battalion training continued, attention was paid to MAP READING for N.C.O.s	15th
ADINFER	11		Training as above. regimental sports were held on the evening of the 10th	16th
ADINFER	12	6-0 AM	C1- 6-0 AM the battalion left ADINFER and moved across country to bivouac at MOYENVILLE. The 19th Brigade was in reserve.	17th
MOYENVILLE	13/14		Training continued as at ADINFER	18th
MOYENVILLE	15	6.30PM	At 6.30 PM the battalion moved into the line relieving the 9th H.L.I. The forward position was a line of OUTPOSTS. These numbered from the RIGHT 1 to 6. D Coy held Posts 1, 2 + 3 and C Coy 4, 5 + 6. B Coy in support and A in reserve B.H.Q. at T.14.a.4.1.	TRENCH MAP Sheet 51/13 S.W. Ed 4A.
LINE	16		Patrolling in tense about this time owing to the suspected retirement of the enemy	19th
LINE	17/18		On the night of 17/18th an inter company relief	20th

SECRET

WAR DIARY 20TH S. BN. ROYAL FUSILIERS

No 3

INTELLIGENCE SUMMARY.

Army Form C. 2118.

Instructions regarding War Diaries and Intelligence Summaries are contained in F. S. Regs., Part II. and the Staff Manual respectively. Title pages will be prepared in manuscript.

(Erase heading not required.)

Place	Date	Hour	Summary of Events and Information	Remarks and references to Appendices
	MAY			
LINE	17/18		ditto. took place, dispositions after relief as follows: — A Coy from 1, 2 & 3 inch B Coy on the left holding Posts 4, 5, 6. C Coy in support and D in rear.	
LINE	19		As above. At 3.0 am 50 or under 2/Lt MORISON, J reported to 5th S.R. for carrying.	WD
LINE	20		The outpost line was evacuated in the afternoon of the 20th. Companies moved independantly to the QUARRY in U.13.c which was the point of assembly for the battalion. At 4.30 pm the battalion advanced in four waves. A Coy on the LEFT and B Coy on the RIGHT leading with C & D Coys in support respectively. The Cameronians were on the right. Zero was at 4.30 PM and the objective the HBG Tunnel line from U.4.a.6.4 to the FONTAINE-CROISILLES ROAD. The battalion was held up 100 yds from the objective by machine gun fire, and then occupied a trench 180 yds long, the	ISR

T.J.134. Wt. W708 —776. 500000. 4/15. Sir J. C. & S.

SECRET

No 4

WAR DIARY 20TH S. Br ROYAL FUSILIERS.
or
INTELLIGENCE SUMMARY.

Place	Date	Hour	Summary of Events and Information	Remarks and references to Appendices
	MAY			
	20		remainder holding a corrected line of shell holes on the RIGHT of this trench. The following officers were wounded Capt DS HODGSON-JONES. Act Capt E.F CHARNLAN, 2/LT A.C. GRAHAM, 2/Lt C H BRYANT 2/Lt S.R. DAVIS, 2/Lt A GARRITY and 2/Lt J MORISON wounded during the time his party was attached to 5th Scottish Rifles.	15th
	21.		The battalion held the new position the following officers and W.O. were mentioned in Despatches under this date. Major F.S MODERA, Capt. D.W HOLLINGSWORTH Capt D S HODGSON-JONES and R.S.M. RAVEN.. The Military Cross is awarded to the officer 2/Lt H. CLARK.	15th
	22		At midnight the battalion was relieved by the 16TH K.R.R.C and proceeded to bivouac in the sunken road in T22 a and T22 c arriving here at 3.0 A.M in the 22ND	15th
	23/25		The battalion in bivouac in sunken road T22 a + c the time being devoted to cleaning clothing and equipment.	10th

SECRET.

WAR DIARY 20TH S. BN ROYAL FUSILIERS. Army Form C. 2118.

No. 5

or

INTELLIGENCE SUMMARY.

(Erase heading not required.)

Instructions regarding War Diaries and Intelligence Summaries are contained in F. S. Regs., Part II. and the Staff Manual respectively. Title pages will be prepared in manuscript.

Place	Date	Hour	Summary of Events and Information	Remarks and references to Appendices
	MAY			
T.22 a + c	26/27		At 9.0 p.m. one company of 3 officers and 85 O.R. was attached to 9th H.L.I. for the purpose of holding the line during a further attack by the 19th & 98th Infantry Brigades. It took place on the 29th.	19th
"	28/29		At 1.0 AM on the 29th the Company attached to the 9th H.L.I. rejoined the battalion. Capt J.W. Hollingsworth is awarded CROIX de CHEVALIER LEGION D'HONNEUR.	19th
T.22 a + c	30.		The unit was relieved in the sector trench by 13TH NORTHUMBERLAND FUS. - 21st DIVISION. The battalion moved at 3-0 pm to MOYENNVILLE.	13th
MOYENNVILLE	31.		Leaving MOYENNVILLE at 3.5 pm we proceeded across country via ADINFER, RANSART. Then by road to billets in BEUGNÂTRE. Total Casualties for month of officers wounded 3, O.R. killed 16, wounded 43, missing 29.	W.P.H.

J.W. Hollingsworth
Capt.
Comm'g. 20th Royal Fusiliers

20th (S) Bn Royal Fusiliers

Army Form C. 2118.

WAR DIARY
or
INTELLIGENCE SUMMARY.
(Erase heading not required.)

Vol 20

SECRET

(2)

Place	Date	Hour	Summary of Events and Information	Remarks and references to Appendices
June 1917. Bellacourt	1/3		Time was devoted to organisation of Companies and inspections	CRC
"	4.		Training commenced, starting each day at 6.15 am and finishing at 4 pm	CRC
"	5.	3pm	Inspection of Battalion in fighting order by the Corps Commander.	CRC
"	6/10		Training as per the A & Rifle Range Practice included in Programme of Work.	CRC
"	11/16		Class advanced Training commenced. 8hr Sleeve Orders + Battn. Field Exercises.	CRC
"	17.	10.30am	Bn Church Parade and Medal presentation by III Corps Commander at BASSEUX. Prospects of MnM Ribbons were :— Capt D.N. Hollingworth 20th R. Fusiliers — Chevalier et Legion d'honneur	
			4/17164 C.S.M. Burn. M.H. — Distinguished Conduct Medal.	
			2/Lt H. Clark — Military Cross.	
			PS 5428 Sgt V.A. Page — Military Medal.	
Rd Nfe PS/13 SW	18.	6am	The Battalion moved via RANSART & ADINFER to Camp "A" MOYENNEVILLE area, arriving at 9am. Commanding Officer + Co Commanders left BELLACOURT by bus at 7.30 am to proceed to reconnoitre front line.	CRC
Camp "A" MOYENNEVILLE AS A,2,H.	19.	7pm	The Battalion left Camp "A" Companies at 300x interval, and moved via St LEGER — CROISILLES to P. The two Bn frontages extended from CURRENT LANE up d.3.6 along HUNTER TRENCH to LUMP LANE U.7.d.18 thence along LUMP LANE to TUNNEL LINE at U.7.b.4.4. Disposition of Companies on front	CRC

19.H. (8 sheets)

2/(S) Bn. Royal Fusiliers.

Army Form C. 2118.

WAR DIARY
or
INTELLIGENCE SUMMARY.

SECRET

(Erase heading not required.)

Instructions regarding War Diaries and Intelligence Summaries are contained in F. S. Regs., Part II. and the Staff Manual respectively. Title pages will be prepared in manuscript.

(1)

Place	Date	Hour	Summary of Events and Information	Remarks and references to Appendices
June 1917 R.R.Hqts SIRSK				
In the Line	19		A Coy on right, C Coy then left, holding HUMBER TRENCH. C Coy holding LUMP LANE. D Coy in support in BIRD-HIND TRENCHES holding night posts at U.7.d.4.2. and U.7.d.1.9. B.H.Q. in PLUM LANE at U.7.d.2.3. Aid Post L QUARRY U.I.A.7.	CRC
In the Line	20/23		Defensive as above. Minimum number of men only left in HUMBER TRENCH & LUMP LANE daily between the hours of 11 am and 12 noon & 7 pm & 8 pm owing to heavy field artillery fire on BTUNNEL TRENCH. All men withdrew to BIRD TRENCH.	CRC
	24	midnight	C Coy withdrew from LUMP LANE – 1 Coy of 12th Londoners occupied – attacked TUNNEL TRENCH from 4 attack in failure owing to heavy punitive gun-fire C Coy reoccupied LUMP LANE	CRC
		morning of 25th	The Germans withdrew. Battalion relieved on time by 1st Queens & 2nd Worcestershire Regt. Reliefs complete by 11:30 am 25/6/17. Battalion moved back to Tent at CAMP "C" MOYENNEVILLE where Batt'n was 2/4th COLBOURNE, G.	
CAMP "C" MOYENNEVILLE (B32d&B32b)	26/27 28.		arrived at night, had by hard roads. To WAYTE, M.T. lightly assembled 27/6/17 but exp. attack on 5th Tanks. Police CRC Tanning carried on, but not intense.	CRC
B.Hqts LENS A.	29.	7 pm	The Battalion moved across country to ADINFER, thence by road to MONCHY-au-BOIS. Transport moved by road via MOYENNEVILLE – AYETTE – DOUCHY-les-AYETTE – ADINFER	

20th Bn. Royal Fusiliers

WAR DIARY
or
INTELLIGENCE SUMMARY.

Army Form C. 2118.

(3.)

SECRET

Place	Date	Hour	Summary of Events and Information	Remarks and references to Appendices
BEING in TRENCHES	June 1917 29.		Arrived at trenches at MONCHY at 10 pm. BHQ 400 x S of the M in MONCHY.	C.B.2.
MONCHY-on-BOIS	30.		Training during the forenoon. Entrenching etc.	C.B.C.
			Casualties for the month. 3 Officers wounded. 2/Lt JONES 21/6/17; 2/Lt COSBOURNE, O. 23/6/17. and 2/Lt WHYTE M.T. 20/6/17 (remained at duty) 3 O.R. killed. 14 wounded. 3 wounded & remained at duty	C.B.C.

L.J. Tegner Lt Col.
(Cmdg. 20th (S) Bn. Royal Fusiliers
30.6.17

1917 July – 1917 Dec

20 H.
(2 sheets)

WAR DIARY 20th (S) B. Royal Fusiliers

Army Form C. 2118.

INTELLIGENCE SUMMARY. SECRET.

(Erase heading not required.)

July 1917

Place	Date	Hour	Summary of Events and Information	Remarks and references to Appendices
MONCHY au BOIS	JULY 1		At MONCHY au BOIS the battalion was in bivouacs	15TH
	2		The battalion left MONCHY au BOIS at 8.30 AM and marched via BIENVILLERS – SOUASTRE – BAYENCOURT – ACHEUX – LEALVILLERS to ARQUÈVES	15TH
ARQUÈVES	3		The march was resumed at 8.15 AM. – THIÉVRES to NAOURS via B.H.Q. was in the chateau. Maj. Y.S. MODERA. M.C. rejoined – TALMAS to NAOURS via the 3rd Via RAINCHEVAL – PUCHEVILLERS	15TH
NAOURS	4	5.15 AM	Leaving at 5.15 AM the battalion marched via WARGNIES – HAVERNAS – VIGNACOURT to YZEUX	15TH
YZEUX	5		From YZEUX the battalion marched to billets at AIRAINES	15TH
AIRAINES	6		The time devoted to cleaning of stores and equipment –	15TH
	7		A draft of 81 O.R. arrived	15TH
	8			
	9		The battalion commenced training in open warfare and special	15TH
	10		classes for Lewis gunners, scouts etc. Rec.el training 2.30 to 4.30 pm	
	11		A draft of 94 O.R. arrived. Training as above.	15TH
	12		Lieut G.C. Zeigler joined and took over command of C Coy.	15TH
	13		Training continued at 7.15 2/Lt G. Colbourne rejoined from hospital	15TH
	16		A draft of 58 O.R. arrived	16TH

(2.)

WAR DIARY 20th (S) Bn Royal Fusiliers. Army Form C. 2118.
or
INTELLIGENCE SUMMARY. SECRET

(Erase heading not required.)

JULY 1917

Hour, Date, Place		Summary of Events and Information	Remarks and references to Appendices
July 1917 ARRAINES	16/18	Training continued as before. A draft of 54 o.r. arrived on the 18th.	WH
"	18/22	As above. On the 22nd Capt. G.H. Jones Millicent rejoined the battalion. Battalion sports were held on the 19th.	WH
"	23rd 24th	On the 24th a draft arrived of 31 o.r.	WH
"	24/29	Training continued as before. The following officers joined the battalion on the 29th :- 2/Lt. Chapman H.D. 1/Butler C.J. Coop. G.S. Kirk H. Lewis W. 1 Barker R.A. Orders received to entrain for DUNKERQUE. All trenches dug for training purposes filled in. A killing party consisting of 2/Lt. MURGATROYD and 4 other ranks left for LONG PRÉ.	WH
"	30th	BRAY-DUNES. D. Coy. left AIRAINES at 4 am and marched to PONT-REMY. Entrained at 8.55am. Detained at DUNKERQUE and moved in barges up canal to Fort at BRAY-DUNES. Battalion less D. Coy. left AIRAINES at 7am. Marched via SOREL & DUNCQ to PONT-REMY. Entraining at 11 am. Arrived DUNKERQUE at 9pm - embarked on barges, slept in barges during night and moved up canal at 6am to BRAY-DUNES. Casualties 4.O.R. wounded (accidentally).	
	31st		

T. Gentry Lt Col
Comdg 20th (S) Bn Royal Fusiliers.

1/8/17.

20th (S) Bn. Royal Fusiliers

19/33

Army Form C. 2118.

WAR DIARY
or
INTELLIGENCE SUMMARY.   SECRET

(Erase heading not required.)

Vol 22

21.H.
(4 sheets)

Place	Date	Hour	Summary of Events and Information	Remarks and references to Appendices
Ref. Map DUNKERQUE I.A.	August 1917			
DUNKERQUE	1.	6.30am	The Battalion less transport, moved in barges along the CANAL de DUNKERQUE, as far as the PONT de GHYVELDE. Disembarked there and marched to BRAY DUNES. H.Q. Details and "B" Coy in huts. "A.C. & D" Coys in tents on dunes. B.H.Q. opposite BRAY DUNES Parish Church. Battalion Transport left DUNKERQUE 11pm July 30th and moving by road reached BRAY DUNES at 4am 1/8/17.	C.R.C.
BRAY DUNES	2.		Companies + H.Q. as distributed as above. Battalion took over the BRAY DUNES coast defences. These defences consisted of several posts between the FRONTIER & BRAY-PLAGE, which the Battalion had to man in the event of a hostile attack from the sea. Training carried on, in the dunes and on the beach.	C.R.C.
"	3/14.			C.R.C.
"	15.	4.10am	The Battalion left BRAY DUNES at 4.10am + marched via LA PANNE and COXYDE to KUHN CAMP at (QUEENSLAND CAMP) 500x S.W. of OOST DUNKERQUE. Transport + Q.M. Stores billets at JENNIOT at (CANADA) Camp ½ mile West of COXYDE. Battalion in huts	
		9am	MINIMUM RESERVE (25 other Ranks per Coy + 5 officers) left BRAY DUNES at 9am and marched to Divisional Depot Bn at GHYVELDE	C.R.C.
OOST DUNKERQUE	16.	7.30pm	The Battalion left camp 7.30 pm and marching via WULPEN and NIEUPORT took	

20th (S) Bn. Royal Fusiliers

WAR DIARY
or
INTELLIGENCE SUMMARY.

Army Form C. 2118.

SECRET

(2)

Place	Date	Hour	Summary of Events and Information	Remarks and references to Appendices
	August 1917			
Ref. Map LOMBARTZYDE 20,000. TRENCH Map				
COST DUNKERQUE	16		over trenches in the LOMBARTZYDE Sector from the 1/4 West Riding Regiment. Only 100 men per Coy were taken up the line. Battalion on a one platoon frontage. Dispositions as follows: "C" Coy holding of front line with 1st Platoon in NOSE TRENCH; 1st Platoon in NOSE SUPPORT; 2 Platoons + Coy HQrs in NASAL TRENCH; "A" Coy in Support with 2 Platoons + CHQ in NASAL SUPPORT; and 2 Platoons in NASAL WALK: "D" Coy in reserve with 2 Platoons + CHQrs in NASAL LANE; — 2 Platoons attached to 57 7 Coy RE (these 2 platoons moved into dugouts in NIEUPORT on the 18th): "B" Coy in tunnel in the REDAN (The Coy carried rations for front line Coy.) Shelled with gas a little while of the night 16/17th	
In the line	17th		Dispositions as above. Rations and water to ARCH BRIDGE by TRANSPORT, Transport and Q.M. Stores moved to COXYDE BAINS. MAJOR F.S. MODERA. MC Commdg. Battn. in the line 4th GL H.F. LEADER with 1st line Transport	CRE
"	18		ditto	CRE
"	19...		Later Coy relief: "A" Coy relieved "C" Coy + "C" Coy took over trenches previously occupied by "A" Coy	CRE
	20/21		ditto	CRE
	21/22		Battalion was relieved in the line by 1st Seo. Rif. Battalion after relief moved into	

20th (S) Bn Royal Fusiliers

Army Form C. 2118.

WAR DIARY
or
INTELLIGENCE SUMMARY. SECRET

(Erase heading not required.)

(3)

Place	Date	Hour	Summary of Events and Information	Remarks and references to Appendices
August 1917				
In the Line	21/22		Support in the REDAN. Dispositions as follows: — A.B & C Coys & D Coy less 2 platoons found in REDAN (M.28.C.90.90.) 2 Platoons of "D" Coy in dugouts in NIEUPORT, B.H.Q. in house at M.28.C.70.85.	CRC
"	22/23		As above. Working parties supplied each night as follows: — 1½ Coys for work under OC left Subsector HOMBARTZYDE Sector. The 2 Platoons of "D" Coy in NIEUPORT for work under O.C. Rt Subsector. C Coy detailed for defence of the REDAN supplied ½ Coy nightly for work on upkeep of NASAL PARADE.	CRC
	25/26		"B" Coy 24 RFus rushed & captured by enemy from 1st Scot Rif. (the Cameronians) GEILEIDE BROOK Post. "B" Coy 24 RFus sent up in support. They garrisoned NASAL TRENCH and held 2 posts on the GEILEIDE stream.	CRC
	26th		As above.	CRC
	26/27th		"B" Coy relieved by "C" Coy the Cameronians and returned to found in the REDAN but remained under orders of O.C. the Cameronians	CC
	27/28th		Relieved in Support by 1st Dorsets. Relief complete by 3:15 am 28/8/17. Moved to KUHN camp	CRC
Rd N4 DUNKERQUE 1A	28		at OOST DUNKERQUE. Left KUHN Camp at 9·30 a.m. and marched via COXYDE to billets at LA PANNE. Transport + QM Stores rejoined Battn. here	CRC

Army Form C. 2118.

20th (S) Bn Royal Fusiliers

WAR DIARY
or
INTELLIGENCE SUMMARY.
(Erase heading not required.)

SECRET

Place	Date	Hour	Summary of Events and Information	Remarks and references to Appendices
Rd. Myo DUNKERQUE LA PANNE	August 1917. 29	9 am	The Battalion, less Transport, entrained at 9am & moved via ADINKERQUE and DUNKERQUE to Pte SYNTHE Station arriving at Billets, Bivo at CHm one mile SSE of Pte SYNTHE	
		10.15am	Transport left LA PANNE at 10.15 am & moved to PETITE SYNTHE by road.	
Pte SYNTHE	30.		Battalion rested. Minimum reserve from GHYVELDE rejoined the Battn:	CRC
"	31	11.45	Battalion entrained on the DUNKERQUE – GRANDESYNTHE road at LE MOULIN & moving via BOURBOURG – St PIERRE – NATTEN arrived at HOULLE at 5.30 p.m. Bm in Billets.	CRC
			Other Ranks:—	
			Estimated Casualties for the Month:— 12 Killed in Action, 49 wounded, 2 missing	CRC
			The following officers joined the Battn: in the field on the date shown against their names:— 2nd Lieut Brooke L Aug 15th	
			" Miles 2S 19a	
			" Smith J " "	
			" Stokes H E " 20th	
			" Major Hockley Capt Batn on attachment by 4th Army 7697/8 9/8/17	
			" 2nd Lt Colborn G G admitted to hosp sick 11/8/17 Returned 27/8/17	
			" Lawler L J " " " 27/8/17	
			" Cock G S " " " 23/8/17	
			" Easter L S O.S. " " D.B. 17/8/17	CRC
			" Lt Lawler L J w/ Royal Fusiliers Army 2 O.S. 1st Royal Fusiliers	

Army Form C. 2118.

20th (S) Bn. ROYAL FUSILIERS.

WAR DIARY
or
INTELLIGENCE SUMMARY.

SECRET.

(Erase heading not required.)

Instructions regarding War Diaries and Intelligence Summaries are contained in F. S. Regs., Part II. and the Staff Manual respectively. Title pages will be prepared in manuscript.

22 H.
(3 sheets)

Place	Date	Hour	Summary of Events and Information	Remarks and references to Appendices
Ref.Map: HAZEBROUCK 5a.	SEPTEMBER 1917			
HOULLE	1/13		Battalion in Billets at HOULLE. Semi-open Warfare training carried out.	
	13		Draft of 31 other ranks joined the Battn. from 39th I.B.D.	
	14		Inspection of Transport by A/G.O.C. 19th Inf. Bde. (Lt. Col. Chaplin.)	
	15	10am	The Battalion left HOULLE at 10 a.m. and marched via GANSPETTE and WATTEN to billets at LEDERZEELE.	
LEDERZEELE	16	7.30am	The Battalion left LEDERZEELE at 7.30 a.m. and marched via NOORDPEENE, ZUYTPEENE, BAVINCHOVE, OXELAERE, and arrived at billets in the STEENVOORDE area at 3 p.m.	
STEENVOORDE	17		The Battalion left STEENVOORDE area and marched via EECKE to billets and tents at THIEUSHOUK.	
THIEUSHOUK	18/19	7am	Battalion in billets and tents in THIEUSHOUK. Training in Musketry and Close Order carried out	
	20		The Battalion left THIEUSHOUK at 7 a.m. and marched via BERTHEN, BOESCHEPE Farm to tents in the N.W. WESTOUTRE area.	
WESTOUTRE	21		Battalion in tents in WESTOUTRE. General Training carried out. Draft of 100 O.R's. arrived.	
	22	8 a.m.	MINIMUM RESERVE (25 other ranks per Coy. and 5 Officers) and newly arrived draft, left N.W. WESTOUTRE area and marched via BERTHEN to Divisional Depot Battn. at MONT-DE-CATS.	
		4.30pm.	A working party of 20fficers and 160 other ranks left camp to proceed to forward area to bury cable, and returned at 7 a.m. 3rd.	
	23	12 noon	40 Other ranks of new draft rejoined Battalion from Divisional Depot Battn.	
		2 p.m.	A working party of 4 Officers and 300 other ranks left camp for forward area to bury cable and returned 9 a.m. 24th.	
	24		Battalion in camp at N.W. WESTOUTRE. 68 Cases of gas poisoning developed in men of the two working parties.	

- 1 -

Army Form C. 2118.

WAR DIARY
or
INTELLIGENCE SUMMARY.
(Erase heading not required.)

Place	Date	Hour	Summary of Events and Information	Remarks and references to Appendices
Ref.Map: YPRES Edn.3 1/10,000 SEPTEMBER 1917	25	5.45 a.m.	The Battalion, less Transport and B Echelon, left N.W.WESTOUTRE area, and marched via HYDE PARK CORNER, LA CLYTTE, CAFE BELGE, ZILLIBEKE track to Railway Dugouts at I.21.a-d; arrived 12.40 p.m. Transport and B Echelon moved to H.35.a-c.	
		2 p.m.	MINIMUM RESERVE left MONT-DE-CATS and marched via BERTHEN, WESTOUTRE, LA CLYTTE, to bivouacs ½ mile S.W. of DICKEBUSCH LAKE.	
Ref.Map: POLYGON WOOD Edn.1a.		4 p.m.	1 Officer and 2 runners from each Coy. reconnoitred the forward tracks towards J.13.c-d, J.19.a-b.	
		11.30 p.m.	Battalion left Railway dugouts and marched to a reserve position at J.19.a.9.6. 2nd Lt. FINCH J.H. Wounded - shell.	
	26	8.30 a.m.	B.H.Q. struck by gas shell; casualties included Lt.Col. LEADER, A/Capt. CLARK, Capt. W. McCONNELL, R.A.M.C., 2nd Lt. HILL W.E., 2nd Lt. PHILIP D.C., 2nd Lt. LEWIS W. (Gas) Lieut. GREENWOOD R.O.(N.Y.D.N.)	
		2 p.m.	2nd Lt. CHAPMAN, H.D went to 98th Bde. as Liaison Officer.	
		3 p.m.	Capt. J.F.H.TEMPLAR took command of Battn. with 2nd Lt. P.J.TOMKINSON as Adjutant.	
		6 p.m.	Battalion under orders of 98th Bde. moved into trenches near STIRLING CASTLE in J.13.d. B Coy. was attached to the 5th Scottish Rifles in Support position at J.14.b.4.	
		11.45 p.m.	Capt. D. HOLLINGSWORTH from MINIMUM RESERVE took Command of the Battn. Capt. TEMPLAR became Acting Adjutant. Casualties included 2nd Lt. CHAPMAN (Gas).	
	27	4 p.m.	Battn. attached to 69th Bde, 3rd Div. B Coy. rejoined Battn. 10 p.m.	
	28	9 a.m.	Battn. relieved and moved into camp in No 1 area West of DICKEBUSCH Rd. Major F.S. MODERA, M.C. returned from leave and took Command of the Battn. Capt. D.W HOLLINGSWORTH became Acting Adjutant.	
Ref.Map: HAZEBROUCK 5a 1/100,000		6 a.m.	Transport marched to the BLARINGHEM area; arrived at LE CROQUET 5 p.m.	
		7 a.m.	MINIMUM RESERVE left bivouacs ½ mile S.W. of DICKEBUSCH LAKE and marched for BLARINGHEM area. Arrived LE CROQUET 6 p.m.	
		10 p.m.	Battn. camp bombed by aeroplanes; 1 other rank killed, 1 other rank wounded.	
	29th	3 p.m.	The Battn. left No.1 area DICKEBUSCH and marched to OUDERDOM.	
		5 p.m.	Battn. entrained and left OUDERDOM. Arrived EBBLINGHEM at 8.30 p.m. Marched to LE CROQUET and moved into billets 10.30 p.m.	

WAR DIARY
or
INTELLIGENCE SUMMARY.

Army Form C. 2118.

(Erase heading not required.)

- 3 -

Place	Date	Hour	Summary of Events and Information	Remarks and references to Appendices
SEPTEMBER 1917	30		Battalion in billets at LE CROQUET. Cleaning.	
			Casualties for the month:-	
			Officers - 9 Wounded.	
			Other ranks - 2 Killed.	
			34 Wounded.	
			70 Gassed.	
			1 Missing.	
			The following Officers joined the Battn. in the field on dates shown against their names:-	
			Hon. Lieut. Stokes P.A. 6.9.17.	
			2nd Lt. Wright G.B. 30.9.17.	
			" Taylor A.H. 30.9.17.	
			" Neish D. 30.9.17.	
			2nd Lt. R.K. KELLER admitted to Hospital sick 20/9/17.	
			A/Capt. A. MURGATROYD " accidentally wounded 22/9/17.	
			2nd Lt. GOULD W.T. returned from Hospital 18/9/17.	
			2nd Lt. COOK G.S. " " 18/9/17.	

                         MAJOR,

1st Oct. 1917.   Comdg. 20th (S) Bn. ROYAL FUSILIERS.

Army Form C. 2118.

20th (S) Bn Royal Fusiliers

WAR DIARY

INTELLIGENCE SUMMARY.

(Erase heading not required.)

Vol 24
SECRET.

Place	Date	Hour	Summary of Events and Information	Remarks and references to Appendices
	October 1917			
Ref Map Sheet 36A 1/40000	1		Battalion in billets LE CROQUET distributed in the squares B18 & C13 with BHQ at B18 B 8.10. Training by Coys carried out in billeting area	CRR
LE CROQUET	2		Battalion in billets as above.	CRR
	3	10.15am	Rehearsal parade for inspection by the Field Marshal Commanding in Chief. Battalion in billets as above – The Battn together with other units of the 19th Infantry Brigade were inspected by the Field Marshal Commanding in Chief at LE CROQUET. 8 OR attached to 19th M.G.Coy as carriers. A Brigade Pioneer Coy was formed 2nd/Lt H.KIRK and 22 OR were attached to this Coy.	CRR
Ref Map Sheet 28 NW 1/20000 HAZEBROUCK 5A VLAMERTINGHE	4	11.30am	The Battalion less Transport left LE CROQUET and marched via LYNDE to EBBLINGHEM station where they entrained at 1.30 pm and moved via STEENVOORDE and ABEELE to VLAMERTINGHE arriving at 6 pm. Transport left LE CROQUET and moved to VLAMERTINGHE by road. The Transport & QM Stores remained at VLAMERTINGHE HQ & BB. The remainder of the Battn marched to a field near Goldfish Dugouts at H12 a 6.5 arrived at 7 pm.	26 H. (7 sheets)

– 1 –

Army Form C. 2118.

WAR DIARY
INTELLIGENCE SUMMARY.
(Erase heading not required.)

Place	Date	Hour	Summary of Events and Information	Remarks and references to Appendices
Ref Map Sheet 28 NW 1/20,000			and bivouced for the night.	CRE
VLAMERTINGHE	5		The Batt. became attached to 3rd AUSTRALIAN DIVISION II nd ANZAC CORPS for duties between our & 2nd Canadian Railway Trps for work on Light Railways, parts having arrived during the night & camp was formed at the field M12 a 8.5	
		11.30 am	A Working party of 5 officers + 237 O.R from A & B Coys reported to 2nd Canadian Railway Troops for work on Light Railways and returned at 6 p.m	CRE
	6		Dispositions as above.	
			On relief of 3rd Australian Division the Batt. became attached to the 66th Division	
		6 am	A Working party of 5 officers & 234 O.R. from C & D Coys reported to 2nd Canadian Railway Troops for work on Light Railways & returned 1.30 pm	CRE
		11 am	A Working party of 5 officers & 215 O.R reported for work as above & returned 6 pm.	CRE
	7	1 am	Winter time came into force	
			Dispositions as above	CRE
		6 am	A Working party of 5 officers + 230 O.R from C & D Coys reported to 2nd C.R.T. returned 12 noon	CRE
		10 am	A Working party of 5 officers + 210 O.R from A & B Coys reported to 2nd C.R.T. returned 2 pm	CRE
	8		Dispositions as above	
		6 am	A Working party of 5 officers + 232 O.R from C & D Coys reported to 2nd C.R.T. returned 11 am	CRE
		11 am	A Working party of 5 officers + 211 O.R from A & B Coys reported to 2nd C.R.T & returned 4 pm.	CRE

-2-

Army Form C. 2118.

WAR DIARY
INTELLIGENCE SUMMARY
(Erase heading not required.)

Place	Date	Hour	Summary of Events and Information	Remarks and references to Appendices
Ref Map Sheet 28 NW 1/20,000	October 1917 9		Dispositions as above	
		6 am	A working party of 5 officers & 252 O.R. from C & D Coys reported to 2nd CRT & returned 11 am	CRC
		11 am	A working party of 5 officers & 210 O.R. from A & B Coys reported to 2nd CRT & returned 5 pm	CRC
VLAMERTINGHE	10		Dispositions as above. Battalion picked in Camp	
	11		Dispositions as above	
		6 am	A working party of 5 officers & 219 O.R. from A & B Coys reported to 2nd CRT & returned at 11 am	CRC
		11 am	A working party of 5 officers & 252 O.R. from C & D Coys reported to 2nd CRT & returned at 4 pm	CRC
YPRES	12	6 am	A working party of 3 officers & 150 O.R. reported to 2nd CRT & returned 12 noon	
		12 noon	The Batt. less transport & Q.M. Details entrained to new Camp at I.24.7.2 Tents were moved	
			on 2 lorries supplied by 2nd CRT	
		2 pm	Transport & Q.M. Details left VLAMERTINGHE marched to new Camp arrived 4.30 pm	
	13	6.45 am	A working party of 6 officers & 450 O.R. reported to 2nd CRT & returned 11 am	CRC
	14	6.45 am	A working party of 6 officers & 450 O.R. reported to 2nd CRT & returned 11 am	CRC
	15	6.45 am	A working party of 6 officers & 450 O.R. reported to 2nd CRT & returned 11 am	CRC
	16	6.45 am	A working party of 6 officers & 450 O.R. reported to 2nd CRT & returned 11 am	CRC
	17	6.45 am	A working party of 6 officers & 450 O.R. reported to 2nd CRT & returned 11 am	CRC

Army Form C. 2118.

WAR DIARY
INTELLIGENCE SUMMARY
(Erase heading not required.)

SECRET

Place	Date	Hour	Summary of Events and Information	Remarks and references to Appendices
Ref. Map HAZEBROUCK 5A 1/100000	October 1917 17	9.30am	The Transport less 2 Cookers & Motor Cart & 4 New Cart proceeded by road to SHANKILL CAMP at NEUVE EGLISE near ASYLUM (YPRES) - VLAMERTINGHE STATION - ZEVECOTEN - LOCRE - DRANOUTRE	
		1.45 pm	The remainder of the Transport left camp & proceeded to SHANKILL CAMP by same route	
		2 pm	The Battalion were relieved by the 10th CAMERONIANS. The Battalion marched to a point on the road between ASYLUM (YPRES) and KRUISSTRAAT where they entrained	CRC
NEUVE EGLISE		5.15 pm	The Battn detrained at NEUVE EGLISE & marched to SHANKILL CAMP. The Battn came under orders of G.O.C. 19th Infantry Brigade and were in Divisional Reserve VIII Corps	CRC
	18		Cleaning in Camp and at Palmer Batt on West side of the NEUVE EGLISE - STEENWERKE road	CRC
	19	9 am	Cleaning & Kit Inspection. Working party of 1 Off. + 400 O.R. for work at HILLSIDE CAMP	CRC
			100 NCO's & men marched for Anti-Aircraft defence	CRC
	20	9 am	Specialist training & training by Coys carried out in Camp	
			Working party of 1 Off + 40 OR reported for work at Hillside Camp	CRC
Ref Map Sheet 28 SW	21	9 am	Sunday. Working party of 1 Off + 50 OR reported for work at PENZANCE LINES T20 B.11.	CRC
	22		Specialist training & training by Coys carried out in Camp Reconnaissance of forward area by C.O. + two other officers Following demicad working parties	

— 4 —

WAR DIARY
INTELLIGENCE SUMMARY
(Erase heading not required.)

Army Form C. 2118.

SECRET

Place	Date	Hour	Summary of Events and Information	Remarks and references to Appendices
Ruyaulcourt October 1917 Sheet 28 S.W.	22		PENZANCE LINES 1 officer + 80 other ranks	
			290 Army Troops Coy RE. 1 NCO + 9 men	
			Main Divisional R.E. Dump DE KENNEBEK 7 Sgt 2 A. 2 NCOs + 20 men	CRE
	23		A pat. of 1 officer + 18 OR reported to Prisoners of War Cage BALLEVUE relieve Canterburys	CRE
	24		Specialist training + training by Coys	
	25		Specialist training. Trench digging + revetting. Consolidation of shell holes	CRE
			Lecture by G.O.C. 19th Brigade on Trench Warfare	
			Prisoners of War tent relieved by 100th Brigade + returned.	
	26/27		Specialist training. Battalion + Ceremonial Drill	CRE
			Draft of 20 OR joined Batn.	CRE
	28		Working parties returned from 290 Army Troops Coy RE from Main Divisional R.E. dump DE KENNEBEK	CRE
	29		Specialist training	
		3.30 pm	Drums + Fifes left camp for PENZANCE LINES. 2nd [WORKS R.H. proceeded]	CRE
			there to take command of all Band Drums + Fifes of the Brigade	

- 6 -

SECRET   Army Form C. 2118.

WAR DIARY
INTELLIGENCE SUMMARY.
(Erase heading not required.)

Place	Date	Hour	Summary of Events and Information	Remarks and references to Appendices
October 1917				
Ref. Map SHEET 28 S.W.	30	5pm	The Battn less transport left camp and marching via WULVERGHEM relieved the 10th MIDDLESEX Regiment in a Reserve position at Bristol Castle and Battn HQ at T6.d.3.4. Dispositions as follows A B & D Coys were distributed in trenches SE of Bristol Castle with Coy HQ A Coy at T6.g.8.2. B Coy V.I.C.I.4. D Coy V.I.C.8.2. C Coy were in an advanced position in U3 central with Coy HQ at U3.a.6.1. This Coy was placed at the tactical disposal of the OC Cameronians (on the line).	CRC
	31		Dispositions as above. Working parties included a party of 6 officers and 200 OR under the command of Major D.W. HOLLINGSWORTH engaged in the construction of a support trench in U5 central.	CRC
				CRC
			Major E. S. MODERA MC was appointed to the Acting Command of the Battn as from 11/10/17 (Authority M.S. Circ G 448/4)	CRC
			The following officers joined the Battn in the field on the dates shown against their names.	
			Lt (Temp Capt) J.H. BOAG RAMC 1st October 1917	
			2nd Lt R.O DARKER 9th October 1917	CRC
			2nd Lt R.K KELLER returned from hospital 10th October 1917	
			2nd Lt J.T SMITH proceeded on Lewis Gun Instructor Course LE TOUQUET 11/10/17 returned 29/10/17	
			2nd Lt RABARKER returned from General Course XL Corps School 12/10/17.	CRC

Blair Thora Lt Col
Comdg 30th Royal Fusiliers

– 7 –

WAR DIARY
INTELLIGENCE SUMMARY.
(Erase heading not required.)

Army Form C. 2118.

SECRET

Place	Date	Hour	Summary of Events and Information	Remarks and references to Appendices
	October 1917			
	11/10/17		Major I.S. MODERA MC. to be a/Lieut Col whilst in command of the Battalion.	GRO
			Casualties for the month.	
			Officers: nil.	
			Other Ranks	
			Killed 1	
			Wounded 10 (5 remain at duty)	
			Missing nil.	GRO

J Stuart Modera. Lieut Col
(Commanding 20th (S) Bn. Royal Fusiliers

20th (S) Bn Royal Fusiliers Vol 2 5

Army Form C. 2118.

WAR DIARY
INTELLIGENCE SUMMARY.
(Erase heading not required.)

Place	Date	Hour	Summary of Events and Information	Remarks and references to Appendices
Ref Map Sheet 28 SW. 1 In reserve	November 1917		Battalion in a Reserve position at BRISTOL CASTLE and Battn HQ at T6 a 3.4 Dispositions as follows A B & D Coys were distributed in trenches S.E. of Bristol Castle with Coy H.Q. A Coy at T6 a 8.2. B Coy U1 c 1.4. D Coy U1 c 8.2. C Coy were in an advanced position in U3 central with Coy HQ at U3 a 6.1. This Company was placed at the Tactical disposal of OC No 2 CAMERONIANS (in the line). The transport were at SHANKILL CAMP at T9 6-3.0	
	2		Working parties included a party of 6 officers & 200 OR under the command of MAJOR HOLLINGSWORTH DSO engaged in the construction of a support trench at D.5 central. Dispositions and working parties as on previous day. Reconnaissance of front line position by Company Commanders. Capt. CT BUTLER wounded.	24 H. 6 inhab. ¼. ¼.
In Line	3/4		The Battn left the RESERVE POSITION and relieved the CAMERONIANS in the front line. RIGHT SECTOR	¼.
	4	1.30 am	Relief completed. Dispositions as follows. Battn front from U11 b 3.5 to U5 b 6.5.	

Army Form C. 2118.

WAR DIARY
INTELLIGENCE SUMMARY.
(Erase heading not required.)

Place	Date	Hour	Summary of Events and Information	Remarks and references to Appendices
Ref. Map Sheet 28 SW	November 1917 4		B.H.Q at V.10.a.0.7. B.Coy LEFT FRONT Coy with H.Q at U.5.k.3.0. D Coy RIGHT FRONT Coy with H.Q at U.5.d.2.7. One Platoon & one Lewis gun and team was attached to D.Coy. 2 Lewis guns & teams from A Coy were attached to B Coy. A Coy (less 1 Platoon and Lewis gun and team) in POLLARD SUPPORT TRENCH with Coy H.Q at U.5.c.2.7. C Coy was in RESERVE trenches with Coy H.Q at U.4.b.33. D Coy the Cameronians were in trenches N of B in BETHLEHEM FARM with Coy H.Q at U.3 central and were at the tactical disposal of the Battn. Relieved by trench tramway from WULVERGHEM to BETHLEHEM FARM.	G.K.
	5		Dispositions as above	G.K.
	6		Battn H.Q. moved to V.4.c.15.10. Signal Office remained at V.10.a.0.7. other dispositions as before	G.K.
	7		Battn. was relieved in the line by the 1st QUEENS. R.W.S Rgt.	
		8.30pm	Post No 11 of LEFT FRONT Coy raided by the enemy, two men missing.	
		10.30pm	Relief complete. After relief Battalion marched via STINKING FARM – WULVERGHEM – NEUVE-EGLISE to KORTEPYP A CAMP T.26.b.7.5	G.K.
	8		Battalion in CAMP cleaning.	G.K.

Army Form C. 2118.

WAR DIARY
INTELLIGENCE SUMMARY.

(Erase heading not required.)

Place	Date	Hour	Summary of Events and Information	Remarks and references to Appendices
Above knee 1917 Ref. Map. SHEET 28 S.W.	9-12		Training carried out in Camp.	
	13		2nd Lieut. G. COLBOURNE appointed Acting Adjutant vice CAPT. C.B. CATCHPOLE who assumed Command of A Coy.	G.C.
STRAZEELE Ref. Map. SHEET 27 S.E. SHEET 36 A.	14	8.30am	The Battalion marched to STRAZEELE via WATERLOO ROAD, RAIELSBERG and BAILLEUL.	G.C.
		1 pm	Arrived in billets. Dispositions as follow: Battn. H.Q. W. 28. A. 30. 4.5; A Coy. H.Q. E. 4. a. 5. 0. ; B. Coy. H.Q. W. 21. b. 0. 2. i D Coy H.Q. W. 28. a. 0. 6.	G.C.
	15-16		Training in Camp.	
Ref. Map. SHEET 28	17	7 pm	Battalion entrained and moved via BAILLEUL - LOCRE - OUDERDON - VLAMERTINGHE - YPRES to H. 24. c. 3. 3. and there debussed and marched to Bivouacs I.10. c. 5. 9.	G.C.
POTIJZE	18		Arrived 2.30 pm. Q.M. Stores and Transport by road to BRANDHOEK. Battalion rested and cleaned camp. Reconnaissance of ZONNEBEKE - POTIJZE Road and M'n Track.	G.C.
	19	10.45am	Battalion marched to billets on YPRES-MENIN Road I.9.a.3.2. Battalion in Brigade SUPPORT	G.C.

WAR DIARY
INTELLIGENCE SUMMARY

(Erase heading not required.)

Army Form C. 2118.

Place	Date	Hour	Summary of Events and Information	Remarks and references to Appendices
November 1917 Ref Map SHEET 28 20.23			Battalion engaged on work in FORWARD AREA.	
Ref Map ZONNEBEKE 7a	24	2.30pm	Battalion moved up to RIGHT SUPPORT. Route ZONNEBEKE - POTIJZE Road - "H" and "K" Tracks. Battalion HQ. SEINE D.16.d.15.35.	
	25		Reconnaissance of defence positions. The Battalion supplied carrying parties to carry ammunition and materials.	
	26		Carrying parties as before.	
	27		Battalion relieved 5th SCOTTISH RIFLES in RIGHT SUB-SECTOR.	
		11.20pm	Relief completed.	
	28		S.O.S. on RIGHT FLANK; heavy barrage by enemy on FRONT Line positions. Estimated casualties; 1 Officer (2nd Lt L.B. SOLOMON) & 50 O.R.	
	29		Dispositions as before.	
	30	7.50am	S.O.S. signal sent up by RIGHT FRONT. The enemy were seen to leave trench towards RIGHT FLANK. No attack on Battalion front.	
		9.45pm	Battalion relieved by 2nd WORCESTERSHIRE REGT. Relief completed.	

WAR DIARY
INTELLIGENCE SUMMARY.
(Erase heading not required.)

Army Form C. 2118.

Instructions regarding War Diaries and Intelligence Summaries are contained in F. S. Regs., Part II. and the Staff Manual respectively. Title pages will be prepared in manuscript.

Place	Date	Hour	Summary of Events and Information	Remarks and references to Appendices
November 1917.	30		Battalion proceeded to billets previously occupied on YPRES-MENIN Road.	E/L
			Lt. Col. MODERA F.S., M.C. remained at "B" Echelon each on 24th	
			Major HOLLINGSWORTH D.W. took the Battalion into the Trenches on 24th	
			Lt. Col. MODERA F.S., M.C. admitted to Hospital sick on 29th	
			Major HOLLINGSWORTH D.W. assumed Command of Battalion on 29th	
			The following Officers proceeded on leave:-	
			Capt. TEMPLAR J.F.H. on 6th	
			2nd Lt. GOULD W.T " 10th	
			" NEISH D " 21st	
			" WHYTE M.G. " 21st	
			" BARKER R.O. " 21st	
			2nd Lieut. FREELAND P. discharged from Hospital on 13th	
			2nd Lieut. FREELAND P. admitted to Hospital sick on 21st	
			Casualties for month:-	
			1 Officer wounded (2nd Lt. L.B. SOLOMON)	
			Other ranks - 29 Killed	
			69 Wounded	
			2 Missing	

G.G. Zieffler Capt. for Major
Comm'g. 20th (S) Bn Royal Fusiliers

SECRET Army Form C. 2118.

20th (S) Bn Royal Fusiliers
WAR DIARY
or
INTELLIGENCE SUMMARY.
(Erase heading not required.)

Place	Date	Hour	Summary of Events and Information	Remarks and references to Appendices
	December 1917			
Ref Map Sheet 28 Brandhoek	1	8.30am	Battn marched from billets in YPRES-MENIN RD via IRISH FARM to ST JEAN STN and thence by train to BRANDHOEK.	GV
		12 noon	Arrived TORONTO CAMP G 18 a 50.60 Transport at G 18 a 15.60	GV
	2-6		Training in Camp Lt Col F.S. MODERA McF reassumed Command of Battalion	GV
POTIJZE RD	7	11am	Battalion marched to Camp on YPRES-POTIJZE Rd I 3 c 9.2 Route BRANDHOEK - VLAMERTINGHE - YPRES and relieved 9th M.L.I. Transport at M 7 c central.	GV
Bde Reserve	8-10		Training in Billetting area	GV
Ref Map Sheet 28 WATOU	11	9.40am	Battn entrans at ST JEAN Station debrans at ABEELE and thence marched to billets in WATOU area. Battn HQ at L 7 a 7.3. A Coy HQ at L 7 b 2.8 B Coy HQ at K 10 b 7.7. C Coy HQ at K 12 a 1.3 D Coy HQ at K 5 d 4.4.	GV
	12-13		Cleaning and improving billets	GV
	14-20		Training in billetting area	GV
	20		Lt Col F.S. MODERA MC admitted to Hospital accidentally injured Capt G.E.R. de MIREMONT 2nd Royal Welch Fusiliers assumed temporary Command of the battalion pending the return from leave of Major D.W. HOLLINGSWORTH	GV
Ref Map Sheet 28 POPERINGHE	21	8.25am	Battalion marched to POPERINGHE route Cross Roads K 24 b 9.0 - ABEELE - POPERINGHE. Transport at Sheet 27 L & I 2. Battn HQ 21 Rue de BOESCHEPE Battn billeted in buildings in vicinity	GV
	22-24		Battn supplied a daily working party of 3 Companies to C.R.E. VIII Corps. Nature of work. Thieung Corps Line	GV

— 1 —

25 H.
(3 sheets)

2nd (S) Bn Royal Fusiliers II.

Army Form C. 2118.

WAR DIARY
INTELLIGENCE SUMMARY.
(Erase heading not required.)

Place	Date	Hour	Summary of Events and Information	Remarks and references to Appendices
	December 1917			
Ref Map Sheet 28 POPERINGHE	25		There were no working parties today.	
	26-27		Working Parties as on 22-24	A
	27		Lt Col S. MODERA M.C. returned from hospital and resumed command of the Battn vice Capt EER de MIREMONT	A
	28		Working parties as on 27th.	A
Ref Map Sheet 27 WATOU	29		Working parties as on 28th	A
		11 am	Battn was relieved by 4th Kings Liverpool Regiment. B Coy & HQ marched to old billets in WATOU area. Route Rue des CHIENS, POPERINGHE - ABEELE Road - Rue de DUNKERQUE L4 & 72 - ST JAN TER BIEZEN - Road Junction L2a 4.7 - Road Junction L10 9.0. A.C. & D. Coys returned direct from work by train to ABEELE and marched to billets previously occupied	A
	30		Sunday	
	31		Lectures to all officers and Platoon Sgts by Coys Commanders and Lt Col LEVY DSO at STEENVOORDE. Training in Battery area	A A
			Casualties for month 1 other rank wounded. – 2 –	

20th (S) Bn Royal Fusiliers

WAR DIARY
or
INTELLIGENCE SUMMARY.
(Erase heading not required.)

Army Form C. 2118.

Place	Date	Hour	Summary of Events and Information	Remarks and references to Appendices
December 1917	29		Major B.W. Hollingsworth assumed command of Battn. during absence on leave of Lt Col Modera M.C.	
	10		2nd Lt Vickers C.E. attached VIII Corps B Works Coy	
	24		" Thorley R.H. returned from Divisional Dump	
	22		Lt Robinson T. rejoined Battn in the field	
	11		2nd Lt Solomon L.B. returned from hospital	
	6		Lt Col Modera P.S. M.C. " " " "	
	19		" admitted to hospital accidentally injured	
	27		" returned from hospital	
	29		2nd Lt Youstmon P admitted to hospital sick	
			2nd Lt Keller R.K. musketry Course 2nd Army School 31/11/17 to 23/12/17	
			2nd Lt Cook G.S. VIII Corps Bombing Course 5/12/17 to 29/12/17	
			2nd Lt Darker R.O. " Gas Course 19/12/17 to 24/12/17	
			2nd Lt Claughton W.T.A. GHQ Lewis Gun Course 6/12/17 to 16/12/17	
			2nd Lt Sutro E.L. VIII Corps Intelligence Course 13/12/17 to 23/12/17	
			2nd Lt Lloyd A.E. 5 Army Musketry School 16/12/17 to 16/12/17	
			2nd Lt Gould W.T. General Course at 2nd Army School 10/11/17 to 16/12/17	
			2nd Lt Taylor A.H. " at 4th Army School 28/12/17 to 29/12/17	
			2nd Lt Whelp " " " " 21/11/17 to 29/12/17	
			2nd Lt Mead General Snipers Course VIII Corps " 21/11/17 to 29/12/17	

B.W. Hollingsworth Major
Commanding 20th (S) Bn Royal Fusiliers

SECRET.

1918 JAN: FEB

20th Royal Fusiliers.

DISBANDED 19/8/FEB

WAR DIARY
INTELLIGENCE SUMMARY.
(Erase heading not required.)

Army Form C. 2118.

Instructions regarding War Diaries and Intelligence Summaries are contained in F.S. Regs., Part II. and the Staff Manual respectively. Title pages will be prepared in manuscript.

Place	Date	Hour	Summary of Events and Information	Remarks and references to Appendices
WATOU Sheet 27	Jan. 1918 1		New Years Day. Battalion holiday.	SL
	2		Training in billeting area.	SL
BRANDHOEK Sheet 28	3	9 am	The Battn entrained at ABEELE STATION, detrained at Brandhoek Station & marched to TORONTO EAST CAMP. G.18.a.15.60. Transport by road to H.7.c. central	SL
In support SEINE	4	8.30 am	The Battn with strength of 80 O.R. per Coy. exclusive of H.Q. embussed, proceeded to YPRES, & marched to WHITBY CAMP. I.8.b.8.6.	SL
		9 am	Transport & Q.M. details proceeded by road to POTIJZE. Remainder of Battn at H.7.c. central where demolition platoon under 2nd Lt. W.T. GOULD, was formed.	SL
		3.30 pm	The Battn marched via YPRES - POTIJZE - ZONNEBEKE road to SEINE. D.16.d.6.4. & relieved 4th YORKS. Regt. in RIGHT SUPPORT	SL
RIGHT SUB-SECTOR HAMBURG	5		The Battn was relieved in RIGHT SUPPORT by 1st QUEENS REGT. The Battn relieved 9th DURHAM LIGHT INFANTRY in RIGHT SUB-SECTOR dispositions as follows:- Battn. H.Q: HAMBURG. D.16.b.5.7.; B Coy- Left Front Coy. with H.Q at D.12.b.17.70; D Coy- Centre Coy. with H.Q. at D.12.a.95.20; C Coy- Right Front Coy: with H.Q. at D.12.c.30.55; A Coy- Support Coy. with H.Q at D.17.a.8.5.	SL SL

26 H Archives

SECRET.

Army Form C. 2118.

WAR DIARY
or
INTELLIGENCE SUMMARY.
(Erase heading not required.)

Instructions regarding War Diaries and Intelligence Summaries are contained in F. S. Regs., Part II, and the Staff Manual respectively. Title pages will be prepared in manuscript.

Place	Date	Hour	Summary of Events and Information	Remarks and references to Appendices
Ref. Map Sheet 28 6/9 RIGHT SUB-SECTOR	January 1918		Dispositions as above.	S/L
WHITBY CAMP	9		The Battn. was relieved in RIGHT SUB-SECTOR by 1st QUEENS REGT. On relief Battn. proceeded to WHITBY CAMP I.8.R.8.6.	S/L
BRANDHOEK	10	11:30am	The Battn. proceeded by Light Railway to BRANDHOEK & thence by march route to TORONTO CAMP EAST. Transport by road.	S/L
	11/12/13		Cleaning and training in Camp.	S/L
	13		Lt. Col. F. STEWART MODERA. M.C. returned from leave & reassumed Command of the Battn.	S/L
YPRES Brigade Support	14		The Battn. proceeded by Light Railway to YPRES. Battn. billetted in cellars in YPRES with Battn. H.Q. at I7.d.9.4. Transport & QM Stores at H.7.c. central	S/L
	14/20		Dispositions as above. Working parties for the forward area provided by the Battn. daily.	S/L
SEINE In Support	21	4:15pm	The Battn. marched via YPRES-POTIJZE-ZONNEBEKE road & JUDAH TRACK to SEINE D.16.A.6.4.4. relieved 1st MIDDLESEX REGT in RIGHT SUPPORT. Battn. HQ. at SEINE & troops in immediate vicinity.	S/L
	22/24		Dispositions as above.	S/L

SECRET.

Army Form C. 2118.

WAR DIARY
or
INTELLIGENCE SUMMARY.
(Erase heading not required.)

Instructions regarding War Diaries and Intelligence Summaries are contained in F. S. Regs., Part II. and the Staff Manual respectively. Title pages will be prepared in manuscript.

Place	Date	Hour	Summary of Events and Information	Remarks and references to Appendices
January 1918				
Ref Map Sheet 28A ALNWICK CAMP	25		The Battn. was relieved in RIGHT SUPPORT by 9th H.L.I. On relief Battn. proceeded to ALNWICK CAMP.	SL
	26		Battn. in ALNWICK Camp resting + cleaning.	SL
Ref Map Sheet 27A ST MARTIN AU LAERT	27	3.40 pm	The Battn. entrained at ST JEAN Station + detrained at ST. OMER + thence marched to billets in ST. MARTIN AU LAERT. Dispositions as follows: Battn. HQ - R.33.d.3.0. A Coy. R.32.b.5.9; B Coy - R.27.c.3.6; C Coy - R.33.a.9.7; D Coy - R.33.b.9.8.	SL
	28/31		Dispositions as above. Training in area. Casualties for the month: Officers - (nil) Other ranks - Killed - 3 Wounded - 12 Missing - 1 The following Officers proceeded on courses:- Lieut. T.H. HARRISON - VIII Corps School 15.1.18 2nd Lt. L.B. SOLOMON " " 15.1.18 " W.S. MILES " " 15.1.18	SL

SECRET. Army Form C. 2118.

WAR DIARY
or
INTELLIGENCE SUMMARY.
(Erase heading not required.)

Instructions regarding War Diaries and Intelligence Summaries are contained in F. S. Regs., Part II. and the Staff Manual respectively. Title pages will be prepared in manuscript.

Place	Date	Hour	Summary of Events and Information	Remarks and references to Appendices
January 1918			The following Officers proceeded on Course —	
			A/Capt. F.W. BOWER — 42° Squadron R.F.C. 13.1.18.	
			2nd Lt. A.E. FLOYD — Intelligence Course — 25.1.18.	
			The following Officers rejoined from Course —	
			2nd Lt. A.E. FLOYD — IV Army Musketry School 10.1.18	
			A/Capt. F.W. BOWER — 42° Squadron R.F.C. 16.1.18	

Edward M[...]
Lieut-Colonel
Commanding 2nd S.B. The Royal [Fusiliers]

Army Form C. 2118.

20th (S) Battn Royal Fusiliers

WAR DIARY

INTELLIGENCE SUMMARY.

(Erase heading not required.)

SECRET.

27.H.
(3 sheets)

Instructions regarding War Diaries and Intelligence Summaries are contained in F.S. Regs., Part II and the Staff Manual respectively. Title pages will be prepared in manuscript.

Hour, Date, Place	Summary of Events and Information	Remarks and references to Appendices
February 1918 Ref Map SHEET 27A S.E. ST MARTIN au LAERT. 1.	Orders received for disbandment of the Battalion personnel to be posted to the 2nd & the 13th Battalions Royal Fusiliers	S/L
2/5	Final match in Inter Platoon Football Tournament for Cup presented by Lt Col F. STEWART MADERA M.C. Result No 9 Platoon 3 goals No 13 Platoon 2 goals.	S/L
5	Training in area.	S/L
	The Battalion was inspected by Major General R.J. PINNEY C.B. Commanding 33rd Division & Brigadier General C.R.G. MAYNE D.S.O. commanding 19th Infantry Brigade.	Farewell in speeches S/L.
6/7	Draft- 5 / 3. Officers & 42 Other ranks proceeded to join 4th Battalion Training in area.	S/L
8	Draft of 6 officers & 222 other ranks proceeded to join 2nd Battalion	S/L
9	Draft of 7 officers & 214 other ranks proceeded to join 13 Battalion.	S/L
	Draft of 29 other ranks proceeded to join 4th Battalion	S/L
	Battalion Headquarters moved to R 33 a 5 6.	S/L
10	Major D.W. HOLLINGSWORTH proceeded to POPERINGHE to assume duties as O.C. Reinforcements VIII Corps.	S/L
14	Surplus Personnel (innavent officers & N.C.O's above the rank of sergeant and trained signallers) to other units. proceeded to VIII Corps Reinforcement Camp. 4 other ranks proceeded to join 2nd Battalion 3 other ranks proceeded to join 4th Battalion. 3 officers & 3 other ranks proceeded to join 13th Battalion.	S/L
15	Transport & transport personnel (Capt. G.F. JONES-WILLIAMS & 34 other ranks) attached to the 14th Infantry Brigade	S/L

20th (S) Batt. Royal Fusiliers

WAR DIARY
INTELLIGENCE SUMMARY.
(Erase heading not required.)

SECRET. Army Form C. 2118.

Instructions regarding War Diaries and Intelligence Summaries are contained in F. S. Regs., Part II and the Staff Manual respectively. Title pages will be prepared in manuscript.

Hour, Date, Place	Summary of Events and Information	Remarks and references to Appendices
February 1916 Ref. Map SHEET 27A S.E. ST MARTIN au LAERT. 15.	There remained unposted the following Headquarter Staff(viz):- LT. COL. F. STEWART MODERA M.C. CAPT. G. COLBOURNE (Adjutant) Hon LT & QUARTERMASTER P.A. STOKES, CAPT. D.L. PITSCHÉ.	Nil.
	Casualties from 1st to 13th February 1916 - nil.	Nil.
	The following officers joined the Battalion in the Field 13-2-16. 2LT B BLAIN 2LT BOWLER and 2LT PYE.	Nil.
	Undermentioned officers and other ranks were posted as follows:-	Nil.
	To the 2nd Battalion Royal Fusiliers. CAPT. C.B. CATCHPOLE, LIEUT. T.H. HARRISON 2LT W.T.A. C LAUGHTON W.T. GOULD M.G. WHYTE G.S. COOK J.T. SMITH W.E. STOKES R.G. DARKER D. NEISH G.V. KENNY-SIVEWRIGHT and 270 other ranks.	Nil.
	To the 4th Battalion Royal Fusiliers. 2nd LTS P. FREELAND E.L. SUTRO S.R. HONEYWILL A.P. CHARLES and 88 other ranks.	Nil.
	To the 13th Battalion Royal Fusiliers. CAPTS. G.G. ZEIGLER F.W. BOWER LIEUT. B.F.A. MARSHALL 2LTS P.I. TOMPKINSON R.K. KELLER A.E. FLOYD R.H. WORLEY W. KIRK W.S. MILES R.A. BARKER A.H. TAYLOR R.H. VICKERS A.B. BLAIN E.M.J. BOWLER and H.A. PYE and 271 other ranks.	Nil.

2b.(S) Battn Royal Fusiliers

Army Form C. 2118.

WAR DIARY
INTELLIGENCE SUMMARY
(Erase heading not required.)

SECRET

Hour, Date, Place	Summary of Events and Information	Remarks and references to Appendices
February 1918.	Those officers and other ranks who are not shown as having proceeded to join their new battalions under various dates as above proceeded direct from leave or courses.	S/L.
	Capt. J.H.F. TEMPLAR struck off strength on proceeding to Senior Officers Course Aldershot.	S/L.

Stuart Moore
16/2/18.
Lieut Col
Comdg. 20th Royal Fusiliers

S.H.
(2 sheets)

20 t° Royal 4to:
fol: 3
Plan 16

22nd

33RD DIVISION
19TH INFY BDE

TRENCH MORTAR BTY
JLY-AUG 1916

19th Brigade.
33rd Division.

19th BRIGADE

LIGHT TRENCH MORTAR BATTERY

JULY 1916

WAR DIARY or INTELLIGENCE SUMMARY

Army Form C. 2118

19th Trench Mortar Batt[ery]
July 1916.

Vol I

Place	Date	Hour	Summary of Events and Information	Remarks and references to Appendices
Givenchy	1 & 2		Working on 12 new emplacements for a Raid on the Northern Craters. 98th Brigade put in 4 Emplacements under the command of 98 T.M.B.	Casualties O.R.
	3		Mortars "keyed" and inspection of Emplacements by A. Group Commander and 2 T.M.O.	
	4		Raid took place. 4 mortars as arranged fired slow from 10.30 P.M. to 12 P.M. under Lt Hammer 98 T.M.B. Keying up a Barrage on Trenches South of Northern Craters. 19 T.M.B. 8 guns, 3 mortars under Lt Morgan fired for 45 minutes on enemy Support trenches Northern Craters. 5 Mortars under Lt Price fired for 35 min. on enemy Saparend trenches behind Northern craters. Total number of rounds fired 2,345.	W. 1 W. 2
	5			
	6		Cleaning and taking over mortars	
	7		Relieved by 112 T.M.B.	
	8		Came to Labourse	
	9		Kept batteries for practice	
	10		Moved Review marched to Bailewisie	
	11		Marched to Beamer.	
	12		Came to Brias South Huers.	
	13		Resting	
	14		Marched to G. Baudel	
	15		Arrived Manning Wood.	
16-17			Staff Say	

Army Form C. 2118

WAR DIARY
or
INTELLIGENCE SUMMARY
(Erase heading not required.)

19 Trench Mortar Battery
July 1916

Place	Date	Hour	Summary of Events and Information	Remarks and references to Appendices
Mametz Wood	19		Supplied carrying party 15 Trenches under Lt. Morgan.	Casualties O.R.
	20		Sent 2 mortars up to High Wood under Lt. Davies for Barrage purposes. Burnied on offensive barrage 2nd Bn. R.W.F. in an attack about 20 rounds fired and enemy Machine gun knocked out. Lt. Davies recommended also Sgt Jones. The Battery also furnished guards and escorts to German Prisoners. This is girt relief up to Lt Davies and his teams under the circumstances but not successful owing to heavy counter attack and damage placed on road. However Lt Davies managed to bring his teams & guns out without any casualties or damage to mortars.	W. M. 2. 1.
	21		Sent up 2 mortars & teams to High Wood for Defence work and were relieved by 7.T.M.B. at 12 midnight.	3 2
	22		Returned to Buire.	
	23–31		Training and supervising.	Total O. O.R. W. 1. 7. M. 1.

W.F. Coy
Capt OC 19 T.M.B.
3rd Aug, 1916

19th Brigade.
<u>33rd Division</u>.

<u>19th BRIGADE LIGHT TRENCH MORTAR BATTERY</u>

<u>AUGUST 1916</u>

Original.

Army Form C. 2118
Vol 2

WAR DIARY
INTELLIGENCE SUMMARY
(Erase heading not required.)

19 T.M.B

Instructions regarding War Diaries and Intelligence Summaries are contained in F.S. Regs., Part II. and the Staff Manual respectively. Title Pages will be prepared in manuscript.

Place	Date Aug.	Hour	Summary of Events and Information	Remarks and references to Appendices
Buire Becourt	1-5		Reorganising & training.	
	6		Took over from 153rd T.M.B.	
	9		2nd Lt Beaulin & Sergt Jones to HQ instructor at XV corps school of grenades.	
	12		Handed over to 100th T.M.B.	
Fricourt	13		Took over from 98th T.M.B.	
	14		Men westherg under Town Major.	
	15		Visited O.C. 98 T.M.B. at Bazincourt & arrange loan of 1 Officer & 8 crews & Stokes.	
High Wood	16		2nd Lt Armstrong 3 Spt. 16 aren to High Wood.	
	17			
	18		Sergt & 2nd Lt Pink relieved 98th T.M.B. 92nd Lt Armstrong. 2nd Lt Armstrong in High Wood. Rounds fired 25, on Wood Lane	1 O.R. wounded.
	19		Action & men in High Wood.	
	20			
	21		1 Beau fired 100 rounds in support of raid on enemy trench to west of enemy Wood. 6 rounds fired on Wood Lane	
	22		Sergt & Lt Pink relieved by 2 Lt Morgan. 6 rounds fired near Wood corner of H Wood.	
	23		Carrying party of 100 others registering new trench N.E. from Wood Lane 6 rounds & 12 rounds on Wood Lane in indication.	
	24		Carrying party of 100 from the 8th Battalion in new trench. 18 rounds fired.	
	25		2Lt Armstrong received 2 Lt. Morgan	
	26		7 Rounds fired on Wood Lane & 12 on H. Wood Trench	
	27	5am	19 T.M.B relieved by 1st T.M.B.	
	28		cleaning guns etc.	
Fricourt	29-30		In support	
	31	1.30pm	Moved to Ribemont.	

A S Riley Capt.
O.C. 19 T.M.B.

33RD DIVISION
19TH INFY BDE

19TH MACHINE GUN COY.
FEB 1916 - JAN 1918

WAR DIARY
INTELLIGENCE SUMMARY

Place	Date	Hour	Summary of Events and Information	Remarks and references to Appendices
In the Field	1916 24 Feb.		The 19th Brigade Machine Gun Company was nominally formed today while the Brigade is in Brigade Rest. The Machine Guns being French stores in the Divisional Group (since 27th December 1915) and half the personnel of the Company being in the Trenches only an Officer and two Sections (2/Royal Welch Fusiliers and 1/Cameronians) composed the actual Company.	
"	5th March		The Company relieved Machine Gun Detachments of 100th Infantry Brigade (8 guns) in the CUINCHY Sector. The 9th Motor Machine Gun Battery remained in in 4 Reserve positions.	
"	7th March		The 1/Middlesex and 2/A.&S.H. and 2/R.W.F. and Sutherland Highlanders relieved the Company from their battalions, viz no 1 completes the Company with the weapons of the 2nd half will remain in the trenches as Infantry. The Company relieved the fun teams on February 9th & the 9th Motor Machine Gun Battery in the reserve positions.	
"	9th March		The three gun positions N.9 of LA BASSEE Canal were relieved by the 114th Brigade or the Brigade front being moved south of the Canal.	

Army Form C. 2118

WAR DIARY
or
INTELLIGENCE SUMMARY
(Erase heading not required.)

Instructions regarding War Diaries and Intelligence Summaries are contained in F. S. Regs., Part II. and the Staff Manual respectively. Title Pages will be prepared in manuscript.

Place	Date	Hour	Summary of Events and Information	Remarks and references to Appendices
In the field	16th March		The Company was relieved by the Machine Gun Detachment of the 98th Brigade with the exception of 4 gun team which remained in army shortage of machine gunners in the 98th Brigade.	
	4th March		The Company relieved Machine Gun Detachment (No 98 Brigade in the Auchy sector with the exception of 4 gun section held by 11th Motor Machine Gun Battery.	
	9th April 10th April		Pte Moulden was wounded in the head in R7 (KINGSWAY) position whilst relieved by the Machine Gun Detachment of the 98th Brigade. The Company still man the four gun position.	
	18th April		The Company relieved the Machine Gun Detachment of the 1st Brigade in the CUINCHY sector.	
	19th April		Sergeant Drum was wounded by shell-fire in S6 (KEY TERRACE) position.	
	4th May		The Company was relieved by the Machine Gun Detachment of the 98th Brigade. The Company moved to rest billets at BETHUNE. Twelve guns were brought out of the trenches.	
	8th May		To remain in Gun Park belonging to the Company were cleaned from the Machine Gun's and the day was spent in	

Army Form C. 2118

WAR DIARY
INTELLIGENCE SUMMARY
(Erase heading not required.)

Instructions regarding War Diaries and Intelligence Summaries are contained in F.S. Regs., Part II. and the Staff Manual respectively. Title Pages will be prepared in manuscript.

Place	Date	Hour	Summary of Events and Information	Remarks and references to Appendices
In the Field	5th May contd		cleaning the guns which were out of the first time since 27th December 1915.	
	6th May	10.30am	Colonel Chaplin temporarily commanding the brigade inspected the transport lines and billets of the Company	
		10.45am	At Hd Qy COLLEGE DES JEUNES FILLES. The Brigade Veterinary officer visited and inspected the horses, lines and harness.	
		2.30pm	Model transport and vehicle were shown by 3/R.W.F. Transport in view of uniformity in Brigade	
	7th May		General cleaning of guns, ammunition and saddlery.	
	8th May		General cleaning of guns, ammunition and harness.	
	9th May		General cleaning of guns, ammunition and limbers.	
	10th May		Brigade Route March. Inspection en route by Brigadier and by Divisional General.	
	11th May		The Company paraded under Section officers to gun drill	
	12th May		The Company paraded under Section officers for gun drill except No 3 Section which went to the Ranges.	

WAR DIARY / INTELLIGENCE SUMMARY

Army Form C. 2118

Instructions regarding War Diaries and Intelligence Summaries are contained in F. S. Regs., Part II. and the Staff Manual respectively. Title Pages will be prepared in manuscript.

(Erase heading not required.)

Place	Date	Hour	Summary of Events and Information	Remarks and references to Appendices
In the field	13th May		The Company was busy working party improving the horse lines and building a Field Oven.	
"	14th May		The Company continued on the work of the previous day.	
"	15th May		The Company paraded under orders of the Company S.M. Officer. In the afternoon the guns etc & packing the Limbers preparatory to cleaning & proceeding to the trenches.	
"	16th May		The Company relieved the 100th Brigade Machine Gun Company in the AVCHY Sector manning 10 guns. The remaining 6 guns were kept in reserve at Company Headquarters at BEUVRY. The Reserve teams were billeted in the Rue of BEUVRY. The Transport took over the transport lines & occupied by Transport of the 100th Brigade Machine Gun Company in BEUVRY.	
"	17th May		The Transport erected a harness room. The reserve teams were occupied in general cleaning & billets.	
"	18th May / 19th May		2nd Lieut J.W. Westfield joined the Company as reinforcement. Working Party proceeded to the trenches in the purpose of building Gun Emplacements in LEWIS ALLEY.	

WAR DIARY
INTELLIGENCE SUMMARY
(Erase heading not required.)

Army Form C. 2118

Instructions regarding War Diaries and Intelligence Summaries are contained in F. S. Regs., Part II. and the Staff Manual respectively. Title Pages will be prepared in manuscript.

Place	Date	Hour	Summary of Events and Information	Remarks and references to Appendices
In the field	20th May		Sergeant Major Snider relinquished the appointment of Company Sergeant Major at his own request, Sergeant Liddle appointed.	
"	21st May	9 a.m.	The reserve team paraded by 9 a.m. for Church Parade	
"	22nd May	1:15 pm	The reserve team relieved the team in the line. Parade at 1:15 P.M.	
"	23rd May		Our artillery carried out bombardments of the enemy's trenches at 4 different periods during which we co-operated with indirect fire from a Stokes Jarvis mounting.	
"	24th May	9 a.m.	Church Parade. A work party was sent to indirect fire position in (Lewis Alley) LEWIS ALLEY and to carry S.A.A. for indirect fire position.	
"	27th May		A field oven was constructed at the huts, BEUVRY S.E.	
"	30th May		Our Reserve teams relieved the guns teams in the line.	
"	30th May		19 men from 5th D.R. joined for duty as reinforcements.	
"	31st May		3 men arrived to join Coy. O.C. 182nd M.G. Coy. was attached for instructions.	

Army Form C. 2118.

WAR DIARY
INTELLIGENCE SUMMARY.
(Erase heading not required.)

Instructions regarding War Diaries and Intelligence Summaries are contained in F. S. Regs., Part II. and the Staff Manual respectively. Title pages will be prepared in manuscript.

Place	Date	Hour	Summary of Events and Information	Remarks and references to Appendices
In the Field	3rd June	—	Relief of teams in line by reserve teams.	
	4th June	9am	Church Parade.	
	9th June		Coy H.Q. moved from BEUVRY to ANNEZIN. 12 guns were relieved by 100th M.G. Coy. 37 S.R. attached men returned to duty.	
	10th June			
	11th 15th		Advanced drill practised.	
	15th June		Reinforcement of 1 Saddler & 1 Driver & 1 Trans. arrived. 12 guns relieved 118th M.G. Coy in GIVENCHY sector. One section with 4 guns was sent to be attached to 100th M.G.Coy.	
	16th June		Coy H.Q. moved from ANNEZIN to ESSARS.	
			4 guns were relieved by the 98th M.G. Coy. SPITBANK team came on and below relief. Capt W.H.G. Pery-Knox Gore proceeded on leave to the U.K. Coy H.Q. moved from ESSARS to BEUVRY – 25 PREOL ROAD. Company was engaged in cleaning guns & re-...ing.	

Army Form C. 2118.

WAR DIARY
INTELLIGENCE SUMMARY.
(Erase heading not required.)

Instructions regarding War Diaries and Intelligence Summaries are contained in F. S. Regs., Part II. and the Staff Manual respectively. Title pages will be prepared in manuscript.

Place	Date	Hour	Summary of Events and Information	Remarks and references to Appendices
In the field	19th June		Company engaged in clearing field boxes and ammunition Returned 2 guns J. 98th M.G. Coy in GIVENCHY section. 2 guns of Coy were relieved in CUINCHY section by 98th M.G. Coy.	
	20th June			
	21st June		Relieved 11 guns of 98th M.G. Coy in GIVENCHY section. 1 Gun damaged by shell fire 1 Broker anvil.	
	22nd		Reinforcement 2Lt. W.Y. Greig.	
	24th June		2Lt. W.Y. Greig wounded in head by Shell fire and removed to 133rd Div Casualty Clearing Station. BETHUNE. Capt. W.C. Pery-Knox-Gore returned from leave	
	25th June		Reserve teams relieved 9 gun teams in the line.	
	27th June		2/Lieut L.J. Grant joined the Company as Reinforcement from the base.	
	30th June		2/Lieut C.B. Dean joined the Company as a Reinforcement from the base. 2/Lieut J.R. Grey evacuated from 33rd Divisional Casualty Clearing Station.	

19th Inf.Bde.
33rd Div.

19th MACHINE GUN COMPANY.

J U L Y

1 9 1 6

Army Form C. 2118.

19 M.G. Coy

1st 6

WAR DIARY
or
INTELLIGENCE SUMMARY.
(Erase heading not required.)

Place	Date	Hour	Summary of Events and Information	Remarks and references to Appendices
In the field	3rd July		Capt. H.J.E. Bacon went to 33rd Div. Hospital BETHUNE.	
"	4th July		Relief of 9 guns by 9 guns. Coy teams in reserve.	
"	5th July		On the night of 5th & 6th July guns cooperated with the 2nd Royal Welsh Fusiliers in their raid on the enemy trenches. (with indirect fire only) The packing gland of one Vickers gun was damaged.	
"	6th July		Pte Bill went to hospital.	
"	7th July		On the night of 7 & 8 July the Coy was relieved by the 188th M.G. Coy. Pte Ford No 3 Sect was wounded.	
"	8th July		The Coy moved from LE PREOL to OBLINGHEM.	
"	9th July		The Coy moved from OBLINGHEM and entrained at YOUDERVILL STATION for AMIENS.	
"	10th July		The Coy detrained at AMIENS and marched to POULAINVILLE.	
"	11th July		The Coy marched from POULAINVILLE to DAOURS. The Division joined the V Corps, Fourth Army.	

Army Form C. 2118.

WAR DIARY
or
INTELLIGENCE SUMMARY.
(Erase heading not required.)

Instructions regarding War Diaries and Intelligence Summaries are contained in F. S. Regs., Part II. and the Staff Manual respectively. Title pages will be prepared in manuscript.

Place	Date	Hour	Summary of Events and Information	Remarks and references to Appendices
In the Field	12th July		The Coy. moved from DAOURS to BUIRE sur ANCRE. Sergeant Paddy No 1 Section went to hospital	
"	13th July		An inspection of guns and limbers was carried out by Section Officers	
"	14th July		The Coy. moved from BUIRE to MEAULTE and bivouaced outside the village at night. Camp shelled but no casualties.	
"	15th July		The Coy. moved up to MAMETZ WOOD. Four Officers were left behind in reserve. Lt. Do MORGAN, Drum RUSSELL, 7. 3 Horses wounded.	
"	16th July		Lt. MORGAN replaced by Lt. DEAN. Lt. W.T. Boughey moved up to front line 1000 yds. behind HIGH WOOD with 2 guns. He returned after four hours. Ptes Yates and Richards gassed from gas shells. Pte Allan wounded.	
"	17th July		Bde. was relieved and Coy had no guns in front line.	

WAR DIARY or INTELLIGENCE SUMMARY

Army Form C. 2118.

Place	Date	Hour	Summary of Events and Information	Remarks and references to Appendices
In the field	18th July		6 guns of Coy. were sent forward to BAZENTIN LE PETIT under 2/Lt DEAN. No guns were fired.	
"	19th July		Relieved by 98th Bde. M.G. Coy, and went back (west side) in reserve.	
"	20th July		To BAZENTIN LE PETIT (west side) in reserve. No 4 Section under 2/Lt Mayfield went forward with the 5th Scottish Rifles in their attack on HIGH WOOD. The guns were pushed forward after the assaulting line had gone forward and managed to get good positions in the wood. These had to be abandoned after the assaulting troops had been forced to withdraw. At 11 p.m. 2/Lt. DEAN with other four guns went forward and took up positions in HIGH WOOD. Casualties for the day were as follows. 2/Lt — wounded. — No 8 Sergt Cavanaghein 1/Cpl Brown wounded; also Pt Stevens killed. Pt Carns, Sgt Healy appointed C.S.M. 118th M.G. Coy.	

WAR DIARY
or
INTELLIGENCE SUMMARY.
(Erase heading not required.)

Army Form C. 2118.

Instructions regarding War Diaries and Intelligence Summaries are contained in F. S. Regs., Part II. and the Staff Manual respectively. Title pages will be prepared in manuscript.

Place	Date	Hour	Summary of Events and Information	Remarks and references to Appendices
In the Field	21st July		Nos. 1 & 4 Sections relieved by Nos. 2 & 3 sections at 3am. The Coy. was relieved late at night by the 151st M.G. Coy. of 51st (Highland) Territorial Division. During the operations of the previous days the guns were worked by teams of only four men under one N.C.O. This was found to be insufficient owing to the long distance guns had to be carried forward, over very difficult ground and often under extremely heavy shell fire. It was impossible for gun teams to carry more than 25 boxes of S.A.A. Belted ammunition when going into action.	
"	22nd July		The day was devoted to cleaning up guns. The Coy. ready to move at a two hours notice.	
"	23rd July		The day was devoted to cleaning up guns and limbers.	

Army Form C. 2118.

WAR DIARY
or
INTELLIGENCE SUMMARY.
(Erase heading not required.)

Instructions regarding War Diaries and Intelligence Summaries are contained in F. S. Regs., Part II. and the Staff Manual respectively. Title pages will be prepared in manuscript.

Place	Date	Hour	Summary of Events and Information	Remarks and references to Appendices
In the Field	23rd July		Reinforcements of 3 2/Cpls. and 25 men arrived from Base	
In the Field	24th July		L/Sergeon Section paraded under Section Major for advanced drill	
"	25th July		Capt H.F. Bacon TL. Strand Returned from Hospital. Capt H.S. Bacon appointed Temporary Town Major. BOITTE Section paraded under Section Major in morning loading parade in morning fire action & rifle helmets inspected. Pte W. Jones tried by field General Court Martial at Cerqy. H.Q. for (1) entering a disorderly house (2) Drunkenness. Lt D. Campbell acted as Prosecutor. Lt W.T. Boughey as a member of the Court	
"	26th July		A draft of 85 N.C.O. and men arrived today. Parade of B Coy at 9.30 a.m. for advanced drill. Langshaw instructed under Pte Hok. Two men went to hospital (on with Scabies.) Lt. A.D.D. BONNOR evacuated from 19th Field Ambulance	
"	27th July			
"	28th July		Coy Parade at 9.30 am	

Army Form C. 2118.

WAR DIARY
or
INTELLIGENCE SUMMARY.
(Erase heading not required.)

Instructions regarding War Diaries and Intelligence Summaries are contained in F. S. Regs., Part II. and the Staff Manual respectively. Title pages will be prepared in manuscript.

Place	Date	Hour	Summary of Events and Information	Remarks and references to Appendices
In the field	29th July		Coy parade at 9.30 am. Continuation of advanced Drill Instruction for new men. 2nd Lts A.T. BROGDEN and W.B. BABER joined Coy.	
	30th July		Church Parades — Church of England — 11 am. Presbyterian — 11 am. Roman Catholic — 9.30 am	
	31st July		A draft of 1 N.C.O. and 8 men arrived. Coy Paraded at 9.30 a.m. in continuation of Advanced Drill	

19th Brigade.
33rd Division.

19th BRIGADE.

MACHINE GUN COMPANY

AUGUST 1916

Army Form C. 2118.

19th Machine Gun Coy

Vol 2 1

WAR DIARY
INTELLIGENCE SUMMARY.
(Erase heading not required.)

Place	Date	Hour	Summary of Events and Information	Remarks and references to Appendices
	3rd Aug 1916		The Company came into its programme of advanced drill for the driver now in instruction in Vickers Gun in the last draft, every morning from 9.30 am till 12.30 am while the Brigade is at BUIRE.	
	6th Aug 7th Aug		2nd/Lt WRIGHT & CLARK from Coy from Base 19th Company moved from BUIRE to L'AMIRE & W.J. FRICOURT.	
	7th Aug		The Company had practice in crawling forward to positions with guns, tripods and ammunition; taking advantage of every possible cover.	
	8th Aug		A similar programme to that of the previous day was carried out.	
	9th Aug		Morning spent in short route march and physical training.	
	10th Aug		Capt & A/Major E. Bacon, 2nd in Command of Coy appointed O.C. 95th M.G. Coy. Morning spent in Gun Drill.	Sgt A/Major E Bacon Comdg 19th Machine Gun Company

WAR DIARY
or
INTELLIGENCE SUMMARY.

Army Form C. 2118.

19th Machine Gun Coy

Place	Date	Hour	Summary of Events and Information	Remarks and references to Appendices
In the field	11th Aug		Coy went on moving under section officers.	
"	12th Aug		Day spent in thoroughly cleaning guns and packing limbers.	
"	13th Aug	4 am	The Coy moved to FRICOURT with the Brigade which is now in support, and left behind with "D" Echelon all other Ranks over establishment strength; also all Lewis Gun officers of the Coy. Worked the Machine Gun Ration in HIGH WOOD. Four others have been in position on that part of front. 2nd Lt ROBERTSON and Coy were on that part of front.	
"	15th Aug 17th Aug		Nothing unusual to note. 2nd Lt. W.B. BABER slightly wounded by splinter from a premature burst. B one 1 even shell, and	
"	18th Aug		admitted to hospital. Attack in afternoon by the 4th Brigade of Division. Coy standing by, ready to move at a moment's notice.	

Hay. KerGon Bflair Coy commandy
19 Machine Gun Coy

WAR DIARY
INTELLIGENCE SUMMARY

Army Form C. 2118.

19th Machine Gun Coy

Place	Date	Hour	Summary of Events and Information	Remarks and references to Appendices
In the Field	19th Aug	2am	Coy relieved 98th M.G. Coy. in HIGH WOOD. Eight guns were placed in front and support line, the remaining Eight in Reserve line near BAZENTIN-le-GRAND Village. Two "Indirect fire" positions were built during day. 6 O.R. wounded during day. (3 wounded (shell fire) and 3 suffering from shell shock)	
"	20th "		4 O.R. Casualties in front line (either wounded or suffering from shell shock.) 1000 rounds per gun (2 guns) in tracks taking the Uhlan Exits.	
"	21st "		2000 rounds per gun (2 guns) fired on new German trench running N.S. from S.11.b.25.10 and tracks behind HIGH WOOD. Lt. A.N.M. WATKINS joined his Coy (Rfg 7.C.Sw)	
"	22nd "		½ Coy under Sgt Clarke & 81 O.R. returned to HQ & Base under charge of Sgt Clarke. ½ Coy in front line relieved by ½ Coy in Reserve line. 4500 rounds fired at new German tr running W & from their & Rd.	SH.D.25.20 to trench thence to Rd
"	23rd "		Sgt. WRIGHT admitted to hospital suffering from	Rfg. Knowles Patton Commanding 19th Machine Gun Company

WAR DIARY
or
INTELLIGENCE SUMMARY

Army Form C. 2118.

19th Machine Gun Coy

Place	Date	Hour	Summary of Events and Information	Remarks and references to Appendices
In the field	23rd		5000 rounds fired at new German trench running N.E. from S.11.d.25.10 and tracks between HIGH WOOD.	
	24th		Right Brigade of Division attacked an enemy 4 guns firing indirect fire from George tree during an artillery bombardment on German trench running N.E. from S.11. from S.11.d.25 to 16,800 rounds were fired during our artillery bombardment. 21,300 rounds during 24 to 5 during 25th. L/Cpl Morrow, Pte. McPherson and Matkas killed on right of 24th. 2 O.R. wounded. Three men killed in previous nights bivouac in QUARRY CEMETRY. 6000 rounds Indirect fire on tracks running N.E. through M.34.d. & SWITCH TR. from S.4.b.5.3 (Rly Map 57c.5w)	
	25th			
	26th	4.45pm	Lt W. T. BUGHEY offered 2nd in Command. 103 Bgde. to Coy. relieved other Coy. 6000 rounds Indirect fire free in SWITCH TRENCH from S.4.b.5.3 to S.5.d.5.4. and tracks through M.34.d.	Letters: Thos Goss Patten, Rowdy 19 Machine Gun Company

Army Form C. 2118.

WAR DIARY
INTELLIGENCE SUMMARY.
(Erase heading not required.)

19th Machine Gun Coy.

Place	Date	Hour	Summary of Events and Information	Remarks and references to Appendices
In the Field	26th Aug		1 N.C.O & 5 men joined Coy from the Base. Pte HAINES tried by Field General Court Martial for "Self inflicted Wounds" (behaving negligently hence a Gun Burst.)	
"	27th Aug		2nd Lt. C. TAYLOR. 13th H.L.I. joined Coy from the Base. The Coy was relieved in the East by the 184th M.G. Coy and returned to FRICOURT. 1 O.R. wounded. 5000 rounds indirect line fired on Elsia Switch TR. from S4.b.5.3. to S.5. central (2 guns) (Ref. Map 57 C Sw.) there was fired from Nood side 23rd.	
"	28th Aug		Guns and Ammunition was thoroughly cleaned. 1 O.R. joined Coy.	
"	30th Aug		Pte HAINES awarded 14 days F.P. No 1. Later promulgated. 1 N.C.O. and 7 men joined Coy from the Base.	
"	31st Aug		Coy moved from FRICOURT to RIBEMONT.	

Major Roper Cotton Cavalry
19th Machine Gun Company.

vol 8

WAR DIARY
INTELLIGENCE SUMMARY

19th Machine Gun Coy

Place	Date	Hour	Summary of Events and Information	Remarks and references to Appendices
Yth	1st Sept		The Coy marched from RIBEMONT to MOLLIENS-AU-BOIS along with the rest of Brigade. An hours halt was made on the way for dinner.	
to	2nd Sept		The Coy marched from MOLLIENS-AU-BOIS to AUTHEUX. Two ordinary Coy halts fell out. There were the first to fall out in Coy since its formation, two hours halt for dinner. Church Service in morning for Wesleyans and Non Conformists. Afternoon spent by remainder in cleaning guns and limbers.	
to	3rd Sept		The Coy marched from AUTHEUX to VILLERS L'HOPITAL. During the above marches the want of a cooker was felt while the battalions in the Brigade were able to have hot meals when the Brigade made the hour or two "hours" halt no above described, the Machine Gun Coy had to content itself with tinned meat.	
to	4th Sept			
to	5th Sept		The Coy marched from VILLERS L'HOPITAL to LINZEUX.	

Captain O.C D. Campbell 2 Lt Adjt
19th M.G. Coy

WAR DIARY
or
INTELLIGENCE SUMMARY
(Erase heading not required.)

Army Form C. 2118.

19th Machine Gun Coy

Place	Date	Hour	Summary of Events and Information	Remarks and references to Appendices
Field	5th Sept		Sgt Wright rejoined Coy from hospital.	
do	6th Sept		The Coy. marched from LINZEUX to HIRECOURT	
do	7th Sept		Parade in morning to clean equipment.	
do	8th Sept		The Coy. marched from HIRECOURT to REBRUVIETTE	
do	9th Sept		The Coy. marched from REBRUVIETTE & BREVILLERS. Pte Biggins was tried in afternoon by F.G.C.M. at 2nd R.W. Fus. Headquarters IVERGNY, under Sec 9(2). Brigade now in VII Corps Third Army.	
do	10th Sept		The Coy. moved from BREVILLERS to POMMIER and had a two hours' halt on the way for dinner. 2nd Lieut. MERFIELD and five Other Ranks left for Third Army Rest Camp, BOUROGNE. Lieut. P.G. Robertson left for England to take up a commission in the 3/7th Argyll & Sutherland Highlanders (T.F.)	
do	11th Sept		In afternoon the Coy. moved into trenches and relieved the 57th M.G. Coy in the HANNESCAMP -	

Captain Comdg 19th Mchy Gun Coy
15th nd. Coy

WAR DIARY
INTELLIGENCE SUMMARY
(Erase heading not required.)

Army Form C. 2118.

19th M.G. Coy

Place	Date	Hour	Summary of Events and Information	Remarks and references to Appendices
In the Field	11th Sept.		Cont'd: [HANNESCAMP] – FONQUEVILLERS Sector. Five M.G. positions in the front line were taken over. Six in the village line while the remaining five were kept in reserve. From 8.30 p.m. – 12.30 p.m. 3 Machine Guns fired Indirect fire on E.29.9.2.9 to E.29.B.15.25. and E.29.C.5.6 to E.29.C.50.65 also E.30.A.20.65 to E.30.A.20.85. Pte 13 Gguns was awarded 28 days F.P. No 1.	(Ref map FONQUEVILLERS) 3000 rds
"	12th Sept		Indirect fire was brought to bear on E.30.A.20.25 to E.30.A.65.50; also E.30.a.20.61 to E.30.a.w.85; T.29.B.W.75 to E.24.D.29.S	3000 rds
"	13th Sept		Indirect fire was used on gap made in wire by our artillery; and E.24.C.75.75. ; E.30a.25.65. to E.30.A.35.35 – 3000 rounds.	
"	14th Sept		Indirect fire was used on gap in wire, on tracks behind the German lines. 3500 rounds were fired	
"	15th Sept		3,500 rounds (indirect fire) were fired on roads and tracks behind German lines; also gap in wire	
"	16th Sept		4,000 rounds (Indirect fire) were fired on Pigeon Wood, La Bray'lle Farm and roads behind German lines	

W Campbell Captain Commdg
19th M.G. Coy

Army Form C. 2118.

WAR DIARY
INTELLIGENCE SUMMARY.
(Erase heading not required.)

19th M.G. Coy

Instructions regarding War Diaries and Intelligence Summaries are contained in F. S. Regs., Part II. and the Staff Manual respectively. Title pages will be prepared in manuscript.

Place	Date	Hour	Summary of Events and Information	Remarks and references to Appendices
In the Field 19th Sept	17th Sept		2000 rounds (Indirect Fire) were fired on Gaps in enemy wire, roads and tracks behind German lines.	
"	18th Sept		4000 rounds (Indirect Fire) were fired on Gaps in wire, Pigeon Wood, La Brayelle Farm, and roads behind German lines.	
"	19th Sept		2/Lt. L.H. MERFIELD and 5 O.R. arrived from Rest Camp. Bdr. LONG N.E. 2 O.R. proceeded to Rest Camp. Pte HAINES No 2 Section proceeded to England on leave. 2000 rounds (Direct Fire) were fired on roads and tracks behind German lines, also gaps in German wire. Coy H.Q. shelled with L.2 How. Shells.	
"	20th Sept			
"	20th Sept		4000 rounds (Indirect Fire) & were fired on roads and tracks behind German lines.	
"	21st Sept		4800 rounds (Indirect Fire) fired on roads & tracks behind German lines. Removed Coy Headquarters from HANNES CAMP to BIENVILLERS.	

W Sanphill 2/Lt /Adj. 19th M.L. Coy Capt Comdg

Army Form C. 2118.

WAR DIARY
or
INTELLIGENCE SUMMARY.
(Erase heading not required.)

19th M.G. Coy

Place	Date	Hour	Summary of Events and Information	Remarks and references to Appendices
In the Field	22nd Sept		3000 rounds (Indirect fire) fired on PIGEON WOOD, La BRAYELLE Fm and roads and tracks behind German lines	
"	23rd Sept		4000 rounds (Indirect fire) fired on PIGEON WOOD, LA BRAYELLE FARM, Gap in wire and roads behind German lines.	
"	24th Sept		Divine Service for five teams in BIENVILLERS. 4000 rounds (Indirect fire) fired on roads tracks behind German lines. Sgt Got arrived from M.G. Advanced course of Instruction at CAMIERS. 2/Lt J. GRANT and Servant 2/Cpl HOSH proceeded to attend Advanced M.G. Course of Instruction at CAMIERS. 2 O.R. also proceeded to Base Camp, BOULOGNE.	
"	25th Sept			
"	26th Sept		1000 rounds (Indirect fire) fired on PIGEON WOOD, La BRAYELLE FARM and Gap in German wire. Capt. PERY-KNOX-GORE was on special leave to the United Kingdom. 1000 rounds were	

W Tampler 2/Lt Adjt
19th M.G. Coy.

Army Form C. 2118.

19th M.G. Coy

WAR DIARY
INTELLIGENCE SUMMARY.
(Erase heading not required.)

Place	Date	Hour	Summary of Events and Information	Remarks and references to Appendices
In the field	26th Sept	Cont =	Fired on tracks and roads behind German lines, the majority of targets being selected according to the information gathered from the Battalion Intelligence Section. Ever-relief of five guns carried out.	
	27th Sept.		Capt Ring has gone promoted Major - the promotion to date from 14/7/16. 4000 rounds (Indirect fire) fired on Pigeon Wood (south side) and tracks and roads behind German lines. Lt MERFIELD went to hospital. The usual number of rounds was fired on German roads, tracks and lines.	
	28th Sept			
	29th Sept		4000 rounds (Indirect fire) fired on woods, roads, tracks behind German lines.	
	30th Sept		The Coy moved from trenches and BIENVILLERS to HUMBERCAMP, on relief by the 167th M.G. Coy.	

W Humphrey 2/Lt Adj.
19th M.G. Coy

WAR DIARY

Army Form C. 2118.

19th Machine Gun Coy

Place	Date	Hour	Summary of Events and Information	Remarks and references to Appendices
In the field	1st Oct		The Coy moved from HUMBERCAMP to LUCHEUX. Parade according to Brigade Time Table 2 O.P.	
"	2nd Oct		arrived from REST CAMP, BOURGNE and 20E departed for same camp.	
"	3rd Oct		Sunday. Parade in fields in morning.	
"	4th Oct		Y.G. Camp marched at Coy H.Q. another wet day and no parades and am	
"	5th Oct		Parades according to Brigade Time Table.	
"	6th Oct		Tactical Exercise carried out by Coy in morning.	
"	7th Oct		Major PERCY KNOX COTE returned from leave. Parades according to Bde Time Table	
"	8th Oct		Coy marched to DOULLENS and took part in Brigade Tactical Exercise. 12 O.P. returned to Base (Surplus).	
"	9th Oct		Parades as usual. Instruction on Gun.	
"	10 Oct		No 1 Section took part in Tactical Exercise at DOULLENS. No 2 Section took part " " at OPPE. Lt J McQUEEN M.G.S. joined Coy from Base Deport 19th M.G. Coy	

Army Form C. 2118.

WAR DIARY
INTELLIGENCE SUMMARY
(Erase heading not required.)

19th Machine Gun Corps.

Place	Date	Hour	Summary of Events and Information	Remarks and references to Appendices
In the Field	11th Oct		Parades as usual. Bn H.Q. and 2 Battalions of Brigade moved up to SAILLY-AU-BOIS. Sgt MAXWELL returned from months furlough.	
"	12th		Moving spare parts of Guns. Coy starting by road to more	
"	13th		Leaving Guns in morning.	
"	14th		No 2 section with 2 officers moved up to BAYENCOURT. One gun placed in trenches; remainder kept at BAYENCOURT.	
"	15th		Divine Service for Church of England denomination.	
"	16th		Parades as usual. Section officers. 2 O.R. left Coy for Course at CAMIERS. 1 O.R. left for School Army School of Cookery. 1 O.R. left for Anti-Gas School.	
"	17th		Parades and Lectures to officers	
"	18th		Coy. moved from LUCHEUX to BEAUCOURT	
"	19th		Coy. moved from BEAUCOURT to MERICOURT. The 19th Infantry	
"	20th		Coy. remained in MERICOURT.	
"	21st		Coy. moved forward to THE CITADEL, EAST of MEAULTE	

Stampier Lt. Coy,
19th M.C. Coy

Army Form C. 2118.

WAR DIARY
INTELLIGENCE SUMMARY.
(Erase heading not required.)

19th Machine Gun Coy

Place	Date	Hour	Summary of Events and Information	Remarks and references to Appendices
—	22nd Oct.		The Coy. moved up to MONTAUBAN VILLAGE.	
—	23rd Oct.		Artificer joined Coy. from the Base.	
—	24th Oct.		The Coy moved up past MONTAUBAN — two sections went into trenches — two were kept in reserve at Coy H.Q. at GUILLEMONT	
—	25th Oct.		1 O.R. killed — ANTELOPE TRENCH	
—	26th Oct.		2 O.R. killed — one in front line and one in reserve. Sgt Humber wounded. MAJOR PERY KNOX GORE O.C. Coy. left Coy on receiving appointment as Corps M.G. Officer.	
—	27th Oct.		Quiet day. No casualties.	
—	28th Oct.		Relief Scheme in the line. Sgt WRIGHT wounded. Attack by 18th Div. Bde. Lieut. D.E. FALKNER joined Coy from 18th Bn. as a/C.O.	
—	29th Oct.		Coy relieved in the F/100 & Mr. Coy and moved to the BRIQUETRIE. No casualties.	
—	30th Oct.			
—	31st		Day spent in cleaning up. W Humphreys Lt [?] Coy	

Vol 10

CONFIDENTIAL

WAR DIARY

OF

19ᵗʰ MACHINE GUN COMPANY

FROM 1ˢᵗ NOV. 1916   TO   30 NOV 1916.

Army Form C. 2118.

WAR DIARY
of
INTELLIGENCE SUMMARY
(Erase heading not required.)

19th Machine Gun Coy.

Instructions regarding War Diaries and Intelligence Summaries are contained in F. S. Regs., Part II. and the Staff Manual respectively. Title Pages will be prepared in manuscript.

Place	Date	Hour	Summary of Events and Information	Remarks and references to Appendices
Bt de Zulu	1st Nov		Day spent in building dug-outs at BRIQUETRIE	
do.	2nd Nov		(MONTAUBAN) Paid men in afternoon. Uneventful day. 33 Other Ranks joined from Laneston to bring up the new Establishment of a Machine Gun Company	
do.	3rd Nov		Coy relieved the 99th M.G. Coy. on the right of 3rd Lt Guards in front one gun in outpost at LES BOEUFS. H in reserve in the FLERS line and 4 at Bn Hd Q. at GUILLEMONT STATION.	
do.	4th Nov		Nothing eventful happened. Heavy shelling but no casualties	
do.	5th Nov		Big attack along front of 5th & 15th British Armies and French 6th Army. Brigade advanced to ridge in front of LE TRANSLOY.	Rhodes Capt

2449 Wt. W14957/M90 750,000 1/16 J.B.C. & A. Forms/C.2118/12.

WAR DIARY or INTELLIGENCE SUMMARY

Army Form C. 2118.

19th Machine Gun Corps

Place	Date	Hour	Summary of Events and Information	Remarks and references to Appendices
In the Field	5/Nov		Front line Guns did some useful work and moved to new positions. Some parties caught by our fire. Our Guns in support did useful work with Lewis fire on the CEMETERY CIRCLE, N. TRANSLOY. 1000 rounds were fired in all that day. Pte. DEMPSTER No 4 Section killed.	
do.	6/Nov		Constructing positions.	
do.	7/Nov		Company relieved by 23rd Machine Gun Company with the exception of one team. She was due to the front line. Fact that the relieving Officer for front line failed to report his arrival to the O.C. Section Coy moved to CARNOY HUTS. Lt. W.C. TAYLOR and one team mentioned above, after having been officially reported missing,	R.W.B. [signature]

WAR DIARY or INTELLIGENCE SUMMARY

Army Form C. 2118.

19th Machine Gun Coy

Place	Date	Hour	Summary of Events and Information	Remarks and references to Appendices
In the Field	8th Oct 1916		Reported at Coy Headquarters at 7 pm. 2 men from Coy missing.	
do	9th "		Coy moved from CARNOY suite to MEAULTE.	
do	10th "		The transport moved out at 1 pm for DAOURS. En route for ROBENLEE.	
do	11th "		Usual day. Parade in morning for Inspection of tube helmets, iron rations & Rifles.	
HQ	12th "		Coy entrained at BOIRE STATION for FRUCOURT approximately 10 mls south of ABBEVILLE. Coy arrived at FRUCOURT in the early hours of the morning. No reveille. Ye MERIEL went in Centre.	
do	13th "		Day spent in cleaning Guns.	
do	14th "		Day spent in cleaning Equipment etc.	

Army Form C. 2118.

WAR DIARY
or
INTELLIGENCE SUMMARY
(Erase heading not required.)

19th Machine Gun Corps

Place	Date	Hour	Summary of Events and Information	Remarks and references to Appendices
In the field	15th Nov		Parades all day. There were Company & Platoon Lectures. Musketry Handling of Arms. Lectures on Loading Fire and Map Reading.	
	16th Nov		Parade in forenoon only.	
	17th Nov		Route march by Company. A great deal of sickness in Coy. - 5 other Ranks being admitted to hospital.	
	18th Nov		Short parade in morning.	
	19th Nov		Divine Service were held for the three different denominations.	
	20th Nov		Lieut. J. CAMPBELL Inverness on leave to the U.K. F.G. Court martial assembled at CITERNE. Pte. Ballum of this Coy was among the accused. Court was adjourned until the 21st inst before Pte Ballum case was heard. He was charged with desertion.	

Army Form C. 2118.

WAR DIARY
or
INTELLIGENCE SUMMARY
(Erase heading not required.)

19th Wiltshire Regt Coy

Instructions regarding War Diaries and Intelligence Summaries are contained in F.S. Regs., Part II. and the Staff Manual respectively. Title Pages will be prepared in manuscript.

Place	Date	Hour	Summary of Events and Information	Remarks and references to Appendices
In the field	21 Mar		Battalion band at F.G. constructed. Parades in morning, inspection P.T., G.A., and Visual Training	
"	22 Mar		Companies were inspected by the G.O.C. Division in the A.M. Construction continued throughout. Six names PH L + Parade 6 officer 235 O.R. Drum presented on leave to U.K.	
"	23 Mar		Parades in A.M. Company, P.T., revolver practice, gun drill and firing stoppages. In the afternoon the Company battled teams defeated the 3rd organisation A.S.C. at first round of the Division Football Competition Set 13. 3-0, in the first round. O/g G.D. Smith 2/Lt Wakefield rejoined from leave in U.K.	
"	24 Mar		O/g G.D. Smith revolver. O/g Smith proceeded on leave to U.K.	
"	25 Mar		Weather bad. Inclement and wet. 2/Lt Grant proceeded on leave to the U.K. 2/Lt Burgess rejoined the Company from a M.G. Course at Camiers	

2449 Wt. W14957/M90 750,000 1/16 J.B.C. & A. Forms/C.2118/12.

Army Form C. 2118.

WAR DIARY
or
INTELLIGENCE SUMMARY
(Erase heading not required.)

14th Machine Gun Corps

Place	Date	Hour	Summary of Events and Information	Remarks and references to Appendices
In the field	26Nov		Weather bad. Church of England and Presbyterian church Parades in the morning, the former at CITERNE and the latter at FRUCOURT.	
"	27Nov		Parades. P.T. and range work, stoppages and rendered further training. Enthusiastic fire and use of dial sights in afternoon. The Company was inspected at noon by Lt Col CLARKE, the Corps Machine Gun Officer. Weather improved. 2Lt. Wilkins proceeded to CAMIERS for M.M.G. Course.	
"	28Nov		Parades. P.T. range, and tactical training.	
"	29Nov		Coys. Company worked in a tactical scheme. Company quiet.	
"	30Nov		Company worked in tactical scheme.	

AWard S. Robertson
Captain
14 M.G. Coy

Army Form C. 2118.

Vol XI

19th Machine Gun Company

WAR DIARY
INTELLIGENCE SUMMARY
(Erase heading not required.)

Place: In the field
Month: December 1916

Date	Hour	Summary of Events and Information	Remarks and references to Appendices
1 Dec.		Company gathered about. Company in new ground. Weather fld.	
2		Weather. Gathered above. C.O. attends a funeral of Turks murder near a culvert aerodrome.	
3		Company parades for bath at HALLECOURT. In consequence there was no divine service.	
4		Gathered work continued.	
5		Gathered work continued. One section employed on road cleaning.	
6		Work done same as on the 5th.	
7		Transport proceeds to forward area by road, senior 2/Lt McQueen in charge, the transport officer being on leave to the U.K.	
8		The Company moves to forward area. Proceeding by rail to AIRAINNES and Entraining there for thereon MERICOURT. Marched from MERICOURT to VAUX. 2/Lt Inglis billeted.	

Army Form C. 2118.

WAR DIARY
or
INTELLIGENCE SUMMARY

(Erase heading not required.)

19th Machine Gun Coy

Place	Date	Hour	Summary of Events and Information	Remarks and references to Appendices
	8th Dec.		Lt Campbell and 2nd Lieut Dean rejoin the Company from leave to U.K.	
	9th Dec.		The Coy. marched from VAUX to Camp 112 — situated on the BRAY – ALBERT road. Lt R.W.S ROBERTSON was exchanged with Second Lieutenant	
	10th Dec.		The Coy. remained at Camp 112.	
			Lieuts Roberton and Taylor proceeded with U.K. on leave.	
	11th Dec.		The Coy. moved from Camp 112 to Camp 17 men took over huts from the French. The Coy. moved via MARICOURT. Lieut D. Campbell was acting Officer	
	12th Dec		The Coy. remained in the Camp	
	13th Dec.		The Coy still in Camp 17. Ptes McIntosh and Biggins to 2 echelon were tried by Field General Court Martial under Sec 9 (a) Army Act. They were convicted. The former awarded 56 days FP No. 1. latter awarded 6 months I.H.L.	St Campbell Lieut Act. 19th M.G.C.

Army Form C. 2118.

WAR DIARY
or
INTELLIGENCE SUMMARY
(Erase heading not required.)

19th Machine Gun Coy

Place	Date	Hour	Summary of Events and Information	Remarks and references to Appendices
	14th Dec.		The Coy relieved the 100th M.G.C. at night. Four Guns only were put into the line. Three sections were billeted at (Camp 20) "B" Echelon was fixed at B.14.C. (Ref. Map 62.C. N.W.)	
	15th Dec.		During the day shape of the communication trenches, communication with the front line guns during daylight was found to be impossible. At this part of the line it was impossible to move about across the open without being sniped at by the German artillery.	
	16th Dec.		Coy relief at night. One other Rank wounded during the relief. Four guns were brought up and placed in the support line. Three men proceeded on furlough to the U.K.	

(Signed) Campbell Rait
Capt. 19th M.G.C.

Army Form C. 2118.

WAR DIARY
or
INTELLIGENCE SUMMARY

(Erase heading not required.)

19th Machine Gun Co

Instructions regarding War Diaries and Intelligence Summaries are contained in F. S. Regs., Part II. and the Staff Manual respectively. Title Pages will be prepared in manuscript.

Place	Date	Hour	Summary of Events and Information	Remarks and references to Appendices
	17th Dec		Very misty day and little shelling.	
	18th Dec		C.Q.M.S. Bayley appointed C.S.M. of 164th M.G.C. Sergeant McAvoy " C.Q.M.S. of 24th M.G.C. Sergeant Duval 63rd M.G.C. appointed C.Q.M.S. of this Coy. Another section relief at night. Lieut A.M.M. WATKINS arrived from M.G. Base courses.	
	19th Dec		Very hard frost and much more shelling. Has made "B" Echelon billets rather tricky during the night.	
	20th Dec		Another section relief. Owing to the wet state of trenches, relief was carried out every 48 hours. Two extra guns were sent up to Coy. dropping line, now making a total of 10 Guns in the line. 2/Lt A.T. BROGDEN returned from leave. Lieut A.M.M. WATKINS and 5 O.R. proceeded on leave to U.K.	B. Murphy Major 19th M.G.C.

2449 Wt. W14957/M90 750,000 1/16 J.B.C. & A. Forms/C.2118/12.

WAR DIARY or INTELLIGENCE SUMMARY

19th Machine Gun Co.

Place	Date	Hour	Summary of Events and Information	Remarks and references to Appendices
	22nd Dec.		Coy. relieved at night by the 98th M.G.C. and moved back - part of the way by bus - to CAMP 17	
	23rd Dec.		Day spent in cleaning up guns, gun etc. were cleaned	
	24th Dec.			
	25th Dec.		Informed visit to camp by G.O.C. Division. During the Company's period of 8 days' trench duty there was only one case of Trench feet.	
	26th Dec.		The whole Brigade moved to CAMP 12	
	27th Dec.		Transport left for VAUCHELLES near ABBEVILLE while the Company entrained for same destination at 6 p.m. at EDGEHILL STN. near BUIRE - SUR- ANCRE. Coy. reached VAUCHELLES same night.	St. Amphus Front M.G. 19th M.G.C.

Army Form C. 2118.

WAR DIARY
or
INTELLIGENCE SUMMARY
(Erase heading not required.)

19th Machine Gun Co.

Place	Date	Hour	Summary of Events and Information	Remarks and references to Appendices
	29th Dec.		Cleaning up. B.O.R. forwarded on Furlough to the U.K.	
	29th Dec.		Parades :- 9 am - 12.30 pm } Br Cleaning } gun gear antitheus etc. 2 pm - 4 pm }	
	30th Dec.		Parades :- Same as for previous day	
	31st Dec.		S. Parades — C.O.'s Parade 10 a.m.	

D Campbell Lieut

for 19th M.G.C.

Vol 12

CONFIDENTIAL

WAR DIARY

OF

19th MACHINE GUN COMPANY

FROM 1st JAN 1917   TO JAN 31st 1917.

Army Form C. 2118.

WAR DIARY
or
INTELLIGENCE SUMMARY
(Erase heading not required.)

19th Machine Gun Co.

Instructions regarding War Diaries and Intelligence Summaries are contained in F. S. Regs., Part II. and the Staff Manual respectively. Title Pages will be prepared in manuscript.

Place	Date	Hour	Summary of Events and Information	Remarks and references to Appendices
In the Field	1st Jan		Parade in forenoon only.	
	2nd Jan		Parade in forenoon. Capt. Phy. In. Gun Drill. In. Sgt. Dill. Sergeant Dixon 63rd M.G. Co. reported for duty and took over the duties of C.Q.M.S.	
	3rd Jan 4th Jan 5th Jan 6th Jan		Parade all day. Those requiring elementary instruction Class started Pte. those not interfered with went on range. Brigade Route March. Transport accompanied the Coy.	
	(7th Jan)		Lieut. S. CAMPBELL appointed O.C. 98th M.G. Co. Lieut. S.G. ARCHIVES, 98th M.G. Co. appointed second in command of the 19th M.G. Co.	MB
	8th Jan		Parade in morning for Phy. Tr. The remainder of the forenoon in all section arrangements	

Army Form C. 2118.

WAR DIARY
or
INTELLIGENCE SUMMARY

(Erase heading not required.)

19ᵗʰ Machine Gun Coy

Instructions regarding War Diaries and Intelligence Summaries are contained in F.S. Regs., Part II. and the Staff Manual respectively. Title Pages will be prepared in manuscript.

Place	Date	Hour	Summary of Events and Information	Remarks and references to Appendices
Field	7 Jan		Church of England Service at 10.30 am at 2 R.W.S. Headquarters.	
	8 Jan		Ordinary training programme carried out.	
	9 Jan		2ⁿᵈ D. Campbell rejoined his post as second in command to the 98ᵗʰ Machine Gun Coy. Lt. R.W.S. Ralston takes up the position of 2ⁿᵈ in Command in Company	
	10 Jan		2ⁿᵈ Lt. O.C. [?] inspects the Company wire transport near Vieux-Berquin. He returned himself as being satisfied with the appearance of the unit. Ordinary work was carried on after the inspection was over. 2/Lt. McGregor proceeded on leave to U.K.	
	11 Jan		Ordinary practice	

Army Form C. 2118.

WAR DIARY
or
INTELLIGENCE SUMMARY
(Erase heading not required.)

19ᵗʰ Welsh [Machine?] Gun Coy

Place	Date	Hour	Summary of Events and Information	Remarks and references to Appendices
Étaples	12 Jan.		Onegale Route march took place in the morning. Rapid firing in the afternoon.	
"	13 Jan.		Ordinary Training programme carried out.	
"	14 Jan.		Church of England service at H.Q. R.W.F.	
"	15 Jan.		Gymkhana meet for the found was to be held this A.M.	
"	16 Jan.		2ᴸᵗ TAYLOR. Attended to CAMIER on a machine gun course. Other stores we returned to Bge H.Q.	
"	17 Jan.		Decamped. Personnel of the Coy. travelled by train to the front and detrained off from VAUCHELLES-LES-QUESNOY at 5.00 A.M. Owned the stores and kits and remained the front of entrainment. PONT-REMY at about 7.00 A.M. Entrained at 10.45 and detrained at BRAY-TOURBIÈRES at about 6.00 P.M. Marched from there to Camp III, where the temporary huts already erected.	
"	18 Jan.		O.C. went up to the line to inspect trenches to be taken over from the	

Army Form C. 2118.

WAR DIARY
or
INTELLIGENCE SUMMARY
(Erase heading not required.)

19 Machine Gun Coy

Place	Date	Hour	Summary of Events and Information	Remarks and references to Appendices
Inter field	19 Jan		Fine. Left at 4.30 A.M. and arrived at 2.00 P.M. Weather cold. Several parties details since yesterday morning and about 54 inches in the ground now. Company moved from Camp 111 to SUZANNE. Lt. MERFIELD and 2Lt. BROGDEN & WATKINS proceeded to the trenches to inspect the line. Company at 4.30 A.M. and joining the Company at SUZANNE in the evening.	
	20.'9		The Company relieved the Machine Guns of the French 35 Byn in front extending from SOMON FARM on the South of the SOMME to 12.C Central. No 1 Sect is the hut at SOMON FARM the river two guns in each side of the canal. No 3 Sect man the right battalion, but No 2 Sect man the left. and No 4 Sect in support in the much of the river. Company left SUZANNE at 2.15 and filed up the French guides to CURLU. 14 guides were supplied for each gun also certain Officers and a Sergeant from each section found about in the early morning and stayed in the trenches with the French during the day.	

2449 Wt. W14957/Mg0 750,000 1/16 J.B.C. & A. Forms/C.2118/12.

Army Form C. 2118.

WAR DIARY
or
INTELLIGENCE SUMMARY

(Erase heading not required.)

19th Machine Gun Coy

Place	Date	Hour	Summary of Events and Information	Remarks and references to Appendices
P.C. Giroux		2.0 g.m	Company H.Q. now temporarily established at P.C. GIRODON. Relief now is complete sweeps. Relief reported correct by runner by 12.00 midnight. 19th T.M.B. supplied an evening party of 32 men. Weather cold. Ground hard and covered with snow. One Section have having half their guns in one night.	
	21.3m		The remaining Bend guns left the line today. Company H.Q. moved to PETIT CARRIER. Shelling not severe. A good deal of German M.G. fire noted entirely on No. 2 rest front. Hostile aeroplane was observed flying from W. to E. at a height of about 1000 feet. Still cold.	
	22 g.m		Had four steel baths. Walking very good. Everything is normal. Nothing to report.	
	23 g.m		P.G. MAJOR No. 2 Sect. wounded in arm by a rifle grenade. Slight wound in belly. Sgt. POTTER reported from 10th M.B. Coy to assume duties of Sect in Command.	

Army Form C. 2118.

WAR DIARY
or
INTELLIGENCE SUMMARY

(Erase heading not required.)

19th M.B. Coy

Instructions regarding War Diaries and Intelligence Summaries are contained in F. S. Regs., Part II. and the Staff Manual respectively. Title Pages will be prepared in manuscript.

Place	Date	Hour	Summary of Events and Information	Remarks and references to Appendices
In the field	24 Jan.		2/Lt CAMPBELL. Officer commanding 2. R.W.F. places Cpl. PRESTON of No 2 Sect under arrest for neglect. Shell fire harassing. Cpl. B. E. FAULKNER travels on leave to U.K. 2/Lt O'REILLY reassumes temporary command of the company. Co. is ordered to reconnoitre the dug-outs from the front system and the plans drawn on the ridge behind BERLINGOTS VALLEY which linked communication, Sc.	
—	25 Jan.		H.Q. shelled this afternoon, shelling leading to the opening itself and in the daynight roof. No 1 Sect runner wounded in the hand. 2/Lt McQueen reports back from leave to U.K. 4 men from the G.S.R. 1 & 4 for the 1st CAMERONIANS are attached to us for this time of duties in the trenches.	
—	26 Jan.		2/Lt McQueen joins 2/Lt Mefield mica No 4 Sect, 2/Lt MEREFIELD suffering	

Army Form C. 2118.

WAR DIARY
or
INTELLIGENCE SUMMARY

(Erase heading not required.)

19th Machine Gun Coy

Place	Date	Hour	Summary of Events and Information	Remarks and references to Appendices
In the field	27 Jan		from our injured fire	
			Weather still cold and fine. Heavy enemy trench mortar fire on the left battalion front. Sgt Cass and Pte TALBOT killed with No 2 Section	
	28 Jan		Nothing of note has occurred.	
	29 Jan		Reorganisation of 98th M.G. Coy reported today to make arrangements about relief which should take place tomorrow night. The relief scheme read in by 2nd Lt A.C. POTTER acting O.C. Coy has been accepted by the Division.	
	30 Jan		The Company was relieved by the 98th M.G. Coy tonight. The relief was very successful, no casualties having occurred and reported complete at H.Q. by 6.30 P.M. The Company has moved to Camp 19. When quarters were enabled	[signature]

2449 Wt. W14957/M90 750,000 1/16 J.B.C. & A. Forms/C.2118/12.

WAR DIARY
or
INTELLIGENCE SUMMARY
(Erase heading not required.) 19th Machine Gun Coy

Army Form C. 2118.

Instructions regarding War Diaries and Intelligence Summaries are contained in F. S. Regs., Part II. and the Staff Manual respectively. Title Pages will be prepared in manuscript.

Place	Date	Hour	Summary of Events and Information	Remarks and references to Appendices
In the Field	31 Jan.		The Coy Commandant has given us front of another but few the men. Chief points to note in this last ten in the trenches. Difficulty in keeping guns from freezing at night in spite of liberal use of glycerine. SC Brigades whenever fire from the centre of them the river, extremely hot fire in the Enemy front system which was able to be observed was very effective, the hostile rifle was wisely unfielded. Enemy retaliation neither became in his trenches nor artillery but did not answer in finding his guns. One of Lt. Grant's guns in the left Brotelin front opened fire in an enemy working party; the party scattered and did not attempt to resume work during the longer.	

Vol 3

CONFIDENTIAL

WAR DIARY

19 M - G Coy

From O.C. 19ᵗʰ M-G Cy.   To Headquarters 33ʳᵈ Div

Army Form C. 2118.

WAR DIARY
or
INTELLIGENCE SUMMARY

(Erase heading not required.)

19th Machine Gun Corps

Instructions regarding War Diaries and Intelligence Summaries are contained in F.S. Regs., Part II. and the Staff Manual respectively. Title Pages will be prepared in manuscript.

Place	Date	Hour	Summary of Events and Information	Remarks and references to Appendices
In the field	1st Oct		Half an hour's P.T. and general cleaning up of guns, wires and equipments. Weather still very cold. Party of Officers & N.C.O's attached was instructed on anti-aircraft demonstration at CHIPILLY. Demonstration cancelled. One N.C.O. attended the Div. Gas School for future instruction in the use of the new Small Box Respirator.	
" "	2nd "		Gun returns & rounds fielded inspected. Cleaning of guns and ammunition continued. Anti-aircraft demonstration held.	
" "	3rd "		Company inspected by Commanding Officer. Company fund.	
" "	4th "		Church Parade for C of E. & R.C.'s & Presbyterians was held in the Camp. Joint rubbing drill was carried out. 2Lt the QUEEN & 3 O.R. did not proceed to the MACHINE GUN COURSE at CAMIERS commencing on the 5th inst, owing to the unit held being closed.	

Army Form C. 2118.

WAR DIARY
or
INTELLIGENCE SUMMARY
(Erase heading not required.)

19 Machine Gun Corps

Instructions regarding War Diaries and Intelligence Summaries are contained in F.S. Regs., Part II. and the Staff Manual respectively. Title Pages will be prepared in manuscript.

Place	Date	Hour	Summary of Events and Information	Remarks and references to Appendices
In field	5 Jan	5 am	Company received the following orders. No. 1 Small Box Respirator. Lt POTTER proceeded to the Left Bge trenches to reconnoitre. In the afternoon the company did their no. 1 test. As the company were changing at the gun schemes at the Div Gym School for the first fifty of the Small Box Respirator. No. 3 size 3 have been issued to date, all men have been fitted. Lt DEAN, T.O. reconnoitred the trenches route to the Left 63 gr Front.	
		6 am		
		7 pm	Sent nothing. P.T. out gave tuition for the trenches in the morning. Sent Russell and rifled since were instructions to reserve trench first line. 2nd Lt QUEEN proceeded to CAMIER on a Machine Gun Course.	
		8 am	Company successfully relieved the 100th M.G. Coy taking up in the left Brigade front. Guns Coys No. 1 & two teams of No. 4 Sect under Lt OSBORNE & 2/Lt TAYLOR respectively in the front line. No. 3 Sect under Lt WATKINS and No. 2 Sect under Lt GRANT in support. Coy H.Q. established at Basil Wood.	

WAR DIARY or INTELLIGENCE SUMMARY

14th M.G. Company

Place	Date	Hour	Summary of Events and Information	Remarks and references to Appendices
			rifle and anti-aircraft gun. Gun with anti-aircraft gun at HOWITZER WOOD. Company moved off from CAMP 14 at 9.30 A.M. and marched to HOWITZER WOOD. Relieved the Lewis Guns and paraded by commenced to relieve them from them in accounts. Relief reported correct by runner at 8.00 P.M. Weather clear and cold.	
In the field 1916			Still cold. Guns quiet. Nothing to report.	
—	—	10 am	Arrange works made for it about to take place in the morning of the 11th. C.O. very busy allotting gun positions and making wire firing angles. Weather still cold and clear. Gun at 80 WATKINS strong point lodged in, Mould's having his Lewis guns. One artillery firing active.	
—	—	11 am	Whilst today will provide them in a few days. Carried out a careful observation with guns at 402 T 3. Situations at rifle fire found by the points 17 d 70·30, 17 d 70·90, 1·8·c·95·70	

WAR DIARY or INTELLIGENCE SUMMARY

Army Form C. 2118.

1¼ Machine Gun Coy

Place	Date	Hour	Summary of Events and Information	Remarks and references to Appendices
			at 1-2-c-9-5-30. Between 6·15 P.M. and 6·40 P.M. No 2 Sect fired 6 mv rounds & No 3 Sect 5 Qvs. Owing to phosgene in the water, and rifle bullets during the first hilt it. in spite of the use of condenser much steam was visible. As morning was misty and this prevented the enemy from seeing our position & the guns which were in dug-up ground, are enemy did not retaliate on No 3 Sect but did see the rifleing in No 2 Sect. After guns were dismantled, One form of ten rifle shells fell in one of the emplacements but no casualties occurred. Some field well, & shell mmmmm being avoided by the rapid ducking of the men. During the night over 11/12 we moved at ten teams from HOWITZER WOOD old R.H.Q. from O. ECHELON to the INTERMEDIATE LINE between new along the ROAD WOOD CREST. Positions were near by dug-outs and in corner of mmmmm. At present there is time a line to him and trenches from their positions. Whilst at middle they transport not thinning gov.	[signature]

2449 Wt. W14957/M90 750,000 1/16 J.B.C. & A. Forms/C.2118/12.

WAR DIARY or INTELLIGENCE SUMMARY

Army Form C. 2118.

Place: In the field / 19[--]

Date	Hour	Summary of Events and Information	Remarks and references to Appendices
14	—	Lt GRANT's position in the MAIN TRENCH. Shelled Enemy O.C. 5th S.R. went to BROGDEN out of his dug out in the BETHUNE PERONNE Rd., setting to enter in any H.Q. This dug out was taken in from the trench near M.G. dug out and burnt out as long as the 100 m.g. lay	
15	—	2nd BROGDEN's night gun in the left Battn. front fired on enemy party of about 20 which appeared at dawn in front of the enemy wire about C.26.b.7. 150 rounds were fired. Gun of the enemy was seen to fall while the use different wire great activity. 9mm Lewis guns which were considered deeper than the gun did not open fire but sent up to our gunners that the enemy target was possible. All remain unshaken. Gun upon all but ceased fire. Water supplies at P.C. VIOLETTE has broken down M/Cpl CLARKE Corps winches gun Officer visited the enter Trench	
16	—	Lt POTTER, commanding the Coy made a reconnaissance of our front in preparation for an attack by our Bde. It one start was which this morning which never and gunnel communicating to them 2/Lt TAYLOR in charge 16 guns in the left B[--] front line general dump	

WAR DIARY
or
INTELLIGENCE SUMMARY
(Erase heading not required.)

Army Form C. 2118.

19ᵗʰ Machine Gun Corps

Place	Date	Hour	Summary of Events and Information	Remarks and references to Appendices
In the field	17.9.16		At midnight Nos 2 & 3 Sections under 2nd Lt GRANT & WATKINS respectively opened fire in FEUILLAC COURT from about C.25.d.28 and C.25.b.32. 2nd Lieut fired 2100 rounds and the latter 17000. This was in conjunction with the 100ᵗʰ and 12ᵗʰ M.G. Coys and an artillery bombardment. All enemy artillery retaliated heavily and promptly on our gun positions and made it necessary for us to harass the line for one hour. Reconnaissance was carried out. Two half sections in the front line were accordingly relieved this morning also two in the INTERMEDIATE LINE. We are now having about 6 officers having influenza, and including C.O., 2 i/c, there are not officers at a.T.O. This made the fact that being in the coming attack [so] difficult, as our guns have to be detailed with reserves and units gunners for which we talked up with the front in the same operation. The N.C.O. going over to "B" Battery, [who] distribute ammunition for [a minute] [appointment and J.O.]	
	18.		all information needed for the attack in HERSEELD Trench. We have two half sections placed at the disposal of the 2ⁿᵈ R.W.F. & 2.0" R.F. who are going over. The two guns went and of the night & left battalion in the front line. We ancrates the Lewis handler. Guns from trenches K.8.19 on firing in barrage on Enemy Communication. Attack postponed at 6.00 P.M.	

WAR DIARY or INTELLIGENCE SUMMARY

Army Form C. 2118.

19th Machine Gun Corps

Place	Date	Hour	Summary of Events and Information	Remarks and references to Appendices
In the field	19 ...		Enemy putting more munitions. Shell bursts were brought back from the enemy shown in the front line to the support trenches.	
	20 —		Enemy guns fired 5 our rounds in conjunction with an artillery bombardment on enemy communications between 4.20 P.M. and 10.5 P.M. Our Brigade Front is extended to the right and two guns have been sent to the new front from the Support line, relieving the 11th M.G. Coy. Relief completed accordingly. All trenches is now held by 23 guns.	
	21 —		All arrangements for the attack as ordered completed. Garrison as in table. Carrying on very great trouble.	
	22 —		Attack cancelled owing to bad conditions of ground at consequent for inability of troops. There is an hour of new tonight.	
	23 —		LT. ROBERTSON with No's of No 3 Sec. made a reconnaissance of position R1, R6, R7, R12, in the INTERMEDIATE LINE which has to be taken up by Bn Brigade in Divn Reserve in case of attack. The Company now relieved by the 98th M.G. Coy. Relief which complete on Transf. H.Q. at 9.45 P.M. Coy went now marched out & rested & lorries & tramp.	

Army Form C. 2118.

WAR DIARY
or
INTELLIGENCE SUMMARY
(Erase heading not required.)

19th Machine Gun Coy

Place	Date	Hour	Summary of Events and Information	Remarks and references to Appendices
Ennefield	24th		CLERY. All the Company except C.O., 2" in C., 2/Lt BOWDEN and four others of No 1 Sect moved CAMP1, SUZANNE before midnight.	
			C.O & 2 in C. reached Camp 1 at 1.15 A.M. 2/Lt BOWDEN sent at 5.30 A.M.	
			Small arms inspection was held at 2.30 P.M. 2/Lt MERIFIELD rejoined from rent Course.	
	25		Divine Service for C of E. at SUZANNE at 12.00 noon. Other denominations at a P.T. parade. Company paraded at 2.45 P.M. Baths from 5.00 – 6.00 P.M. LT GRANT proceeded to CAMIER for a Machine Gun Course. 2Lt McQUEEN rejoined from M.G. Course.	
	26		Guns and ammunition cleaned in the morning. a/Capt CAMPBELL returning to the Company taking command. 2/Lt PORTER takes over the duties of 2nd in command.	

Army Form C. 2118.

WAR DIARY
or
INTELLIGENCE SUMMARY
(Erase heading not required.)

19ᵗʰ Machine Gun Company

Instructions regarding War Diaries and Intelligence Summaries are contained in F.S. Regs., Part II. and the Staff Manual respectively. Title Pages will be prepared in manuscript.

Place	Date	Hour	Summary of Events and Information	Remarks and references to Appendices
In the Field	27		General cleaning up of guns and gear. All supervision noted, tests and out and handed in.	
	28		Owing to the thaw, the roads are in an appalling condition; a special party, in front all men available, was chosen over by the Brigade and set to work on the roads from 9 to 4.30.	

J. Porter M.

2449 Wt. W14957/M90 750,000 1/16 J.B.C. & A. Forms/C.2118/12.

Army Form C. 2118.

WAR DIARY
~~INTELLIGENCE SUMMARY.~~
(Erase heading not required.)

Vol 14

19th Machine Gun Company

WAR DIARY
for
MARCH 1917.

WAR DIARY or INTELLIGENCE SUMMARY

Army Form C. 2118.

March 1917.

19th M.G.C.

Place	Date	Hour	Summary of Events and Information	Remarks and references to Appendices
In the Field	2nd		Gun drill and practice with ancillary arriving [marches] during the morning, working party of 30 men for the Brigade also [reported] to attend meal in the novels. A captive balloon near the camp was brought down in flames at about 5 p.m. One observer descended with apparent safety in a parachute.	
	3rd		Preparing for trucks during morning. Sixteen guns to be in the line again. Regt. Bomb. of SUZANNE at 1115. Relief carried out in daylight excepting No 1 Section at OMIECOURT, on account of the SOMME, which could only be approached by dark. Relief quite satisfactory. All guns in our front [Bouchav] German shelling. 8" shrams made a unsuccessful attack on our left.	
	4th		Very quiet day. Morning of 119th Company turned up in the morning to get details of the line.	
	5th		Over 3 positions from 9.05 Company on the left, the front-line position over two officers positions were taken over.	
	6th		O.C. "19th" Coy arrived to arrange all about 8 relief. Capt G.E. Falkner returned from leave and took over 2 a/c command of the Coy Lieut [Longhull] reverted to Section Officer and Lieut G.C. Potter [went] to Section Officer.	Humphreys acg 19th M.G.C.

WAR DIARY or INTELLIGENCE SUMMARY

Army Form C. 2118.

19th M. C. Co.

Place	Date	Hour	Summary of Events and Information	Remarks and references to Appendices
Yses	7th March		The C.O. and 2i/c went round from - line trenches. Quiet day.	
	8th March		The C.O. and 2i/c went round from - line trenches. Very quiet day. Some snow showers. Visibility was excellent between showers. The Germans in early morning had man a small revet on one of our saps. Repair relieve some myster by 119th Inf Bde	
	9th March		The Coy. was relieved during the afternoon by the 119th M.G. Co. The relief was quite satisfactory. On completion of relief the Coy. moved back to Camp 1.	
	10th March		The Coy. moved from Camp 1. to Camp 12 marching via BRAY and ETINHEM. Camp 12 was found to be in a very bad state. Lieut A.B. BONNOR joined Coy from Base Depot.	
	11th March		Batten billets were found in the village of CHIPILLY. The Coy moved from Camp 12 to their new billets in CHIPILLY.	
	12th March		Day was spent in cleaning up guns and a few limbers.	

Blampinguine Roy 19th M.G.Co.

Army Form C. 2118.

WAR DIARY
or
INTELLIGENCE SUMMARY.
(Erase heading not required.)

19th M.G.C.

Place	Date	Hour	Summary of Events and Information	Remarks and references to Appendices
Field	13th March		The Coy. was inspected by Major-General Pinney, C.B. G.O.C. Division, and was complimented on its smart appearance. The Men's accoutrements shot while cleaning the rules	
do	14th March		Officers made list of deficiencies in tools, clothing &c. Equipment not owned by men. All Box Respirators were handed in to Q.M. Stores.	
do	15th March		The Coy. had a Route march.	
do	15th March		The following promotions to Sergeant were made:— L/Sgt Connel, Corpl Tickell, Corp Preston. to Sergeant. a/Lsgrad. Lance Sergeant. a/Lsgrad.	
do	16th March		Officers made out list of deficiencies in gun equipment and under equipment. Parades.	
do	17th March	9-9.45am	Phys. Tr.	
		10-11am	War Orders 88 &c.	
		11-12 noon	Instruction in gun & section sergeants. Cleaning of arms and wet C.M. All available officers attended a mil. Conference at D H.Q. Rampurpuiragan 19th July 16	

Army Form C. 2118.

WAR DIARY
INTELLIGENCE SUMMARY.
(Erase heading not required.)

19th M. G. C.

Instructions regarding War Diaries and Intelligence Summaries are contained in F. S. Regs., Part II. and the Staff Manual respectively. Title pages will be prepared in manuscript.

Place	Date	Hour	Summary of Events and Information	Remarks and references to Appendices
Hill	18th March		Church Service :- L/Cpl. Parons at B.H.Q. at 9.30 a.m. The Coy. was allotted baths from 11 a.m. – 1 p.m.	
do	19th March		Coy route march. Awards :- L/Cpl Tukes g. awarded Bronze Medal – Italian decoration – for inspiring valour. Limber Drill was Lieut. Rev. S. Robertson.	
do	20th "		Parades :- one section on Range. Remainder parade in morning for Phy. Tr. Aiming Practice and Anti-gas Drill afternoon – Letting up & Stoppages.	
do	21st "		Range finders – 2 per section – parade separately. Range practice – 2 per section – parade separately. Stoves recently treated with sulphur were washed. All Horse Rugs & blankets were disinfected by detachment of Div. Sanitary Section. Bampfylde Lieut. 19th m g C.	

Army Form C. 2118.

WAR DIARY
INTELLIGENCE SUMMARY.
(Erase heading not required.)

19th M.G.C.

Instructions regarding War Diaries and Intelligence Summaries are contained in F. S. Regs., Part II. and the Staff Manual respectively. Title pages will be prepared in manuscript.

Place	Date	Hour	Summary of Events and Information	Remarks and references to Appendices
Field	22nd March		Coy parade in morning. Coy inspected (along with Transport) by G.O.C. Brigade in field East of CHIPILLY CHURCH.	
do	23rd March		Coy held Route march.	
do	24th March		Coy paraded for Phys. Tr. C.O's parade	
do	25th March		Clocks advanced one hour on night of 24th = 11 p.m. Church service.	
			G.H.Q parade at Coy P-12 at 11 am. Presbyterian do at Camp 13 - at 11 am. After the service the G.O.C. Division presented three Battns of the Brigade present; also the medal ribbons. 1 M.G.C. and 2 M.B. Presbyterians 1 M.G.C. and 2 M.B.	
do	26th March		Very wet day. Route march postponed. Sections carried on Field work. Companies near the Serving Officers.	
d	27th March		Brigade Route march. No Transport except Pack animals. Dumphlin Lint Coy 19 M.G.C.	

Army Form C. 2118.

WAR DIARY
INTELLIGENCE SUMMARY.
(Erase heading not required.)

19th M.G.C

Instructions regarding War Diaries and Intelligence Summaries are contained in F.S. Regs., Part II. and the Staff Manual respectively. Title pages will be prepared in manuscript.

Place	Date	Hour	Summary of Events and Information	Remarks and references to Appendices
Field	29th March		Capt Col Falkner and Lieut Col Peter Fraser 3 days' leave to ROUEN and PARIS respectively.	
do	28th Mar.		Parades. 9-10 am – Phys Tr. 10-11 am – Gun Drill 11-12 noon – Arms Drill (recruit S.B.) N.C.Os taken on the range in morning	
do	29th Mar.		Brigade Route March	
do	30th Mar.		Parades 9-10 am – Phys Tr 10-11 am – under Section Officers' arrangements 11-12 noon – Arms Drill (recruit S.B.) No 2 section on the range in morning 2-3 pm - Belt filling 3-4 pm - Lectures by Section Officers	
do	31st March		Company Tactical Scheme under Lt. D. Humphries (Special attention being paid to advancing under cover.) Pack animals were used to carry guns and tripods.	

D. Humphries
Acting 19th M.G. Co.

Vol 15

CONFIDENTIAL

War Diary

of

19th Machine Gun Company

From 1/4/17   To 30/4/17

Army Form C. 2118.

WAR DIARY
INTELLIGENCE SUMMARY
(Erase heading not required.)

19th MACHINE GUN COMPANY

Places	Date	Hour	Summary of Events and Information	Remarks and references to Appendices
Field	1st April		Church Services in Coy. lines at 11 A.m. at Camp P 12.	
"	2nd April		The Company prepare for move the following day. The Coy. less Transport, marched to CORBIE along the canal bank. Lieut Robertson was Billeting Officer. Billets were taken over from the 100 B. M. G. C. The Transport of Coy. was brigaded with remaining Transport of Brigade and marched to CORBIE along road running S. of Canal.	
"	3rd April		The Coy. moved to MONTONVILLERS N.W. of CORBIE. Officers billeted in the school.	
"	4th April		The Coy. moved to BEAUVAL. Billets found. 33rd Division Their Army.	
"	5th April		The Coy. moved to LUCHEUX arriving there in the evening.	
"	6th April		The Coy. did not move. Morning was spent in cleaning limbers.	
"	7th April		The Coy. moved to SAULTY. Billets very poor. 2nd Lieut. E. C. W. Stokes joined Coy. from Grantham to replace Stamper Lieut Holf 19th M.G. Co.	

Army Form C. 2118.

19th MACHINE GUN COMPANY.

WAR DIARY
INTELLIGENCE SUMMARY.
(Erase heading not required.)

Instructions regarding War Diaries and Intelligence Summaries are contained in F. S. Regs., Part II. and the Staff Manual respectively. Title pages will be prepared in manuscript.

Place	Date	Hour	Summary of Events and Information	Remarks and references to Appendices
Field	7th April		Lieut A.C. Potter recommended for exchange on account of his long period of service in the field	
"	8th April		The Coy. moved to BAILLEULMONT. Capt Talbot and Lieut Bingley made reconnaissance of the forward area. Horse, rations and forage were drawn from Three days. Rations and forage were drawn from BAILLEUVAL at night in preparation for forthcoming operations	
"	9th April		The Coy. did not move. Further preparations were made during the day for the forthcoming move of Division to the forward area. A Brigade Store was formed in the village of BAILLEUVAL, to which were sent all surplus stores, greatcoats & haversacks mens clothing etc. The great Offensive began in morning and the news of the increases won during the day were received with great joy by all ranks.	
"	10th April		The Coy. did not move. Particularly stormy day.	Templeux Luit Fay, 19th m.g. Co.

A5834 Wt. W4973/M687 750,000 8/16 D. D. & L. Ltd. Forms/C.2118/13.

WAR DIARY
INTELLIGENCE SUMMARY

Army Form C. 2118.

19th MACHINE GUN COMPANY.

Place	Date	Hour	Summary of Events and Information	Remarks and references to Appendices
Field	11th April		The Coy. under short notice to move forward. At 5 pm the Coy. left for the forward area and arrived at its destination BOISIEUX - au - MONT about 11 pm. "B" Echelon moved at same time, arriving at its destination BLAIREVILLE about midnight. All the first Line Transport i.e. 8 gun limbers & S.A.A. limbers accompanied the personnel selected for the coming operations. "B" Echelon covered 25% of Water Carts, Cooks Carts and Headquarters limber. "B" Echelon & "Spare Guns" in Officers and men, were left behind with "B" Echelon as "Spare Reinforcements".	
do.	12th April		The CO and 2nd Lieut Brown reconnoitred the new front. In the afternoon the Coy. moved up to HENIN-sur-COJEUL and the first line Transport returned to BLAIREVILLE. 12 guns were placed in reserve positions East of HENIN. "B" Echelon and 1st Line Transport moved up to	
do.	13th April		BOIRY-BECQUERELLE. Guns remained in places in the previous night.	

D. Humphrey Capt
19 MG Co

WAR DIARY
INTELLIGENCE SUMMARY

Army Form C. 2118.

Place	Date	Hour	Summary of Events and Information	Remarks and references to Appendices
Field	14th April		The Coy moved forward in the early hours of the morning and established Headquarters 200 yards west of the HINDENBURG LINE at 7 h a.m. Sub. Lt. (Reg. No. 7102) No 4 Section under Lieut A.D. Bonner was detailed to assist the attack by the 5th Seo Rifles. Lieut Bonner received wound during the attack. Pte. 1 Clark wounded at night.	
do	15th April		Capt G.S. Falkner, Lieut & Others near our account of two fires at "B" Echelon, Lieut Campbell i/c of Coy. Inner Coy Hd.Qrs. at night. Pte Jackson wounded in morning.	
do	16th April		20th Royal Fusiliers attacked in morning. One section under Lt. McQueen went forward with 20th R.F. The attack was unsuccessful. Another section under Lieut A.T. Brogden did excellent work with "The Cameronians". Corporal Hinton and two O/ his Sect. were wounded in action while following up a bombing attack in the HINDENBURG FRONT TRENCH. 3000 rounds Small Arm ammn fired by the Section. The Coy was relieved at night by the 98th m.G. Co.	D[?]am[?]gree m.a.i. 19th m.G.C.

Army Form C. 2118.

WAR DIARY
or
INTELLIGENCE SUMMARY.
(Erase heading not required.)

19th MACHINE GUN COMPANY.
No..........
Date..........

Instructions regarding War Diaries and Intelligence Summaries are contained in F. S. Regs., Part II. and the Staff Manual respectively. Title pages will be prepared in manuscript.

Place	Date	Hour	Summary of Events and Information	Remarks and references to Appendices
Field	16th April		and moved back to Dunkin Road west of MERCATEL.	
do.	17th April		As some of the men did not return from trenches untill 8 am the whole Coy. was given a rest that day. First Reinforcements at B Echelon cleaned the guns & their respective sections.	
do	18th April		Day spent in cleaning up &c. Capture and Watkins reconnoitred some of the positions held by 100th M.G. Co.	
do	19th April		Inspection of Iron Rations, Arms &c.	
do	20th April		Inspection of Arms & Clothing.	
do	21st April		Coy moved up near 100th Bde H.Q. 1 wire section under orders for 100th M.G. Co. digging emplacements at night in preparation for forthcoming operations.	
do	22nd April		Three sections of Coy placed in position for firing indirect line.	
do	23rd April		Big attack at 4.45 am. Preceded by very heavy bombardment. Which fine barrage played on German trenches.	Stamford Lint Roy. 19th M.G. Co.

Army Form C. 2118.

19th MACHINE GUN COMPANY.
No......
Date............

WAR DIARY
or
INTELLIGENCE SUMMARY.
(Erase heading not required.)

Instructions regarding War Diaries and Intelligence Summaries are contained in F.S. Regs., Part II. and the Staff Manual respectively. Title pages will be prepared in manuscript.

Place	Date	Hour	Summary of Events and Information	Remarks and references to Appendices
Field			at 2330 and kept up for 1½ hours. Later at 6/am. a barrage was seen & rom trenches and roads were searched. Barrage kept up for 1½ hours. Altogether 8,000 rounds were fired during the day in assisting both attacks. 10 officers & 800 OR. were captured by 98th Inf. Bde.	
do	24th April		Three sections of Coy relieved the 98th m.g. Co. in the line. The remainder of personnel joined "B" Echelon.	
do	25th April		The Coy was relieved in the line by the 11th M.G. Co. and joined "B" Echelon at BOIRY - BECQUERELLE.	
do	26th April		The Company moved from BOIRY - BECQUERELLE to HENDICOURT in the morning, there was no accommodation but plenty of material and limbers were erected. Seven carpenters were drawn from Brigade.	

R Wulffleck 30/4/1917
19th M.G. Coy

Army Form C. 2118.

WAR DIARY
or
INTELLIGENCE SUMMARY.
(Erase heading not required.)

Instructions regarding W = Diaries and Intelligence Summaries are contained in F. S. Regs., Part II. and the Staff Manual respectively. Title pages will be prepared in manuscript.

19th MACHINE GUN COMPANY.

Place	Date	Hour	Summary of Events and Information	Remarks and references to Appendices
In field	27/4/17		Company moved from HENDICOURT to BAILEULMONT in the morning. G.O.C. Division attended the Company march past and complimented the C.O. in its appearance. 2/Lt CAMPBELL proceeded to M.G. Course at CAMIER. 2/Lt ROBERTSON assumes his duties of adjutant in his absence.	
In field	28/4/17		Deficiencies of gun equipment checked in the morning. Lecture continued in the afternoon. VII Corps M.G. Officer visited the Company & went to see afternoon and discussed the tactics adopted in the recent offensive.	
In field	29/4/17	30—	Divine service for all denominations in the morning. Company had letters and wrote home in the afternoon. Ordinary training & movement of hands carried out. P.T., Gun Drill, arm drill, Lectures, 1 G.A. in the afternoon. a Brigade Conference assembled at BAILLEUVAL to discuss recent operations near FONTAINE-LES-CROISELLES. G.O.C. Division presided.	

R.W.A. Robertson 2/Lt & Actg. Adj't
19 M.G.Coy

Army Form C. 2118.

WAR DIARY
INTELLIGENCE SUMMARY.
(Erase heading not required.)

19th Machine Gun Company

WAR DIARY

for

MAY 1917

Army Form C. 2118.

WAR DIARY
or
INTELLIGENCE SUMMARY.

(Erase heading not required.)

19th MACHINE GUN COMPANY.

No. ....
Date ....

Instructions regarding War Diaries and Intelligence Summaries are contained in F. S. Regs., Part II. and the Staff Manual respectively. Title pages will be prepared in manuscript.

Place	Date	Hour	Summary of Events and Information	Remarks and references to Appendices
Field	1 May		Ordinary Training Programme carried out. P.T., Gun Drill, Arms Drill, Visual Training, the of Ground etc.	
"	2 May		Company moved from BAILLEULMONT to ADINFER in the afternoon. The billets is much varied and there are no arrangements but the men soon erected shelters which are sheets of corrugated iron supported on building material. Twenty rounds S.A.A. were delivered to us at 10.00 P.M., namely 50,000 rounds S.A.A. was delivered to us at establishment completing our establishment.	
"	3 May		Training programme continued. Advanced Drill, Fire direction & use of cover. M.G. Belts were drawn to be exchanged from the VII Corps M.G.O. to be filled and placed in empty S.A.A. boxes for the purpose of establishing any advanced dumps when in action.	

R.W.A./Robertson Lt. M.G.C.
for O.C.

A5834 Wt. W4973 M687 750,000 8/16 D. D. & L. Ltd. Forms/C.2118/13.

Army Form C. 2118.

WAR DIARY
or
INTELLIGENCE SUMMARY.
(Erase heading not required.)

19th MACHINE GUN COMPANY.

No. ....
Date ....

Instructions regarding War Diaries and Intelligence Summaries are contained in F. S. Regs., Part II. and the Staff Manual respectively. Title pages will be prepared in manuscript.

Place	Date	Hour	Summary of Events and Information	Remarks and references to Appendices
Field	4 May		Belts drawn from Corps M.G.O. one filled and old belts overhauled under section arrangements.	
	5 May		Tactical scheme carried out in the morning. Company does P.T. before breakfast. VII Corps M.G.O. visits the Company.	
	6 May		Divine services for C. of E. and R.C. at 2.R.W.F. H.Q. Parade at 9.30 a.m.	
	7 May		Parades. P.T., inspection of stoppages, firing of stoppages, number positions and tactical scheme, Defence of Flanks in morning. Divisional Rifle Meeting held in the afternoon near AYETTE. one Company entered two teams. In the 1st race, 4 firings for riders of N.C.O.'s we were REDSHANKS winner Pte HAVEL who gained 7th in a field of 65. In 4th race, 4 firings for officers (officers charges, SCOTTIE winner Lt. BROWDEN wt. finished 8th in a field of 40. 30 & N.C.O.'s and men and all officers but one were allowed to attend. Our afternoon was excellent and the afternoon was enjoyed by all.	
	8 May		Parades this event on the the 7th but cancelled in consequence of Company moving in A.M.	

RWJ/Robertson Major
for O.C.

A5834 Wt. W4973 M687. 750,000 8/16 D. D. & L. Ltd. Forms/C.2118/13.

WAR DIARY or INTELLIGENCE SUMMARY

Army Form C. 2118.

19th MACHINE GUN COMPANY

Place	Date	Hour	Summary of Events and Information	Remarks and references to Appendices
Field	8th Aug		Usual drill held in afternoon	
		9.45 P.M.	Orders for a Brigade tactical scheme came in. Punctual times for 6.30 A.M. arrangements made.	
		10.45 P.M.	Tactical Scheme Cancelled.	
	9th Aug		2Lt GRANT proceeds to 3rd Army Inf. School for a course of instruction. Parades, P.T., Range and number practice and advance guard scheme. Capt FALKNER, Lt BROGDEN, Lt WATKINS & 2Lt HARRISON attend a Divisional M.G. Conference.	
	10 Aug		Brigade tactical scheme took place today. 1st Coy consisting of 5" S.R. set four of two sections took part. The practice consisted of (a) march to a point of assembly. (b) advance under shell fire (c) deployment under M.G. fire (d) assault (e) consolidation of captured position. Bg. Gen MAYNE expressed himself satisfied with the company, one of the schemes. On reaching two sections carried out the usual training under their section officers.	

6 WA / R Leeston 2Lt & AAdj
for O.C.

Army Form C. 2118.

WAR DIARY
or
INTELLIGENCE SUMMARY.
(Erase heading not required)

19th MACHINE GUN COMPANY.
No............
Date............

Place	Date	Hour	Summary of Events and Information	Remarks and references to Appendices
Field	11 May		Warning order is received that Division will probably move to the forward area tomorrow. Everything is made ready for the move.	
	12 May	6.20 A.M.	The Company march to HAMLINCOURT. Entry. Cross country route used. Transport moved at 9-00A.M. Company arrived at 9-00A.M. Transport at 9-30A.M. Attempted to bivouac in an open field which we invite shelter. Ground sheets are drawn from G.3 gds. Weather fine and hot. In the evening 2 off STOKES reconnaissance the best covered routes to CROISELLES with a view to making a counter attack should the enemy advance.	
	13 May		Divine Service for C of E at MOYENNEVILLE at 10.00 A.M. and R.C. on site of old Church (burnt at the same place at 9.00 A.M. Lt McQUEEN acts as member on a F.G.C.M. in the afternoon. Capt FALKNER visited the O.C. 100th M.G. Coy in the line. We were probably relieve the 100th Coy on the 15/16."	

C.W.A/Blackburn
Lieut F.A/824

Instructions regarding War Diaries and Intelligence Summaries are contained in F.S. Regs., Part II. and the Staff Manual respectively. Title pages will be prepared in manuscript.

Army Form C. 2118.

WAR DIARY
or
INTELLIGENCE SUMMARY
(Erase heading not required.)

19th MACHINE GUN COMPANY

Place	Date	Hour	Summary of Events and Information	Remarks and references to Appendices
Field	14 May		6 relieving parades carried out. P.T., driving practice, cleaning & care of communicating Drill in A.M. Wilkinson and Stoppages in afternoon am. P.M. 2t McQueen & 2Its HARRISON and STOKES reconnoitre the dispositions of the 100 Coy in line. The Coy will relieve 100 M.G. Coy tomorrow.	
	15 May	A.M.	The Company including transport and "B" Echelon move to T 20 d 54 x 100 M.G. Coy H.Q. Although we are relieving the 100 Coy resting in the line, the 100 Coy is remaining at their old H.Q. In consequence thereof we are sheltering to take over. Bivouacs are erected.	x Reference TRENCH MAP 51 B S.W. Edit 4.A
		4.00 P.M.	No 2 Sect under Lt McQUEEN relieves the support sect of 100 Coy.	
		5.30 P.M.	No 2 Sect relief reported complete.	
		8.00 PM	No 1 Sect under 2/Lt STOKES relieves the front line sect of 100 Coy	
		10.45 P.M.	No 1 Sect relief reported complete.	
			The Division is to attack FONTAINE-LES-CROISELLES at about 2 A.M. 17th May. 93rd Bgd is making down HINDENBURG LINE on LEFT. 100 Coy is now under orders to further attacks on H.L. in front of FONTAINE, and Hampton Line tonight D.S.	

A5834 Wt. W4973 M687 750,000 8/16 D. D. & L. Ltd. Forms/C.2118/13.

Army Form C. 2118.

WAR DIARY
INTELLIGENCE SUMMARY.
(Erase heading not required.)

19th MACHINE GUN COMPANY

Place	Date	Hour	Summary of Events and Information	Remarks and references to Appendices
Field	16 May		The attack will be made through the 19th Bde who will remain in their front position forming a reserve line if the attack is successful. On establish of 19th Bde will advance to the extreme right forming a defensive flank. This Company will have one section giving covering fire from the region of 35 Div front.	
		1.30am	Guns that ordered.	
		5.30am	Capt FALKNER & Lt WATKINS reconnoitre positions for Vickers guns on right flank.	
		2.00pm	WO4 Section under LT MERFIELD go forward to U 25 A 29 × to dig positions. Gun positions reconnoitred in morning.	*Reference TRENCH MAP. 51B S.W. Edit 4 A.*
		5.30pm	Operations due for 17 inst are postponed Brig. Gen. MAYNE visits Coy H.Q.	
			It is reported that the enemy intend to return to DROCOURT-QUEANT line, the movement to be completed by 20 inst. If enemy have not retired by then operations stated for 20–17 inst take place on 20.	

D Campbell Lieut for OC

Army Form C. 2118.

16th MACHINE GUN COMPANY.
No...........
Date...........

WAR DIARY
or
~~INTELLIGENCE SUMMARY.~~
(Erase heading not required.)

Instructions regarding War Diaries and Intelligence Summaries are contained in F. S. Regs., Part II. and the Staff Manual respectively. Title pages will be prepared in manuscript.

Place	Date	Hour	Summary of Events and Information	Remarks and references to Appendices
		10.30 P.M.	No 4 Sect returns less 1 N.C.O and 2 men who are remaining at the position.	
	17 Aug.	11.00 A.M.	Gas alert off.	
		2.30 P.M.	I.O.R. reports from 33rd Depot Battn.	
	18 Aug.	9.0 A.M.	9.O.R. report from 33rd Depot Battn. Inter-Section relief.	
		7.00 P.M.	2Lt HARRISON with No 3 Sect relieves No 2 Sect with 2Lt MCQUEEN in support line. No 2 Sect relieves No 1 Sect with 2Lt STOKES in front line.	
		10.30 P.M.	Relief complete. No casualties.	
		11.30 P.M.	Lts WATKINS and MERFIELD with one team of No 4 Sect proceed to T17A92ˣ to fire in SENSE RIVER VALLEY where the enemy are reported active.	
	19 Aug	12.30 A.M.	Night firing team returns after firing 2 over rounds.	
		4.30 A.M.	Enemy aeroplane seen flying low over our front line, fired on by our anti-aircraft M.G.s but without result.	

Stampher
Lieut Atty
16 G.C.

A 5834 Wt. W 4973 M 687. 750,000 8/16 D. D. & L. Ltd. Forms/C.2118/13.

Army Form C. 2118.

19th MACHINE GUN COMPANY.

WAR DIARY
INTELLIGENCE SUMMARY.
(Erase heading not required.)

Instructions regarding War Diaries and Intelligence Summaries are contained in F. S. Regs., Part II. and the Staff Manual respectively. Title pages will be prepared in manuscript.

Place	Date	Hour	Summary of Events and Information	Remarks and references to Appendices
Field	19th May (continued)		No.3 Sect under 2/Lt HARRISON is sent to 100ᵗ M.G. Coy for instructions fire. Position from which they are to fire is in advance of our outpost line. Capt FALKNER proceeds to 19ᵗʰ Bde about places having to fire his guns in such an unused position.	
		8.15 P.M.	No.1 Sect under 2/Lt STOKES leaves Coy H.Q. to relieve No.3 Sect in the support line on relief No.3 Sect proceeds to its indirect fire position. No.4 Sect under 2/Lt WATKINS and Lt MERFIELD leaves for its indirect fire position in the right flank.	
		10.30 P.M.	No 3 Sect reported in position by runner.	
		11.7 P.M.	Watkins are acknowledged by Telephone.	
			Zero has been again put forward for I.O.R. was received Telegr. and new zero is going has been 18 minutes without leave.	
	20 May 12.40 A.M.		Watkins again acknowledged by Telephone	
		4.20 A.M.	Capt FALKNER leaves Coy H.Q. for 19ᵗʰ Bde H.Q. where he is to remain during the battle.	
		5.10 A.M.	Zero.	
		9.50 A.M.	First report of the battle comes in. 53.R. are in their objective, 100ᵗ Bde are in.	

S Campbell Lieut 2/L
A.F.C.

WAR DIARY
INTELLIGENCE SUMMARY

(Erase heading not required.)

Army Form C. 2118.

19th MACHINE GUN COMPANY.

Place	Date	Hour	Summary of Events and Information	Remarks and references to Appendices
Quéant	20 Aug (continued)		HINDENBURG Front Line. Situation at 98th Bde much obscure.	
		10.30 p.m.	Lt DEAN proceeds to U.K. on Staircase Course for U.P.A.	
		2.0 p.m.	Lt CAMPBELL sent in command of two emplacements, rejoining from M.G. course at LAMIER.	
		5.0 p.m.	Returns sent to W01 Sect as usual.	
		6.30 p.m.	A Detail Gun of newer model to 100th M.G. Coy for emergency action to W03 Sect. 100th Bde relieves emergency actions to be used, intimation to this action made to under the command of O.C. 100th M.G. Coy to the command of 100th M.G. Coy to Hindenburg Support Line attached to 19th Bde.	
		7.30 p.m.		
		9.00 p.m.	Runner from W03 Sect reports 12,000 rounds fired and one U.T. ammunition in On work leg a bullet. Otherwise everything is all right.	
		10.30 p.m.	Artillery fire having quieted down, rations are sent up to W02 Sect.	
	21 Aug	12.05 a.m.	CAPT FAULKNER returns to Coy H.Q. from Bde H.R. Runner arrives from W3 Sect. Did not fire during the attack as was impossible to see the troops in front owing to nervous conditions. Gun crews not suffering next up to HINDENBURG FRONT LINE. are recovering from gases and returned near CROISELLES.	

Army Form C. 2118.

WAR DIARY
or
INTELLIGENCE SUMMARY.
(Erase heading not required.)

19th MACHINE GUN COMPANY.

Place	Date	Hour	Summary of Events and Information	Remarks and references to Appendices
	21st May (cont.)		12 Belt boxes, rations and water were sent up to them.	
		6.00 p.m.	Capt FALKNER & Lt CAMPBELL left Coy H.Q. to see No 4 Sect. new positions	
		10.00 a.m.	1 O.R. reported killed by No 4 Sect.	
	22nd May		Quiet day. The Coy was relieved at night by the 149th M. G. Co. and all Guns & teams returned to Coy HQ in the Railway Embankment	
	23rd May		Visits. Harrison and Stokes reconnoitred the reserve line along with the Brig-General. No 1 Section took up positions in the reserve line during the day. All posts were Companies with a reserve platoon and posts were strengthened. Information that Cpl Heaton was awarded the D.C.M. for gallantry in the operations of 23rd April.	
	24th May		Coy resting in Railway Embankment & playing football and cricket.	
	25th May		Informed of the death of Corporal Heaton D.C.M. and Pte Woodard, who died, wounds 20/5/17. Captain Lines took over at 19th M.G. Co.	

WAR DIARY
INTELLIGENCE SUMMARY

Army Form C. 2118.

1916 MACHINE GUN COMPANY.

Place	Date	Hour	Summary of Events and Information	Remarks and references to Appendices
Field	26th May		Preparing to go up to trenches. The Coy relived the 149th M.G.C. No 3 section suffered very badly on going up to the Hindenburg Line. 1 OR wounded during the relief.	
	27th May		Day of an attack on HINDENBURG SUPPORT trench by the 19th and 98th Inf Bde. ZERO was 1.53 p.m. The following were the dispositions of the Company during the attack:- Ref. Sheet 57.B.S.W. (1) No 1 Section was on the left about T.11.A.65.85. This Section employed long range direct overhead fire and during the afternoon and night 27th/28th fired about 12,000 rounds. This was mostly barrage fire although one or two small targets were engaged. (2) No 4 Section was on the right about U.19.C.22 and employed indirect overhead fire some 10,000 rounds were fired. (3) No 2 Section was mostly reserve - One 1 Gun team in town. Place as usual Centre. One gun of No 2 Section was placed at U.19.C.?? to fire to Ol BAN??	

Army Form C. 2118.

WAR DIARY
INTELLIGENCE SUMMARY.
(Erase heading not required.)

Place	Date	Hour	Summary of Events and Information	Remarks and references to Appendices
Field	27 May 17		near the stumps about U.13.D.8.8. in order to enfilade valley and showed any targets present themselves. No targets however were seen and no rounds were fired over the section.	
			No 3 Section. — 2 guns under Lieut T.W.S. Robertson had been placed under the orders of OC 2nd R.W.F. on the right. 2 guns under Lieut G. Harrison had been placed under the orders of OC 1st Camerons on the left. No 1 gun on the left did very useful work in covering the retirement of our infantry after the attack had failed. The gun undoubtedly prevented the enemy from leaving their trenches in large numbers to force back small parties who did move the parapet to hastily retire to the cover of their trench. An enemy machine gun was also successfully engaged after it's last made numerous attempts to mount the gun in support places along the parapet. The ~~gun~~ Bosch in charge was either killed or wounded. No 2 gun moved forward under OC Camerons under Lt Harrison & worked a point about 60 from	

A5834   Wt. W4973 M687 750,000 8/16   D.D. & L. Ltd.   Forms/C.2118/13.

WAR DIARY
INTELLIGENCE SUMMARY
(Erase heading not required.)

Army Form C. 2118.

Place	Date	Hour	Summary of Events and Information	Remarks and references to Appendices
Field	27th May Cont.		when our infantry began to retire. Repeated efforts were made by this gun to fire but failed in each case owing to infantry masking its fire. No. 3 Gun did excellent work when the infantry had come back. Lieut ROBERTSON brought his gun into a new position from which she could keep open fire and seriously affect his was himself killed by bullets from machine guns which he was bravely directing the fire of his guns. Lieut ROBERTSON's death cast a gloom over the whole Company. He was a keen, capable and efficient officer and was beloved by both officers and men. The Officer had been on active service for the long period of 20 months.	
	28th May		The C.O. marked fresh new guns. The Coy. was relieved at night by the 100th N.I.Y. Co. and moved back to bivouacs at MOYENVILLE. Lt Robertson was interred at B.O. 45 d 2.2 S. at 6 P.M. Capt Falkner and Lt Compton present at the burial service. Stretcher bearers buried with him.	

Army Form C. 2118.

WAR DIARY
or
INTELLIGENCE SUMMARY.
(Erase heading not required.)

Instructions regarding War Diaries and Intelligence Summaries are contained in F. S. Regs., Part II. and the Staff Manual respectively. Title pages will be prepared in manuscript.

[Stamp: 19th MACHINE GUN COMPANY]

Place	Date	Hour	Summary of Events and Information	Remarks and references to Appendices
Field	29th May		The day was spent by the Coy in cleaning up.	
	30th May	9.45 a.m	The Coy paraded at 9.45 a.m. for Baths at BOYELLES.	
		2.30 p	The Coy paraded for cleaning guns and making up deficiencies in gun gear &c.	
	31st May		In morning preparations were made for move to Rest Area.	
		3 p.m	Coy. left for BAILLEULMONT.	
			Same billets were taken over as occupied during last rest.	
			Lieut S. H. MERFIELD left for U.K. on leave.	

Dauphin
Lieut
for O.C. 19th M.G.C.

Army Form C. 2118.

19th MACHINE GUN COMPANY.

No.....................
Date..................

WAR DIARY
or
INTELLIGENCE SUMMARY.
(Erase heading not required.)

Place	Date	Hour	Summary of Events and Information	Remarks and references to Appendices
Field	June 1st		Coy paraded at 9am for limber cleaning.	
"	2nd		Coy paraded under depot arrangements. O.C. Coy attended a Brigade Conference at 11.30 a.m. to discuss training programme.	
"	3rd		C.E.T. Service at Recreation tent at 10.30 a.m. Lieut. D. CAMPBELL appointed O.C. 56th M.G. Coy. Lieut. L.A. LAUNDER to 11 O.R. join Coy from Base Depot.	
"	4th		Coy paraded according to training programme. C.O.'s pass out at 3 p.m. Capt. G.P. VAERNER proceed on leave to U.K. (10/6/17) " " " " (16/6/17) 2 O.R.	
"	5th		LIEUT. H.T. BRODDEN resumed command of Company. LIEUT. D. CAMPBELL left the Company to take over command of 56th M.G. Coy. LIEUT. T.A.N.M. WATKINS appointed 2nd in Command (pro tem) Company paraded according to training programme. C.H.Q.P.M.B.L.S. visited the men.	

Army Form C. 2118.

WAR DIARY
or
INTELLIGENCE SUMMARY.
(Erase heading not required.)

19th MACHINE GUN COMPANY.

Instructions regarding War Diaries and Intelligence Summaries are contained in F.S. Regs., Part II. and the Staff Manual respectively. Title pages will be prepared in manuscript.

Place	Date	Hour	Summary of Events and Information	Remarks and references to Appendices
In the Field	June 6		Company paraded according to training programme. Instructional class formed under 2/Lieut. G. Harrison for newly joined recruits. The whole company bathed between the hours of 9 & 12 noon. The Scotland pronounced now 1 month's hard to U.K. (Winnipeg-ies) Divisional Band played in village & were during the evening weather very hot.	
	June 7		Paraded according to programme. Received news of attack by 2nd Army on YPRES Sector — news very encouraging. The Armentières front sent Lieut McQueen as organiser have programme of wire diagrams and opposition of trenches made by 19 t Bde. Weather unsettled, thunderstorms and light showers.	
	June 8		The company went for a stiff route march (9 miles). Received further encouraging news of YPRES attack. Returned to training. The company in the fullness of day	

WAR DIARY
or
INTELLIGENCE SUMMARY.
(Erase heading not required.)

Army Form C. 2118.

19th MACHINE GUN COMPANY.

Place	Date	Hour	Summary of Events and Information	Remarks and references to Appendices
In the Field	June 9 L		Company inspected by Brigadier at 9.30 a.m. Company drawn up in openeds sections in the eight fundred informs before the inspection the General spoke to each to the Officers and expressed himself as being greatly pleased with the smart and soldierly appearance of the men in their appearance and their turn out. The Company have great reason to rate themselves and the General was highly appreciative to all concerned.	
	June 10 L		Church Services held for all denominations	
	June 11 L		Paraded according to programme. Prayers heard inspection of rifles. Company much training for the offensive.	
			Coys. Commander summoned to that for interior relative inspection of Service gear & every equipment tomorrow.	

Pilling Lt. for O.C.

Army Form C. 2118.

WAR DIARY
or
INTELLIGENCE SUMMARY.
(Erase heading not required.)

19th MACHINE GUN COMPANY.
No..........
Date..........

Place	Date	Hour	Summary of Events and Information	Remarks and references to Appendices
Lyte Fields	June 13th		Paraded morning to Programme. Ers Return expected 11.5; Table "C" on the range. Weed semi-final of open events.	
	June 14		Inter evidence during morning. The show commenced at 2 pm. The profit was very well arranged. Audience enjoyed every item, especially Boxing Competence had the most applause. Entrances had been controlled by SE. Hurley, prevented the public. Chaplin to SE Hurley prevented the judges. The Royal Welsh Fusiliers band was in attendance.	
	June 15		The match of the Services took place press at 7 pm - NCE. Lewin being deciding the winners.	

A. Brogden Lyt
for O.C.

WAR DIARY
INTELLIGENCE SUMMARY

Army Form C. 2118.

19th MACHINE GUN COMPANY

Place	Date	Hour	Summary of Events and Information	Remarks and references to Appendices
Enfield	June 16		Paraded according to programme. Instructional class jointed in range. Port & Lakke C.	
	17		Coy paraded for Divine Service at BASSEUX at 10 a.m. Calls Commanded after the service presented Ribbons to officers and other ranks of the 19th Bde group. Cpl Dykes of this Coy was presented with the Italian Bronze medal Ribbon. Played final of four-a-side Brigade football match. Lost to R.F.S. by own goal.	
	June 18		The Coy marched to MOYENEVILLE Camp E. Relieving the 61st m.g. Coy. Lieut + T BROGDEN (acting company commander) of the OC 110th Coy reconnoitred the line with him in advance of arrangement for the relief tomorrow.	SB SW tent 4a
	19		Relieved the 110th Company in the line at 2 p.m. relief completed by 7 p.m. 4 guns in the Front line, 4 guns in the intermediate line, 4 guns on the second System Trench mah. 4 guns in reserve at Coy Headquarters 7.20 p.m. The remaining 4 guns held in reserve. W. line 4 a.m.	
	20		Captain Falkner returns from leave. Captain Falkner v/h BROGDEN vormother.	
	21		Lieut J.C. GRANT proceeded on leave to U.K.	

T.W.Brogden Lieut for O.C.

Army Form C. 2118.

19th MACHINE GUN COMPANY.

WAR DIARY
or
INTELLIGENCE SUMMARY.
(Erase heading not required.)

Instructions regarding War Diaries and Intelligence Summaries are contained in F.S. Regs., Part II. and the Staff Manual respectively. Title pages will be prepared in manuscript.

Place	Date	Hour	Summary of Events and Information	Remarks and references to Appendices
In the field	June 21st		Lieut. J. McQUEEN proceeded to No 3 Company A.S.C. for instruction in Transport Duties. Method of the report from the Army that casualties from shots occurred by the Second system are unknown.	
		22nd	The 4 Guns in Posh in the Divisional reserve. The 100th Company who are in Divisional Machine Gun Officer Major Hutchinson M.C. of the 100th M.G. Coy is appointed Divisional Machine Gun Officer. 2/Lt HARRISON reconnoitring the ground in the afternoon during four emplacements (for indirect fire) during the night.	
		23rd	The Brigade is to attack. 7.30pm 2/Lt LAUNDER is moved up to the front line with two Guns & Launch under the orders of O.C. 1st Devons. His orders are to consolidate after the capture has been taken. 9 pm 2/Lt HARRISON with No 3 Sections moved up to the indirect fire positions. 10.30 Capt Halkew moves the Brigade when he has the remain during the Battle.	
	24th	12 a.m.	Zero. The attack was unsuccessful. 2/Lt HARRISON fired 10,000 rounds sundered fire.	
		3 am	A German Machine Gun was seen firing from Tunnel Trench. A gun of No 1 Section under Lt. STOKES engaged the above. 8 of 250 rounds were fired.	
		3 pm	2/Lt LAUNDER is withdrawn from the front line. He was not called upon to do any thing last night.	

R. Morgan Lt for O.C.

Army Form C. 2118.

[Stamp: 19th MACHINE GUN COMPANY]

WAR DIARY
or
INTELLIGENCE SUMMARY.
(Erase heading not required.)

Instructions regarding War Diaries and Intelligence Summaries are contained in F. S. Regs., Part II. and the Staff Manual respectively. Title pages will be prepared in manuscript.

Place	Date	Hour	Summary of Events and Information	Remarks and references to Appendices
In the field	JUNE 24th	3pm	No 3 Section is withdrawn from the trenches for purposes of relief, and was relieved by the 100th M.G. Coy, who arrived at 6 p.m. The relief complete by 10 p.m. No. 2 Section relieved the 100th Coy in the forward posts in the second System. The remaining sections fell back to Bank E, MOYENNEVILLE	
	25th		The morning is spent with Gun cleaning &c G.Y 7-15.	
	26th		Training was carried out as usual. 1st parade as usual. Drill parade was pleased with it. The Brig. General inspected the Arms drill (10.3.) in the afternoon.	
			The Company was fallen out in the Second System.	
	27th		No 4 Section relieved No 2 Section in the morning as usual.	
			Training was carried out as usual.	
			Trainers was carried out for Lewis	
	28th		Lieut Weathers returned from leave.	
			Training in the morning as usual.	
	29th		Nos. 1,2,3 Sections, H.Qrs + Transport were relieved by the 64th Company, on relief complete they moved to MONCHY-AU-BOIS	
	30th		The morning was spent cleaning up etc. 100th Coy in the relief moved down from the No 4 Section was relieved by the 100th Coy at MONCHY	

A. P. Brogden Lieut for O.C.

Army Form C. 2118.

WAR DIARY
or
INTELLIGENCE SUMMARY
(Erase heading not required.)

Place	Date	Hour	Summary of Events and Information	Remarks and references to Appendices
In the field	1st July 1917		The Company still in MONCHY. Church Parade C of E 10-45 a.m. R.C. 9-15 a.m. Pres. Moral. 10-45 a.m. Passes were allowed to Bienvillers.	
	2nd July		LIEUT. MAC QUEEN returned from leave with the A.S.C. The Company moved by road to ACHEUX via BIENVILLERS, SOUASTRÉ, BAYEN COURT, SAILLY, BERTRANCOURT. Arrived with the Company was gone at 11-30 am to 1-30 PM. The Glorious Beaut march of with the UK.	
	3rd July		LIEUT. DEAN returned from leave. The Company moved by road to TALMAS via LEAL VILLERS, ARQUÈVES, RAINCHEVAL, PUCHEVILLERS. Very hot march.	
	4th July		The Company moved by road to BELLOY via NAOURS, VIGNACOURT. Wet morning much cooler. Very good Billets. Re arrangement of Sections. No 1 Lieut. LAUNDER & STOKES. No 2 Lt. GRANT & DEAN No 3 Lts. HARRISON & LIDIARD. No 4 Lieut. WATKINS & MERFIELD. Transport Officer Lieut MAC QUEEN.	
	5th July		The Company moved by road to BETTENCOURT via ZEUX, BOURDON, HANGEST & CONDE. Very cool march. The Divisional General called to see Billets &c.	
	6th July		The morning was spent cleaning Limbers, Guns &c. The Brig-General called to see Billets	

Ambrose Lieut for O.C.

Army Form C. 2118.

WAR DIARY
or
INTELLIGENCE SUMMARY.
(Erase heading not required.)

19th MACHINE GUN COMPY. Y.

Place	Date 1917	Hour	Summary of Events and Information	Remarks and references to Appendices
In the field	7th		Parades from 9-30 am until 11.45 am. Inspection of Kit & Gun Drill.	
	8th		Under orders to move & from Volunteer Church Parade. 6h.'s 11-30 am at AIRAINES R.C. Village Church. Our Movement AIRAINES arrangements made to take 2 officers & OR to AMIENS by motor lorry. There them acted as Base Depot footer to No.1 Section. Cpl Muson r-joined of 7-. 8 am - 11 am. Limbs Drill.	
	9th		Parades 6-30 - 7-. "Called". The Brig-General self off. Brigade Route March 9-30 am - 10 to 11 am. Gun Drill 6-30 am returned	
	10th		Parades 6-30 & 8 am to 11 am. Mechanism Stoppages Imm Drill.	
	11th		Lieut A. T. BROGDEN attended a Court Martial on Cpl. LOVELL of the company. The case adjourned.	
	12th		Lieut MAC-QUEEN proceeded to U.K. on leave. The Company was paid training carried on as usual until 11 am. at 2-30 Pm	

A. Brogden Lieut

A584. Wt. W4973 M687. 750,000 8/16 D. D. & L. Ltd. Forms/C.2118/13.

WAR DIARY or **INTELLIGENCE SUMMARY**

Army Form C. 2118.

299th MACHINE GUN COMPANY.

Place	Date 1917 JULY	Hour	Summary of Events and Information	Remarks and references to Appendices
In the field	12th		Lieut A.T. BROODEN attended the adjournal Court Marshal on A. LOVELL of this company.	
	13th	6 a.m. 8.50 am 10.30 am	Route march. Lt off returned 8.50 am. Training carried on afterwards until 10.30 am. Training of the company on allowed in any village on the NCO's men of the company.	
	14th		Brigade Ball/thing Own without a truss. Training Lieut Stokes succeeded on Can the Phy. Training, Use of cover & Visual Training match was arranged between the company & 19th Brig. HQ's. The company won A. Funnel polo Service for Ex. E. on Ground near our Transport lines. R.C & Ats. Volantry	
	15th	11 am.	Training until 11 am. Phy Training is Tactical Scheme.	
	16th	11 am.	Training until 11 am. Phy. Training, Picketing of Lenders, Lewis Drill. Lieut Chan attended as a member of a Court Marshal of the Bodyguards of the Governor. The first day of the Divisional Horse Shoes. The company won a Prize for Pack Saddles. Lamps were arranged to convey officers to N.C.O's to the shoes. The company from allotter Ox carts.	
	17th			A.T. Brooden Lieut

Army Form C. 2118.

WAR DIARY
or
INTELLIGENCE SUMMARY
(Erase heading not required.)

19th MACHINE GUN COMPANY.

Place	Date	Hour	Summary of Events and Information	Remarks and references to Appendices
In the field	JULY 18th		The company marched to the Divisional Horse Show returning in the evening. The company ran the coconut cart with them. The men threw clumes on the General & men had a very enjoyable stay — Sergt Newbery, Sergt Duncan were detailed to attend a Course of Machine Gun Work at CAMIERS	
	19th	11 a.m.	Gun Drill, Arms Drill, Saluting	
		2.30 P.M.	Day Firing. Training 2 Sections on Range with Guns Revolvers, 2 Sections training as usual	
	30th		Use of Ground, Methods of Indirect fire & quickly picking up of Targets. Lieut Stokes returned from leave from England. A Divisional Event was carried out. Lieut AT BROGDEN acted as Company Commander 2/Lt HARRISON acting as 2 i/c in Company	
	31st		Training as usual. Day Firing 2 Sections on Range with Guns & Revolvers, 2 Sections use of cover & Lieut AT BROGDEN & 2/Lt HARRISON returned from the Divisional event	
	22nd		Divine Service. All John Ferry left C. at Aucun. L/C Longhorn Pnrs Stewart Ayann the 2nd Royal Welsh Fus held some Battalion Sports in the afternoon the Company won three prizes in the open events	
				ATBrogden Lieut

Army Form C. 2118.

WAR DIARY
or
INTELLIGENCE SUMMARY.
(Erase heading not required.)

Instructions regarding War Diaries and Intelligence Summaries are contained in F.S. Regs., Part II. and the Staff Manual respectively. Title pages will be prepared in manuscript.

19th MACHINE GUN COMPANY

No..................
Date.................

Place	Date	Hour	Summary of Events and Information	Remarks and references to Appendices
I.B. Julu	JULY 22nd		Lieut J MCQUEEN returned from leave from U.K. Lieut LAVNDER admitted Dock Hospital	
	23rd		Training as usual. Phys. Training, 2 Sections on Range with Guns (Stoppages) Revolvers. 2 Sections Gun Drill in Box Respirators, Making of Range Cards	
	24th		Training until 11 a.m. Phys Training, 2 Sections on Range with Guns Revolvers 2 Sections Gun Drill in Box Respirators, Making of Range Cards. Lieut AN M WATKINS had to report to the ADMS at Qn. H.2. for Medical examination for transferring to Indian Army)	
	25th		Training as usual. Phy Training Range (Rifle Practise) The Brig. General called. Sergt Edward (Transport) 1.M 50 Pte BRYDEN with reference to his application for a commission.	
	26th/27th		Parade as usual. Phy Training 8th 11 am. Under Section Officers arrangements Training as usual. In Armourer Serjt offrs Saw a Gun test at WPDM. El	
	28th		Phy Training; Mechanism Care of Guns, Aiming Drill Stoppages	A Wjordan Lieut

A5834 Wt. W4973/M687 750,000 8/16 D. D. & L. Ltd. Forms/C.2118/13.

Army Form C. 2118.

WAR DIARY
or
INTELLIGENCE SUMMARY.
(Erase heading not required.)

19th MACHINE GUN COMPANY.
No..................
Date..................

Place	Date	Hour	Summary of Events and Information	Remarks and references to Appendices
Nieuport	28th July 1917		A. Staff General Carol Maxhee assembled at Headquarters the Company & the Brig of Cpl. Worship Lung & the company Cpl. General who audited the GAMERS on a Mghno Gun Corps Centre section. Nearing this had all volunteer service. Suff.	
	30th		Hams James the Captain from Hd Base. The Company's No. 1/14 coys to Guards would station our segments & the building.	
	31st		with the DUNKERQUE. Lieut Horrin in charge left at 12-15 am. 31st/8 & arriving at POINT REHY Retiring for DUNKERQUE. The Company entering at 8.55 am Arr. at Dunkerque at 5.30 P.M. leaving Dont Bem at Mandlin by canal to BRAY DUNES The Company Hd. arriving there by 10.45 P.M.	

R.M.Bogden Lieut

Army Form C. 2118.

WAR DIARY
or
INTELLIGENCE SUMMARY.
(Erase heading not required.)

19th MACHINE GUN COMPANY.

Place	Date	Hour	Summary of Events and Information	Remarks and references to Appendices
	1st		[illegible handwritten entries]	
	2nd			
	3rd			
	4th			
	5th			
	6th			

Army Form C. 2118.

WAR DIARY
or
INTELLIGENCE SUMMARY.
(Erase heading not required.)

Instructions regarding War Diaries and Intelligence Summaries are contained in F. S. Regs., Part II. and the Staff Manual respectively. Title pages will be prepared in manuscript.

18th MACHINE GUN COMPANY.
No.......... Date..........

Place	Date	Hour	Summary of Events and Information	Remarks and references to Appendices
In the field	1917 AUGUST 6th		The Company was took at 2.30 pm and Lieut Watkins Sergt Ash & Sergt Parker proceeded to 48 Squadron R.F.C. to attend an aircraft course and the duties of L.A.A Brigade R.F.C.	
	7th		Company moved up at 8.10 am with march discipline and inspection by Major Furney. Gun drill on Box Respirators. Musketry. Gun & Lewis Carriage & all different Ranges. Gun drill. Lecture. Gun Cam. Ranges. Gun Car. Range and Musketry. HD with XV Corps tractors. Range practice was arranged for	
	8th		7.15 am to 8.15 am. HD with Rifle Range for recreation. Battery Sergt at 1.15 pm.	
	9th		7.15 am. HD with Rifle. Gun drill. Lectures – 3 officers and 6 other ranks proceeded to U.K. on leave to the U.K.	
	10th		11 am. Lewis Range Firing & Rifle Range Firing Tug of War. The Company moved off at 9.15 am. The Brig-General was present from please at the outpost of 1 M.G. corps Huts in the wood. O.C.G. 18 Gun Company & ABBEVILLE to attend a Transport course at	

A5834 Wt. W4973/M687 750,000 8/16 D. D. & L. Ltd. Forms/C.2118/13.

WAR DIARY or INTELLIGENCE SUMMARY

Army Form C. 2118.

Place	Date	Hour	Summary of Events and Information	Remarks and references to Appendices
Sch.	1917 AUGUST 10th		Coys at their transport lines	
	11th		Lieut. H.H. Hill returned from Divisional Gas Course. 2/Lt Walker proceeded on 14 days leave to UK. The Coy Commander inspected transport of the Coy.	
			Brigade Headquarters.	
			Hounds 7.15am & 12 noon. The transport & Br. Reserves Unit Pigeon Loft Gun Classes were inspected by the R.H. Brigade	
			Coys 7. Lectures were the first two hours of the first night.	
		8.30 pm. M.M.R.B.A.Y. was opened to officers at 9.30 am. R.E 9am	
	12th		Church Parade by C.O.'s was attended by Brigade & Company Commander.	
			The transport officer attended a Brigade Conference.	
			2/Lt C. W. Boyd's drew from stores the 48th Squadron R.F.C. for a course in aerial gas work.	
	13th		Company took work about eight miles. The Company moved off at 8.30 am.	

WAR DIARY or INTELLIGENCE SUMMARY

Army Form C. 2118.

190th MACHINE GUN COMPANY

Place	Date	Hour	Summary of Events and Information	Remarks and references to Appendices
Inkerfield	August 1916			
	15th		Powder 7.15 to 11 A.M. From 9 A.M. to 11 A.M. the Coy fired a barrage into the area. Returned observers of fire. Weather very fine & hot.	
			The Coy paraded with the Canadians. The Coy left BRAY DUNES at 5 A.M. (and reached Inkerfield WIED 27 at 10.30 A.M. The march discipline was very good. Lt MERFIELD went ahead & found a billet.	
	16th		Col FAULKNER spent the day to ascertain the lines and railway.	
			Clerks & staff will be 19th M.G. Coy paraded for class of guns & ammunition from 9.30 A.M. to 11 A.M.	
	17th		Lt WATKINS and Lt LIDDIARD went up for reconnaissance & returned at 11 A.M.	
	18th		The Coy relieved the 199th M.G. Coy in the line. The relief commenced at 7 P.M. & completed at 11 P.M. Lt MERFIELD & Lt DEAN and No 1,2 sections complete at 11 P.M. Lt B. Section at WIED 27.	

WAR DIARY or INTELLIGENCE SUMMARY

Army Form C. 2118.

Place	Date	Hour	Summary of Events and Information	Remarks and references to Appendices
Intrjed	Aug 19th		D.C. Coy relieved No 3 & 4 sections in the line.	
	20th		L. Coy relieved No 3 & 4 sections in the line and changed all avail. guns had out by No 3 section. Also visited C.O. of the Royal Fusiliers re arrange any details of operations. From 7.15 to 8.25 P.M. 5000 fired on to cross roads & trench junctions of German communication trench. One gun put out of action by our splinters in the trench & might very good.	
	21st		Visited my Divisional Machine Gun Officer who recommended the positions also made a reconnaissance of ground during day. Gun on enti-aircraft fired 200 rounds & 17 aircraft. [illegible signature]	
	22nd		Relief — this section took place last night. D.C. Coy noted guns on right of Bn. front. L. Aff's & St. Hn.fn. started fire from as before. Intensive firing commencing at 7 P.M. and reliefs complete reported at 10.30. Fired 5,600 R.ds indirect fire on to German communication trenches, cross roads also 1,800 rounds fired at aircraft. Night very quiet.	

WAR DIARY or INTELLIGENCE SUMMARY

Army Form C. 2118.

19th MACHINE GUN COMPANY.

Place	Date	Hour	Summary of Events and Information	Remarks and references to Appendices
In the field	Aug 23rd		Selected positions for the guns on the proposed forward line. Sections worked at different positions and carried forward different types and 5000 rounds of various natures of German ammunition. 2250 rounds fired at aircraft. Two SAA reported from the 248th Coy. Relief handed over to No 2 Section having stood to. One gun of this section put 5½ action by a direct hit. In all 5250 rounds of ammunition expended on German trenches.	
	24th		O.C. Coy visited sections also visited guns of the 9th Coy conferring re fire to front. Arranged a plan for the disposition of the guns in connection with a proposed raid on the enemies trenches. Also arranged with Capt. BELEBY 248 Coy to cooperate. At 1630 conference at Brigade headquarters explained proposed work of the machine guns in this raid. In all 5500 indirect fire on enemies communications	
	25th			

Army Form C. 2118.

WAR DIARY
or
INTELLIGENCE SUMMARY.
(Erase heading not required.)

19th MACHINE GUN COMPANY.

Place	Date	Hour	Summary of Events and Information	Remarks and references to Appendices
Inflyfield	Aug 26th		A gas attack made on the 98th Bde front also a road on 91st Bde front. Our front trenches/section fired 5500 rounds on to trench junction and road. The enemy communication during the night. No section heavily shelled also the gas sentry reported that there was some gas shells. Returned by Jan. 14th Corps. the line Rly Cottage communication at 1.15 P.M. that quiet confirm reported at 11.30 P.M. Our fully confirm to nowhere. Enemy sh[ells] in Pa Panne quarters.	
	27th		Arrive at 12 P.M. no parades	
	28th			
	29th	10.30am	The Coy moved by buses to PONT DE NYNTHE arriving at 10.30 a.m. Breakfast provided by road assumed at 2.30 am.	
	30th		Coy Parades; Changing Lewis and gun drill section armaments. Lt Keller R.W.S. reported for duty and was temporarily posted to No 4 section	

J Grant Major

Army Form C. 2118.

WAR DIARY
or
INTELLIGENCE SUMMARY.
(Erase heading not required.)

12th MACHINE GUN COMPANY.

Place	Date	Hour	Summary of Events and Information	Remarks and references to Appendices
Billyfield	Aug 31st		The Coy paraded ready to move at 10.15 a.m. moved off at 10.20 a.m. marching to GRAND (POINT DE SYNTHE) Billets reaching their destination at 5 P.M. The Billets situated at LE COSTHOL near MOULLE were fairly plenty & accommodation for Officers, men and transport.	

J. Grant Major

CONFIDENTIAL.

Vol 20

WAR DIARY
OF
19TH MACHINE GUN COMPANY.

19th
MACHINE GUN
COMPANY.
No............
Date... 1/10/17...

Month 30-9-17.

From 1-9-17

J. Grantke A/Capt.

Army Form C. 2118.

WAR DIARY
or
INTELLIGENCE SUMMARY

(Erase heading not required.)

Instructions regarding War Diaries and Intelligence Summaries are contained in F.S. Regs., Part II. and the Staff Manual respectively. Title pages will be prepared in manuscript.

Place	Date	Hour	Summary of Events and Information	Remarks and references to Appendices
Inglefield	Sept 1st		Coy parades 9.30 to 12 noon. Cleaning of guns + personal equipment after action arrangements. 2/Lt Kelland posted for duty with No 4 Section.	
	Sept 2nd		Church Parade Coy R 9.30 am Bn Church Parade 10.30 am R.E. 11 am 7.30 to 7.45 am Physical training gam 11 am under section arrangements. Arms drill under Coy Sergt Major from 11.15 to 12 noon. A Court of Inquiry assembled to enquire into the loss of	
	3rd		1 Bicycle and Spare parts	
	4th		Bn foot Route March. Coy paraded at 9.25 am. Transport played No 3 section football rendered on a draw	
	5th		Coy parades 7.30 to 7.45 Physical training 9 to 11 am under section arrangements. 2/Lt McKenzie reported and posted to No 4 section for duty. Two guns mounted for anti aircraft duty, mounted at E.P.M. and dismounted the following morning at 6 am Bt Sykes detailed to build anti aircraft position	

WAR DIARY or INTELLIGENCE SUMMARY

Army Form C. 2118.

(Erase heading not required.)

Place	Date	Hour	Summary of Events and Information	Remarks and references to Appendices
Julyfer	Sept 5th		2/Lt McCosh arrived and was posted for duty with No 2 Section	
	6th		2/Lt Hamilton attended as a member of C.C.M. held at Hd Quarters. Coy Parades 7.30 to 7.45am + 9am to 12 noon.	
	7.		Nos 1 & 3 sections left MOULLE with their transport wagons & proceeded by road. The sections marched to WATTEN where they entrained. They detrained at ABELEE & proceeded by motor lorry to DICKEBUSH where they hutted in a field SOUTH and (?) of the running half of the Coy remained at MOULLE having parades under officers arranged by 9am to 12 noon. Lt Grant was left in charge of detachment.	
	8th		Nos 3 & 4 sections camped moved to field at Northrest of village. Nos 1 & 2 section Coy parades in Physical Training, Arms Drill and Bayonet Drill.	
	9.		Nos 1 & 2 sections Church Parade R.C. at 8.45am C of E at 10 am. Bathing 11am Lt Mitchell + 2/Lt McCosh recommend Nos 3 & 4 Coys front returning at 5 P.M.	

WAR DIARY
INTELLIGENCE SUMMARY
(Erase heading not required.)

Army Form C. 2118.

Place	Date	Hour	Summary of Events and Information	Remarks and references to Appendices
Wizernes	Sept 1918	11	Nos 1 & 2 sections Coy Parader Weather full overnight. Took Route March, passing about ½ mile from 2.30am to Coy parade.	
	12		C.O. Lt Harrison & Lt McKenzie met attached of 13th M.G. Coy & recommended the line. Patrol 50 O.R. carried 150,000 rounds of S.A.A. from VALLEY COTTAGES to JEFFREY Dump	
	13		Dump tp. Lt Askus + 2/Lt Liddell took charge of 500 O.R. who carried further 150,000 rounds of S.A.A. to JEFFREY DUMP. Nos 2 & 4 sections marched from MOULLE to ARQUES on their way to other line. Weather fine.	
	14		Lt Maynard recommoitred roads & land for transport his head. Nos 3 & 4 sections with their transport marched from ARQUES to BOESCHEPES a distance of 28 miles. They had a midday halt for 1½ hr at 1 o'clock & after Hazebrouck. They marched through the town. The Billets not all that was hoped. Accommodation was remarkably good. A remark to this effect in the D.M.G.O was accompanied by nasty fire overnight	

WAR DIARY
or
INTELLIGENCE SUMMARY.

Army Form C. 2118.

Place	Date	Hour	Summary of Events and Information	Remarks and references to Appendices
Inkped Sept	15th		The C.O., Lt Stokes & Lt Harrison reconnoitred gun positions, dumps & dugouts. Sun O.R. departed whilst his 1st gun position No 2 / 4 sections with transport marched (BOESCHEPES to DICKEBUSH. No fall out after the present day's long march.	
	16th		D.M.G.O. reconnoitred lines with Lt Harrison.	
	17th		Hun Coy. stationed at DICKEBUSH. No Parades. Lt Kaveft, 2Lt McKengie & Lt Moyfeld reconnoitred gun positions.	
	18th		The Coy moved into the line at 3AM. Lt Harrison, Lt Deacon, 2Lt Kavell & 2Lt McKengie remain at B. Echelon Casualties this day Coy with transport moved forward TO R TO P our (VALLEY COTTAGES). On reaching "VALLEY COTTAGES" change from into enemy barrage + withdraw 2 Casualties to VALLEY COTTAGES whilst guns & the	

Place	Date	Hour	Summary of Events and Information	Remarks and references to Appendices
	Sept 19		War ordered and transport returned to DICKEBUSH. The Coy then moved with Albans. The remainder of the unit's strength in charge of the officer & cooks & reminding parties & lines hut but at [Chuck out?] from heavy shell fire. Bn myself & Stokes detached as Batn. Commander res. Some rain during the night.	
	20th		Think most of a little….. there half an hour an…. of demands of day. 5.40 a.m. All spirits in position by 5.35 a.m. Fire to 5.40 a.m. until 6.15 a.m. but account of infantry was not warned until …… they took up their position advancing through position. At 7.30 a.m. completed firing it moving forward at 7.50 a.m. Capt Edmund B. Myself, Lt [Heathers?] & 25 [Bunch?] & concentrated forward positions small engineer…… that the 2nd objection had been taken. After reporting the situation moved forward & [overlooked?] the [temperature?] + Alln. for cover for the men. Orders received D.M.G.B. to be prepared to fire on SOS lines by 5 P.M. On completion of work & laying of lines & …… telephone to dug outs (B.O.S. & HQ) telegraphed …… about 4.45 P.M.	

WAR DIARY
or
INTELLIGENCE SUMMARY.
(Erase heading not required.)

Army Form C. 2118.

Place	Date	Hour	Summary of Events and Information	Remarks and references to Appendices
	Sept 20th		and the enemy fired about 3 shells per gun. Casualties this day 1 O.R. killed, Capt Fellows seriously wounded, 2 Lt. Bickoff slightly wounded + 2 O.Rs wounded.	
	21st		Fired all day. All guns fired on SOS lines from 4 am. Approximately 2500 Rds indirect. HE shrapnel & Stokes recently captured positions for harassing Battery positions for 33rd Div. operations throughout. 15 attempts by Div & ft artillery to neutralize enemy 19.2 + 248 Guns at 11 am. At 2.30 pm recommenced hostile fire. German counter attack E & S.E of 721 e extended A Coy fired 1500 rounds per gun on front indicated. At 4 P.M. massive apparently dispersed. Another counter attack attempted by enemy about 7.15 PM. SOS signals seen. A & D & B sections swift shoot 2000 rds for gun in the first 3 for shrapnel is 54 wounded + the whole Coy fired for about 4 minutes at rate of a half round per minute	

Place	Date	Hour	Summary of Events and Information	Remarks and references to Appendices
A	Sept 22nd		Artillery fire decreased & there was no enemy aircraft during day. 1 Casualty this day. Received relief orders from Bn Hdqrs at 12.15 a.m. withdrew by DICKEBUSH HUTS (All Coys) & then to VALLEY COTTAGES.	
	22nd		by 4 A.M. No casualties this day. Fine weather. Men settled in dug outs. Bt Decon Rifle ranges for transport. Rifles - Bn rest and re-equipt.	
	23		Working parties of 32 men who were an officer supplied for duty. These were distributed between the four companies. Detailed for range work, much in the way hours. The ammunition state of each Coy, Bt GHQ Bt, Harlem recommend position & the kind of Rifle 33rd. Dist Stokes Ammunition. All coys went to the Range in early morning. Grenade training were refilled to clear gun pit & graded hedges for new rifle Fire well. Stokes gun pit graded hedges for new Rotation inspection at 4 P.M.	

WAR DIARY
or
INTELLIGENCE SUMMARY.
(Erase heading not required.)

Army Form C. 2118.

Place	Date	Hour	Summary of Events and Information	Remarks and references to Appendices
	August Sept 23		Pte LEWTHWAITE absent from the 5th M.G. Coy. states that whilst out on Communication Wiring fatigue, Pte Lewthwaite, Grant and Pte McCosh moved up together. Pte McCosh wounded on way up, whilst he reconnoitred. Pte McCosh having early morning returning in a mist.	
	24			
	25	1:10 am	The Coy moved up to the firing hand at 1:10 am, to its position by down also to in position before the retaliation to the practice barrage which was let place at 6 A.M. A battalion from D.M.G.O. for operations carried out on 23rd inst:- 2nd & 3rd M.G. Companies of 23rd ERSATZ. machine Guns from 2nd & 3rd M.G. Company of 23rd ERSATZ Regt. state they were unable to think at present on M.G. Barrage owing to defficient Gr [illegible] Dug outs. This Regt Garrison the front attacked by 23rd Div with [illegible] the 9th Field company operated separately.	

WAR DIARY
or
INTELLIGENCE SUMMARY.

(Erase heading not required.)

Army Form C. 2118.

Place	Date	Hour	Summary of Events and Information	Remarks and references to Appendices
	Sept 25		Emplacements were dug before dawn. Fired on S.O.S. at 5 P.M. 6,080 rounds were fired. The whole of one gun's team casualties.	
	26		Zero hour was 5.50 a.m. Thankful Barrage was fired at 5.50 a.m. 5.57 a.m. 16 guns 15,000 rounds were fired. The second half was fired 5.57 a.m. to 7.25 a.m. 50,000 rounds fired. Pt. Atkins was killed whilst direct the fire of his gun team. Our casualties this day. At 5.15 P.M. Infantry was spotted on the Enemy's extreme front in the vicinity of POLDERHOEK (and GHELUVELT until 5.45 P.M. when S.O.S. signals were answered by fire from all 16 guns (3,239 rounds were fired.)	
	27		4.0 a.m. to 4.55 a.m. Harrassing fire. 4.55 a.m. S.O.S. 6.15 & 8 A.M S.O.S. Intermittent fire 2,2 0,000 rounds fired.	

Army Form C. 2118.

WAR DIARY
or
INTELLIGENCE SUMMARY.
(Erase heading not required.)

Place	Date	Hour	Summary of Events and Information	Remarks and references to Appendices
	Sept 28		The Coy. with drew at 11 am and returned to B. Echelon	
	29		Entrained for EBLINGHAM arrived at 5.35 am and marched to billets at BLAINGHAM	
	30		The Coy. paraded for change of underwear, gum and equipment at 9am to 12 noon. (Commanding Officers inspection at 2.30 pm	

H Grant R.

WAR DIARY
INTELLIGENCE SUMMARY

Place	Date	Hour	Summary of Events and Information	Remarks and references to Appendices
Authuille	Oct 2nd		The Bde paraded for preparation inspection by Brigadier for the inspection by the Commander-in-Chief. Afternoon Kit inspection and C.O.'s chief parade	
	3rd		The Bn paraded at 9.30 a.m. and was inspected by the Bde. parader, afterwards for inspection by Commander-in-Chief, the infantry thereof filed at 12 noon followed by a march past in column of route. The Bn of 32 men allowed at officers of establishment were attached to each Coy. for earth than men are attached to the Coy for Cpt. and instruction in the Vickers and German Machine Guns.	
	4th		Coy paraded which were from 9-12 consisted of (1) Physical drill 7.30 -7.45 (2) Barrage drill and Limber tracking from 9-12. Lieut. Mayfield took the 32 attached men on the gun. Lieut. Shallard took the new N.C.O.s in map reading, and in the afternoon went off billeting for the Company to La Val D'Acquin.	
	5th		Moved by road from Blanyham to La Val D'Acquin arriving about 3 o'clock. Orders to move again to the Bosquin Area arrived	

Army Form C. 2118.

Army Form C. 2118.

WAR DIARY
or
INTELLIGENCE SUMMARY.
(Erase heading not required.)

Instructions regarding War Diaries and Intelligence Summaries are contained in F. S. Regs., Part II. and the Staff Manual respectively. Title pages will be prepared in manuscript.

Place	Date	Hour	Summary of Events and Information	Remarks and references to Appendices
In the field	6th	at 6.30 p.m.	Leave but sent in to Brigadier. Lieut MacQueen left with transport at 6 o'clock to proceed by road stopping at Blaringhem for the night. Lieut Mayfield went by 11 a.m train from Wizerne as billetting officer to Bailleul.	
	6th		Pontoon followed by train leaving at 1.30 p.m. Billets were in camp at Goutepus. Guides from 42nd Bay were at station to lead boy to billets. Weather unsettled and very cold.	
	7th		B.O. and Lieut Mayfield proceeded up the line to reconnoitre, reporting at 42nd Brigade H.Q. at 11 a.m., from where they got a guide for 42nd M.G. Coy H.Q. H.Q. of M.G. Coy just on the right of Mesnin, excellent dug out. Brigadier came over to see B.O. in the morning and asked for a fresh leave list. Lieut MacQueen arrived with transport in the afternoon. Weather fine, line very quiet.	

A5834 Wt. W4973/M687 750,000 8/16 D.D. & L. Ltd. Forms/C.2118/13.

Army Form C. 2118.

WAR DIARY
or
INTELLIGENCE SUMMARY.
(Erase heading not required.)

Instructions regarding War Diaries and Intelligence Summaries are contained in F. S. Regs., Part II. and the Staff Manual respectively. Title pages will be prepared in manuscript.

Place	Date	Hour	Summary of Events and Information	Remarks and references to Appendices
In the field	8th		Operation Orders for relief given to each Platoon Officer. C.O. and Lieut Milne Quier proceeded up to the line to reconnoitre. Lieut McCannon and Lieut Mayfield who proceeded up the line at 2 p.m. via Brigade H.Q.'s. Reconnoissance to move to Penzance Camp. Sergt-Major sent forward to billet Company.	
	9th		Relief of 2nd Company in the line. Relief complete at 12.30 a.m. Weather very wet and night pitch dark. C.O. proceeded on leave. Lieut Merrifield took over second in command and Lieut Grant took 1st Command. 90th Machine Gun Coy put five guns in the line under Lieut Rennie. Capt Gallacher late Company Commander awarded the Military Cross and Sergt Guthrie awarded the D.C.M. by the Brig G.	
	10th		Four German planes flew over at the height of 3000 ft. and dropped bombs near Company H.Q. They were driven by our anti-aircraft fire. H.V. Mellor was witness also to Coy H.Q. Weather very clear.	
	11th		Coy R.O. heavily shelled. D.H.Q G.O. came up to arrange next explosion of defence. Enemy aircraft dropped on hand near one of our positions. 50 rounds were fired. Weather fair.	

Army Form C. 2118.

WAR DIARY
or
INTELLIGENCE SUMMARY.
(Erase heading not required.)

Instructions regarding War Diaries and Intelligence Summaries are contained in F. S. Regs., Part II. and the Staff Manual respectively. Title pages will be prepared in manuscript.

Place	Date	Hour	Summary of Events and Information	Remarks and references to Appendices
In the Field	15/10/17		Lt MIRFIELD proceeded on leave. 2/Lt KALLEND took over 2nd in Command. Positions reconnoitred by Section Officers for new zyphers of defence. Scales fire during day but during night.	
	16/10/17		4 Officers of 2nd L.M.G. Coy came to make reconnaissance of ground. D.A.G.O. & C.O. of 10th M.G. Coy arrived. Coy R.O. went around. Inspect activities of sections & positions with him also went round to report to action. Enemy shelled 40's Position and thereof to must 16 report heart. Section Rear.	
	16/10/17		Enemy Stellt on position during the morning. D.M.G.O. came to Coy R.D. re situation & positions. Live Gun's during afternoon. Enemy having Stellbaum Position	

(A7093) Wt. W12539/M1293 75,000. 1/17. D.D. & L., Ltd. Forms/C.2118/14.

Army Form C. 2118.

WAR DIARY
or
INTELLIGENCE SUMMARY.

(Erase heading not required.)

Instructions regarding War Diaries and Intelligence Summaries are contained in F. S. Regs., Part II. and the Staff Manual respectively. Title pages will be prepared in manuscript.

Place	Date	Hour	Summary of Events and Information	Remarks and references to Appendices
IN THE FIELD	14/10/17		and communications during night. Operation orders sent to Colonel O'Brien about Relief. Weather fair.	
	15/10/17		Col. H.O. heavily shelled during morning. C.O. of 10th moved to take over at 4 o'clock p.m. Relief started at 5.30 p.m. and completed at 9 p.m. Company went to Hints 108 C 8.9.0 for rest. Weather showery.	
	16/10/17		Reorganization of Company. 2nd Lieut. Prout O/C Company cleaned kits & equipment.	
	17/10/17		France: Bests Jr. near river Craighern jour 9.30 to 10.15. Various inspections for want of cleaning	
	18/10/17		Company paraded for inspection by Brigadier at 9.15 am. Men afterwards cleaned equipment.	

WAR DIARY
or
INTELLIGENCE SUMMARY.
(Erase heading not required.)

Army Form C. 2118.

Place	Date	Hour	Summary of Events and Information	Remarks and references to Appendices
IN THE FIELD	19.10.7		Company parade under Coolen Arrangements - men cleaning - chasing of deficiencies - applied new pained under Major f. Sutton instruction in M.G. work. Watt F. Claypeale.	
	20.10.7		Company parade. 9 am inspection of car figure. 10am L.A. 11am - 12 noon remedial drill. Attendance parade under Major for fractes instruction. Meeting was asked between Captain Officers & Sgts. to expect into and arrange plots for the men. 2/Lt PARKER went on Course of Instruction into R.F.A. Captain Parata Church Parade. 10.30 am service in Church. Service Menu Eglise R.C. at 10.15am for men on Coast Coated to bed.	
	21.10.7		Coys Average Guard. Two frames at 9 am for the Queen and details taken about Coolie.	

(A7092). Wt. W12836/M1293. 75,000. 1/17. D.D. & L., Ltd. Forms/C.2118.14.

Army Form C. 2118.

WAR DIARY
or
INTELLIGENCE SUMMARY.
(Erase heading not required.)

Place	Date	Hour	Summary of Events and Information	Remarks and references to Appendices
In the Field	5/10/19		O.C. H.Q. to K.R. L/c Sergt. Rose and Pte. Clarke at 6am 2/10/19 under M.O. by Air.	
	7/10/19		Company Parade: 6.30 - 6.45 am Physical Training under Orderly Officer. 9am - 11am T.O.E.T and Bolero Arrangements. Instructors in ?harge. Tools were now made use of. Major Thompson, L/c moved in aft. & that afternoon went to Roundon Lines. He moved & advanced B.Reserve. O.C. annual Lunch Roundout.	
	13/10/19		O.C. inspected Company at 9am. Owing to bad weather Section to place in huts. Company Parades 9.30 am - Room Inspection. Arrangements. ¼ Gun Teams under L/c LOCKHART Lt and Att. Aircraft Pictures from 248 Company.	

WAR DIARY
or
INTELLIGENCE SUMMARY.
(Erase heading not required.)

Army Form C. 2118.

Instructions regarding War Diaries and Intelligence Summaries are contained in F.S. Regs., Part II. and the Staff Manual respectively. Title pages will be prepared in manuscript.

Place	Date	Hour	Summary of Events and Information	Remarks and references to Appendices
IN THE FIELD	24/9/17		Lt GRANT went on leave. 2/Lt PARKER arrived back from course of Instruction with Albany. Company Parade. Gun Infantry Co. 9am - 6.30am Arm Drill 10.30am - 11am D.A. 11 - 11.30am Musketry. 11.30am - 12noon Gunland. Promotion made - Cpl KEMPSELL Bte 2/Lt/Sgt (near H Cpl GILLESPIE thence Stationed 30-9-17 L/Cpl WEBB to be acting Corpral vice Cpl KEMPSELL L/Cpl 4/9/Sept 2-9-17 2/9/17 H/Cpl STAFFORD to be return Corpral Lampard Stationed 4/9/17 L/Cpl H/Cpl HUSH Lampetry Paid H/Cpl. Vice H/Cpl STEPPS. H/Cpl Lampard 2-9-17. TRANSPORT moved to PENZANCE LINES.	
IN THE FIELD	25/9/17		Company Orders Company Orders. Physical training 9-11am Tender Lecture Arrangements for Owner of CARRIERS, Ration, Ammunition Brigade Stone, Signalling Gear and the G School. Lt. MORFIELD moved Chief Guardian Transportation Lict to HILLSIDE CAMP	

WAR DIARY
or
INTELLIGENCE SUMMARY.
(Erase heading not required.)

Army Form C. 2118.

Place	Date	Hour	Summary of Events and Information	Remarks and references to Appendices
IN THE FIELD	26/10/17		Company Orders. Coys a.m. — Yours afternoon. 9-9.30 a.m. Preparation of Rifles for Stoppages. 9.15 a.m - 12 noon Lewis an Range by attached men. Gun. C.O. visited 2/Lt. LOCKHART on the line.	
	27/10/17		LIEUT. MERFIELD took out 2nd I/c. Parade as usual. 2/LIEUT. LOCKHART. and No. 4 section came out of the line relieved by 100th Inf. Bde. M.G. Coy. Belt boxes handed out. Limbers went to GOOSEBERRY FARM to bring out kit. Company was paid.	
	28/10/17		Church Parade. Attached men fired on range under 2/LIEUT. KALLEND. Attached men fired on range under 2/LIEUT. BALSHAW. Pt. JENKINS made unpaid 2/Cpl.	
	29/10/17 →		LIEUT. HARRISON returned from course at CAMIERS. Reputators inspected by Sergt. ROSE. Classes fired on range under 2nd LT. KALLEND. 2/LT. BALSHAW proceeded on a course with the R.F.A.	

WAR DIARY
or
INTELLIGENCE SUMMARY.
(Erase heading not required.)

Army Form C. 2118.

Place	Date	Hour	Summary of Events and Information	Remarks and references to Appendices
In the field	29/10/17		Sgt HUNT. L/Cpl REEDMAN and Cpl PHIPPS returned from course at Lozinon.	
	30/10/17		1/Cpl STAFFORD promoted a/Corporal. 1/Cpl McINTOSH to be paid. Box Respirators inspected. C.O. Inspected Company in Drill Order. C.O. and LIEUT HARRISON went up the line to reconnoitre. Parades as usual. The Company held a concert in the evening. L/C Armstrong and Pte LINCOLN returned from leave. Pte Palmer went on leave (10 days). Weather dull and showery.	
	31/10/17		Pte WILD proceeded on leave (15 days). We relieved the 98th M.G. Coy in the line by 12 guns, the other 4 guns were supplied by the 248th Coy. Relief completed by 7.30 p.m. Very quiet. Equipment came up most of the way by trolley. Weather fine.	

Confidential

War Diary

19th Machine Gun Company

To November 30th 1917

For Capt and the
OC 19 MG Company

Army Form C. 2118.

WAR DIARY
or
INTELLIGENCE SUMMARY.
(Erase heading not required.)

Instructions regarding War Diaries and Intelligence Summaries are contained in F. S. Regs., Part II. and the Staff Manual respectively. Title pages will be prepared in manuscript.

Place	Date	Hour	Summary of Events and Information	Remarks and references to Appendices
Ypres	November 1st		C.O. visited front line.	
	2nd		Bn. Officers awarded the Mil. Cross. E. Sgt Paull awarded D.C.M. Rifle-men awarded for gallantry in full in War 25/26. During the attack on YPRES. Bt. Parker held 1st Battn at Coy. H.Q. task of very onerous nature & although acted in two positions & all this enabled the Coy to form from the R to a position during the day & caused much discomfort to the enemy.	
	3rd		On a party coming thro' our front, by D.M.G's was carried out by all sections. E.A. was attended to by Pte Pitt an American of the Bn. Coy applied medical comforts to the line until H.Q. Ambulance [?] arrived. Heavily shelled the Coy during the morning.	
	4th		R.6 am misted gun position front of the enemy 24 Ploy	

Instructions regarding War Diaries and Intelligence Summaries are contained in F. S. Regs., Part II. and the Staff Manual respectively. Title pages will be prepared in manuscript.

WAR DIARY
or
INTELLIGENCE SUMMARY.
(Erase heading not required.)

Army Form C. 2118.

Place	Date	Hour	Summary of Events and Information	Remarks and references to Appendices
	4th		Battalion relief took place during the night. Two spies captured in MESINES (Weather very misty)	
	5th		Lt. Conn returned to Bde H.Q. and Lt. Stanhope another American officer joined for instruction (Weather misty)	
	6th		Lt. Lowe R.F.A. returned to duty with his battery. C.O. & the American officer made a reconnaissance of the line. 2/Lt McAdam reported to the Coy for duty & was posted to No 2 Section. Two American officers visited Coy H.Q. 2/Lt Lockhart reported to Coy H.Q. for relief orders	
			Bde relief took place less the M.G. Coy	
	8th		All gunpositions changed at last moment. Coy relieved by 10th Coy. Relief reported complete at 8.45 pm. Coy returned to BULFORD CAMP	
			GAPARD FM Section H.Q. blown in by shell fire. Two E.A. were brought down by Machine Gun fire of this Coy	

WAR DIARY
INTELLIGENCE SUMMARY

Place	Date	Hour	Summary of Events and Information	Remarks and references to Appendices
9th		12.	The Coy started at Bulford Camp, Nos paraded the Coy here from Ireland, in the line the previous night, fitted 16th Machine Gun Coy	
		11 a.	Coy proceded when inspected Chamberlain the drawing of differences and equipment of section equipment ( ) Coy paraded. Chief Church Parade at 10 am Lieut Col. Clarke paraded and left next morning for France	
		12.2	Parties in the town Cpl ... included for paths at WULVERGHEM between the lines & ... 9 Sec. Runners out. The entrenchments, Thoroughly Laws arrangements (attached every night) in Coy Hqrs Instructed under Cpt Smith Second Lt for Cleaning C of E Supplied and fixed Cpt Grant Ball pipes Bullets Sec Balls Grant Communication Drill. ... Rifles by Lieut (C. St ... Smith) ... Section Drill Bullets .... 2 ... section V. H. 2.	

Army Form C. 2118.

WAR DIARY
or
INTELLIGENCE SUMMARY.
(Erase heading not required.)

Place	Date	Hour	Summary of Events and Information	Remarks and references to Appendices
Butterfield	14th		The Company moved from BULFORD CAMP to COULX BOIX from CAPLE G. 1.15 P.M.	
	15	2.30	Company inspected by C.O. Physical training, arms drill and attended Gas inflation testing Water filter.	
		16th	Company moved from CAEUX CROIX to POT ZE at PAM Sdg arrived at 3.15pm. Transport under 2/Lt PARKER arrived 2.15pm S/Lt KALEND succeeded Lt Coy as Billetting Officer.	
	17		C.O. with Lt MERFIELD, Lt HARRISON, 2/Lt McKENZIE Reconnoitred Line. 2/Lt PARKER Reconnoitred Route. SEINE CORNER.	
	18		2, 3, 1st Section relieved to "A" Coy (1st Queens) Canadian M.G. Coy Relief Complete at 8.15pm.	
	19		Lt GRANT 2/Lt KALEND Joined Coy at TYNE COTT. Lt McQUEEN Returned to Base.	
	20th		Harassing fire and observed out Ty No 3 2+1 Battens. Two enemy Lights fired Gas shell struck shell effects the enemy fired putting in Phosphorous ammunition with effects.	

Army Form C. 2118.

WAR DIARY
or
INTELLIGENCE SUMMARY.
(Erase heading not required.)

Instructions regarding War Diaries and Intelligence Summaries are contained in F.S. Regs., Part II. and the Staff Manual respectively. Title pages will be prepared in manuscript.

Place	Date	Hour	Summary of Events and Information	Remarks and references to Appendices
	2.1.18		Casualties this day 3 killed 3 wounded. One grey gelding with the Battalion.	
	2.1.18		Coy relieved in the line by the 2/4 Coy. Relief complete by 9 a.m. The Coy returned after Rs. Relief at POILE; there were no further wounded by Coy during relief.	
	2.2nd		Coy Commander Cheve - Instruction it goes not check or rather handed to Instruction at equipment (1st Coy. hand first duties in transport duties for all the Coys transport companies.	
	2.3rd		Inspection of action of & Instructions and the movement of armament equipment to meet Comp. in preparing entrenchments to meet Coy's requirements would in up the field to act & carried out the 1st Coy for Coy handed Coy. Improvements + Gas Drill.	
	2.4.18		Rd fit performed with the line of Franks assemble.	
	2.5.18		Coy. getting the 105th Coy another in at—2.5th/2/18.	
	2.6.18		The Coy believed that 105th Coy in the line. 2/6 BALSHAM wounded while taking over trench position. Relief reported.	

Army Form C. 2118.

WAR DIARY
or
INTELLIGENCE SUMMARY.

(Erase heading not required.)

Instructions regarding War Diaries and Intelligence Summaries are contained in F. S. Regs., Part II. and the Staff Manual respectively. Title pages will be prepared in manuscript.

Place	Date	Hour	Summary of Events and Information	Remarks and references to Appendices
	27th		complete at 7am. Coy transport detained for duties till few entrained.	
	28th		Battalion all morning having children trains of No 3, 4 & 5 Platoons found for shell fire. Stokes sent hits on Coy H.2. There was sniping of holding reluctants. We have only there known firing.	
	29th		at H1 expired with a drone with 3 enemy (Ints of 5 enemy) Capt Mellhuish Coy officer & D. Coy ord. lengths 2nd Luite sniper E. A. Haskell. downwind have ghrie fire of the section thus the third hence letters ends of the above & others. Thurs the withdrew until 6 H.2. (5th batts) concrete details of relief & time. Coy June 3 (Kirkcudbright)	
	30th		Coy Milton in the front H.H the 2/4th Engs fully complete left btw at 10am S.O.S further down & this was on 30th rept closed front this emerged. Journey ?dun relief	

for Col. Comdt.

War Diary

19th Machine Gun Coy.

From Dec 1st 1917

To Dec 31st 1917

Army Form C. 2118.

WAR DIARY
or
INTELLIGENCE SUMMARY.
(Erase heading not required.)

Place	Date	Hour	Summary of Events and Information	Remarks and references to Appendices
POPERINGHE	Dec 1st 2nd 3rd		Grades Camp Improvements. Grades 9.00 a.m. to 12 noon. Getting gun pits ready for trenches 2.0 p.m. to 3 p.m. Coy Parade. Falls in YPRES Attack very cold.	
	4th	12.30 a.m.	Parade 12.30 a.m. No 2 section under Lt. McKenzie, No 3 section under Lieut. Clarke, No 4 section under Lt. Rochfort, went up the line to relieve the 101st M Gun Coy in B B Group. positions. Lt Grant acted as O.C. B Group.	
		12.30 a.m.	At 12.30 a.m. enemy airplane dropped two bombs near camp. At 9.30 a.m. Lt. McGowan transported reinforced for duty. Weather fine. Hostile airplane very active. Shelled Ouderdom Salvation Army Huts at MANN CORNER at 3 a.m.	
	5th 6th		Grades of Engineer Camp Improvements. E.A. dropped four bombs near Coy H.Q. One plane was brought down, my plane lost.	

WAR DIARY
or
INTELLIGENCE SUMMARY

Army Form C. 2118.

Place	Date	Hour	Summary of Events and Information	Remarks and references to Appendices
POPERINGHE	7th		All ranks felt rested [much] better off. Capt SCHNEN [Reinforcements] arrived from base. Further enemy work. Rifle fire.	
	8th		Glorious but rain all day. A. B. Battery + Lewis Gun Col returned to the Bn [strength] 2/+ off & 56 1/r Gl-Bn. The Battn taking over A. B. Stations [Reliefs] completed by 4.30am 9-12-17. No casualties during the relief.	
	9th		The Battn rested and cleaned up. Moved to BEAUVOORDE mar SLEEVOORDE & relieved 1/4 Div. Rifle.	
	10th		C Coy returned to POPERINGHE by 150 Lm. G. Boy. Coy entrained at St JEAN at 5.30pm. detrained at OHEELLE and marched to billets. Transport proceeded by road under Rev e Queen.	
SLEENVOORDE	11th		[Parades] 9.0am & 2pm. [Rather] much [cleant]	
BEAUVOORDE WOOD	12th		[Parades] 9.0am & 12 noon. Chauncey of gun pict-equipment. Rather much [cleant] [muster] [cleant] killed thru guns [remaining] [movement] [&] [the morning] [long]	

Army Form C. 2118.

WAR DIARY
or
INTELLIGENCE SUMMARY.
(Erase heading not required)

Place	Date	Hour	Summary of Events and Information	Remarks and references to Appendices
BEAUVOIR DE VOED	13th & 14th		Troops in charge of Section Instructors of Physical training. Coy Leaders of Tactical. General musketry mobile Coy Drill. Major Brackett & Physical Training class returns will.	
	15th		Battalion classes formed. A/S Lieut M.E.'s Registered and attached men drill in E.O.'s detailed as instructors. The DIVISIONAL General visited the Coy and inspected them at work.	
	16th		Church Parades C/F — with others B.E.F. Officers handed S.	
	17th	10.50am	Towards Brightwalton under B. Pr. Rochelle	
			Coy paraded for this morning transport parade of Brigade	
	18th	10.45am	Afternoon	
			Coy Route march Cpt. Southwaite lectured Rfln.	
			Officer of the 2nd R.W.F. to machine gun tactics	
			N.C. section Suffered them to demonstrate return and mount. It given the afternoon off to by officer	
			Lunching Must only be a given fresh try of hands etatics	

(37092) Wt. W28391/M1493 75,500 1/17. D. D. & L., Ltd. Forms/C.2118.14

WAR DIARY
INTELLIGENCE SUMMARY

Army Form C. 2118.

Place	Date	Hour	Summary of Events and Information	Remarks and references to Appendices
STEENVOORDE	19^d		After a careful study of the map of Grenades gun F.B and lecture Officers Meuvin C Os	
	20^d		Col. may Reading + use of compass	
			Grenades Intelligence Summaries — reconnaissance	
	21st		Stokes 3" Rifle C Kriegspiel Revision of a Relief	
			C.O. instructed Coy M.S. HL. John followed by Route	
			march. The C.O. Returning by Stilhorn marched across	
			country. Coy ordered C Col. Attached Officers	
	22nd		Coy Sports & instructional lectures destd.	
			Coy Spears + — major + regiments all junior in C Os	
			command. Johns made C. Of M.	
	23rd		Coy paraded for demonstrations C. of T. 11.45 am R Co	
			D. Co 2.0 pm	

Army Form C. 2118.

WAR DIARY
or
INTELLIGENCE SUMMARY.
(Erase heading not required.)

Instructions regarding War Diaries and Intelligence Summaries are contained in F. S. Regs., Part II. and the Staff Manual respectively. Title pages will be prepared in manuscript.

Place	Date	Hour	Summary of Events and Information	Remarks and references to Appendices
BEAUVOIR DES WOOD	24th		Parade. 9 a.m to 12 a.m. Physical drill, Range and close order drill. Weather very cold and frosty.	
	25th		Voluntary service for b of k. at 10.30 a.m. Xmas Christmas dinner at 6 p.m. followed by a concert. Weather still frosty and snow fell.	
	26th		Parade 10 a.m. - 6.0. Each Company for a short route march. All the Company went to the Divisional Baths in the evening. Weather very cold and frosty.	
	27th		Half Company paraded at 9 a.m for inoculation, remainder did C.O's. Range work and belt filling. Weather cold, snow still on the ground.	
	28th		Half Company paraded at 9 a.m for inoculation. The not inoculated parties carried out hill work. Major HUTCHINSON and the men to S.O. with A Company. Snow fell slightly.	
	29th		Remainder of the transport went to be inoculated	

Army Form C. 2118.

WAR DIARY
or
INTELLIGENCE SUMMARY.
(Erase heading not required.)

Place	Date	Hour	Summary of Events and Information	Remarks and references to Appendices
[illegible]	30th		My [illegible] for dinner, dinner at 9.15 am	
	3 A.C.		Capt. handed full [illegible] the boys [illegible] Radio [illegible] [illegible] arrangements B [illegible] Settlers the Boys [illegible] [illegible] arrangements Settlers Roberts on off to the [illegible]	

[signature]

Army Form C. 2118.

WAR DIARY
or
INTELLIGENCE SUMMARY.
(Erase heading not required.)

19th MG Coy

Vol 24

Place	Date	Hour	Summary of Events and Information	Remarks and references to Appendices
STEENVOORDE	1/7/8		1. O.R. to Hospital	
"	2/7/8		3. O.R. to Hospital	
BRANDHOEK	3/7/8		Company moved from STEENVOORDE AREA to RIDGE CAMP. BRANDHOEK	APP. 1
POTIJZE	4/7/8		Co. moved from RIDGE CAMP to No 3 M.G. CAMP. POTIJZE + relieved 245 Co in front line system. LT AL STERN assumed command of Co. vice best Anderson to D. in M.D. 9.P.S. as ofc D.M.G.O.	APP 2.
"	5/7/8		In the line	
"	6/7/8		In the line. 2 O.R. to Hospital	
"	7/7/8		In the line. 3 O.R. Reinforcements from BASE.	
"	8/7/8		Relieved by 19th M.G. Co. 2 O.R. returned from hospital	APP 3.
POTIJZE	9/7/8		Company moved back to "A" Echelon. 3 O.R. to hopsec	
"	10/7/8		2 O.R. evacuated sick	
"	11/7/8		3 O.R. to Hospital	
"	12/7/8		Co. relieved 248th M.G.C in support position in the line. LT A.M.DOBSON assumed command of the Company vice LT AL STEEL on leave to U.K.	APP 4
IN THE LINE	13/7/8		In the line. 1 O.R. wounded in action	
"	14/7/8		In the line. 1 O.R. transferred back to his Battalion	

M. Dobson Lieut
for

Army Form C. 2118.

WAR DIARY
or
INTELLIGENCE SUMMARY.
(Erase heading not required.)

Place	Date	Hour	Summary of Events and Information	Remarks and references to Appendices
IN THE LINE	15/8		In the line	
"	16/8		On the night of the 16/8 were relieved by 19th Machine Gun Co. in the line	APP 5.
POTIJZE			4 O.R. Reinforcements from base.	
"	17/8		1 O.R. to Hospital	
"	18/8		1 O.R. to Hospital	
"	19/8		1 O.R. to Hospital	APP 6
IN THE LINE	20/8		Relieved 19th Machine Gun Co. with the line 2 O.R. from Hospital	
"	21/8		2 O.R. Hospital. 1 O.R. from Hospital. In the line	
"	22/8		Inter Relief of forward gun positions. (A & B relieved by C D Sections). In the line	
"			1 O.R. evacuated sick	
"			2 O.R. from hospital	
"	23/8		Relieved by 19th Machine Gun Co. in the line 2 O.R. evacuated	APP 7
POTIJZE	25/8		1 O.R. from hospital	
"	26/8		2 O.R. evacuated. 2 O.R. returned to their units.	
"	27/8		Company entrained at ST JEAN 3.30pm for ST OMER. From there by route march to Rest billet at VALD'ACQUIN arrived 2.15 a.m	APP 8.
"	28/8			

A. M. DeBa Lieut
for O.C. 19 M.G.Co.

WAR DIARY
or
INTELLIGENCE SUMMARY

Army Form C. 2118.

Place	Date	Hour	Summary of Events and Information	Remarks and references to Appendices
M. DACQUIN	29/8		General Cleaning Equipment etc.	
"	30/8		Transport arrived in M. DACQUIN area, Now complete 11.45 a.m.	
"	31/8		Training as per programme.	

M. Orban Kent
for O.C. 194 M.T. Coy.

33/19

Lo: Roy: Tros: from 58
Vol: 2

101/784

Q.H.
(4 sheets)

Dec 10/15
Jan 14/16

XXXIII 2/32

(19)

2 Dr Welsh Jus

Vol XX

2/33

J R Welsh Ins

Vol XXI

www.ingramcontent.com/pod-product-compliance
Lightning Source LLC
Chambersburg PA
CBHW080809010526
44113CB00013B/2350